Collins *practical gardener*

KITCHEN GARDEN

Collins *practical gardener*

KITCHEN GARDEN

LUCY PEEL

First published in 2003 by HarperCollins*Publishers*

77–85 Fulham Palace Road, London, W6 8JB

The Collins website address is:

www.collins.co.uk

Photography by Tim Sandall

Cover photography by Tim Sandall

Photographic props: Coolings Nurseries, Rushmore Hill,
Knockholt, Kent, TN14 7NN, www.coolings.co.uk

Design and editorial: Focus Publishing, Sevenoaks, Kent

Project editor: Guy Croton

Editor: Vanessa Townsend

Project co-ordinator: Caroline Watson

Design & illustration: David Etherington

For HarperCollins

Managing Editor: Angela Newton

Art Direction: Luke Griffin

Editor: Alastair Laing

Illustration: David Graham

Production: Chris Gurney

A CIP catalogue record for this book is available from the
British Library

ISBN 0007146566

Colour reproduction by Colourscan

Printed and bound in Great Britain by The Bath Press Ltd

Contents

Introduction

Why are kitchen gardens so appealing? Is it because, deep, deep down, we are still primeval beings always searching for food, which makes the sight of a plot of land bursting with herbs, fruit and vegetables – nature bountiful – so satisfying? Or maybe it is the deep calm engendered by the sense of order in a well managed kitchen garden which so attracts us. Whatever it is, there can be few people who can hand on heart say that they do not love the sight of a well planned, well stocked kitchen garden.

In the past, the growing of vegetables was driven mainly by necessity. The creators of beautiful cottage gardens were not primarily trying to create a work of art. All their hard work was in response to need. The fact that their creations were beautiful as well as fruitful was, to a large extent, a happy accident.

Similarly, the monks who toiled in Medieval monastery gardens growing herbs, fruit and vegetables did so to produce medicines to treat the ill and food to feed the poor, as well as the religious community. The layout of their gardens, which we find so attractive, came about through their need to use the available space to its full advantage – it was beauty with a purely practical purpose.

Nowadays, kitchen gardening is driven by an entirely different force. We do not *have* to grow our own fruit, herbs

Cherry 'Morello'

Dwarf bean 'Purple Queen'

and vegetables – there are few shortages, and much of the food available is cheap. All the food we want is there waiting to be delivered to our door at the click of a mouse.

However, we do it for the joy of growing something, the thrill when we harvest it and because we want to enjoy super-fresh food, packed full of flavour and nutrition and, vitally, unadulterated with the mass of chemicals to which supermarket food is so often subjected. We want to know what we are eating.

With this in mind, it makes sense to follow an holistic, organic approach to gardening. Obviously, it is up to each gardener to decide what to do with their own plot of land; however, it seems self defeating to put a lot of effort into your kitchen garden, only to treat its produce in the same way as the commercial growers treat theirs.

It is impossible to pretend that looking after a kitchen garden is effortless. There is a lot of hard work involved, from planning and preparation, to planting and maintenance. However the rewards and satisfactions are so enormous that all the effort will be repaid a thousandfold. There is nothing as satisfying as picking one's own produce and bearing it triumphantly to the table. Try it and see.

How to Use This Book

This book is divided into three main parts. The opening chapters guide you through all areas of garden practice, from assessing your site, through general care and pruning to harvesting, storing and freezing. A comprehensive plant directory follows, with individual entries on over 150 of the most commonly available vegetables, fruits and herbs, listed by category of produce. All the tastiest and most versatile fruits and vegetables are included, covering many different styles of cultivation and uses. This section also includes details on the miniature varieties of many plants. The final section of the book covers plant problems. Troubleshooting pages allow you to diagnose the likely cause of any problems, and a comprehensive directory of pests and diseases offers advice on how to solve them.

care charts provide an at-a-glance summary of the crop's specific needs. (N.B. Where more than one vegetable or fruit appears on the page, the chart may cater for both plants)

detailed descriptions give specific advice on care for each plant, including planting and pests and diseases

colour-coded tabs on the side of the page denote categories of plant and help guide you easily around the book

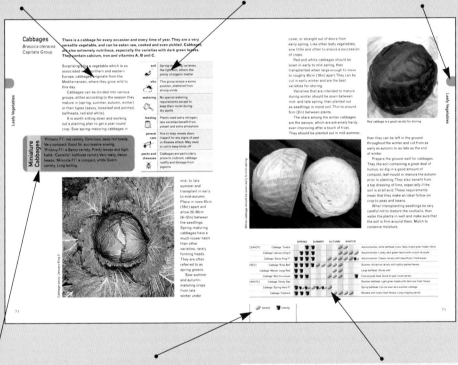

mini crop boxes provide useful recommendations for the best varieties of miniature vegetables available, whenever this is the case

a key at the bottom of the page explains what each symbol means

variety charts list recommended varieties for most genera of vegetables and fruits or the best individual species. These display key information to help you choose your ideal plant, showing:

• when to sow or cultivate the plant during the year
• when to transplant vegetables
• when to harvest the vegetables or fruits
• periods when repeat sowing and harvesting are possible
• additional comments from the author
(N.B. Where more than one vegetable or fruit appears on the page, the chart may list varieties for both genera)

Assessing Your Garden

As with any project in the garden the planning stage is absolutely vital. Survey, analysis and design are the keys to success, and no time spent on these is ever wasted.

Choosing a Site

What success you achieve from your kitchen garden will largely be determined by its position and the state of the soil. The ideal position for a kitchen garden is sunny and sheltered, with good drainage and light, slightly acid to neutral soil. There should be easy access to water and, if possible, to a compost heap, tool shed and greenhouse.

If your garden is too small for a choice of plots then it is a question of improving on what you have. It is amazing what can be achieved with judiciously-placed wind breaks, pruning to allow in the sun, along with serious digging and conditioning of the soil. Why not grow your fruit, vegetables and herbs among the flower beds or in containers?

You should always make use of vertical structures in the garden – buildings, fences and walls – as supports for climbing vegetables, such as beans or tomatoes, and fruit trees. As well as being decorative, walls and fences retain heat and so are ideal for numerous heat-loving fruit trees, such as apricots, peaches and pears.

Do not worry if the site is not level. If the slope is very steep, then the answer is to step it, creating a number of flat terraces; or if this is too difficult, to plant the crops across rather than up and down the beds.

Look at the direction of your prevailing winds and erect some protection. Growing plants put so much effort into standing up to wind that they will not yield much of a crop.

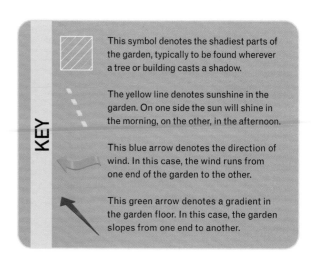

KEY

This symbol denotes the shadiest parts of the garden, typically to be found wherever a tree or building casts a shadow.

The yellow line denotes sunshine in the garden. On one side the sun will shine in the morning, on the other, in the afternoon.

This blue arrow denotes the direction of wind. In this case, the wind runs from one end of the garden to the other.

This green arrow denotes a gradient in the garden floor. In this case, the garden slopes from one end to another.

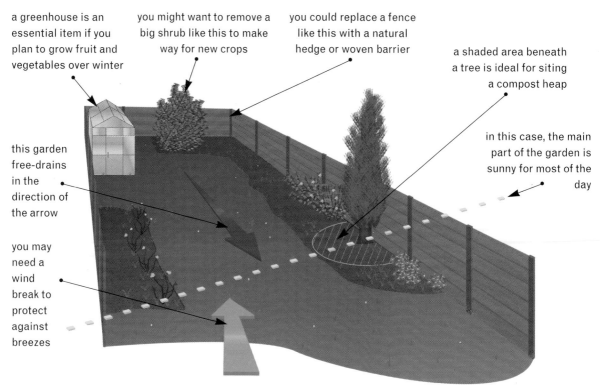

a greenhouse is an essential item if you plan to grow fruit and vegetables over winter

you might want to remove a big shrub like this to make way for new crops

you could replace a fence like this with a natural hedge or woven barrier

a shaded area beneath a tree is ideal for siting a compost heap

in this case, the main part of the garden is sunny for most of the day

this garden free-drains in the direction of the arrow

you may need a wind break to protect against breezes

Working with the Soil

Once you have chosen the perfect site for your kitchen garden and decided upon the basic elements of hard landscaping, it is time to turn your attention to the soil.

The quality of your soil will be the ultimate deciding factor as to the success of your kitchen garden. If your soil is poor then however much effort you expend on planting, watering, weeding, fighting off pests and diseases is only wasted time. Your crops need to be fed – and the soil is the source of their food, strength, health and bounty.

So learn to understand your soil. On a very basic level you need to know its physical type – is it a heavy soil, such as clay, or a light soil, such as sand or loam – and its chemical characteristics, whether it is acid, alkaline or neutral.

It is important to know the physical characteristics for two reasons. Firstly, to give you an idea of how easy the soil will be to work and how much effort you will need to expend on digging. If the soil is light and sandy, it will obviously be a much easier proposition than heavy clay soil which forms large clumps. Secondly, the lightness or heaviness of the soil will have a bearing on the drainage qualities, and the type of soil will indicate how fertile it is likely to be.

Soil types

There are a surprising number of different soil types but each contains sand, silt and clay particles and it is the quantities of these particles which determine the soil's texture. There are loam, chalk, limestone, peat and silt soils, then the combinations of the main types – for example, sandy loam, clay loam and silty loam. All have their advantages and disadvantages.

A simple way to find out what type of soil you have, is to take a handful of moist soil, rub it between your fingers and see how it feels. If it is dry and gritty and runs through your fingers then it is sandy. If it stains your hands and can be squeezed into a ball, it is clay.

Clay is sticky when wet and hard when dry, which is why it is referred to as a heavy soil, because it is literally heavy work to deal with. These characteristics mean clay soil requires more work on the digging front and is very slow-draining. On the other hand, it is often full of nutrients, although plants are hampered in the first place by the difficulty of making root systems, which are vital for their uptake of nutrients. To improve the texture of clay soil you will need to dig in a lot of horticultural

grit, or organic matter such as leaf mould or shredded bark, which help to open the soil up.

Light or sandy soil needs frequent watering and a regular injection of good organic material because it is very free draining, and so nutrients are quickly washed away by the rain. On the plus side, sandy soil warms up quickly, which is ideal for early crops, and because it is so light, digging in the improving organic matter should not be especially heavy work.

Chalk and limestone soils tend to be alkaline and are also very free draining, although often sticky immediately after rain. They are also quite shallow, in other words there is not a great depth of topsoil to work with, and the fact that water soaks through them so easily means they are poor at retaining nutrients, so need constant applications of organic matter and fertilizers.

Peaty soil is made up of such a huge amount of organic material that it will be extremely wet and acidic. However, if you put the effort in and improve the structure and fertilize a peat soil, you will achieve excellent plant growth.

Every fruit and vegetable gardener's favourite soil is loam, which occupies the middle ground between clay and sand, containing just the right balance of the two. It is neither too heavy nor too light, so is easy to work with without the risk of becoming waterlogged or overly dry. It tends to be deep and fertile, holding nutrients well, with a healthy helping of humus (the decayed vegetable products which keep the soil well drained and light).

SOIL

The range of 'soils' and improvers available can seem vast. As a general rule, use soil-based mixes for perennials and soilless mixes for temporary displays. Soil improvers include grit for drainage, and blood, fish and bonemeal – as well as organic matter – for providing vital food and nutrients.

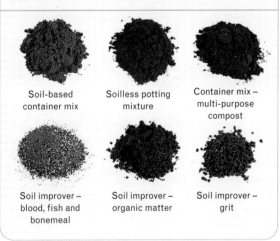

Soil-based container mix	Soilless potting mixture	Container mix – multi-purpose compost
Soil improver – blood, fish and bonemeal	Soil improver – organic matter	Soil improver – grit

Chemical composition

Once you have worked out what type of soil you have, you need to ascertain whether it is acid, alkaline or neutral in its chemical composition. This is important as most vegetables prefer a neutral soil. Certain soils are almost invariably a particular chemical type, for example peat is acid, while chalky and limestone soil tends to be alkaline; however sand or clay soils can be either.

Chemical composition is measured on the pH scale, with a low reading of below pH7 indicating an acid soil, anything higher indicating that the soil is alkaline, and a neutral soil registering as pH7.

Finding out the pH value of your soil is a simple matter thanks to the existence of soil tester kits, which you can buy from any nursery or garden centre. The tester kit will display the various pH levels up the side of the container. A sample of your garden soil is added to the tester and shaken. You can then match the particular colour reading to the corresponding colour on the kit which will tell you your soil's pH value [A].

Other tester kits can tell you in more general terms whether your soil is acidic, alkaline or neutral. A sample of soil is added to a test-tube, shaken and matched against a colour chart which shows the varying degrees of acidity or alkalinity of your soil [B].

For a more pinpoint measurement, sophisticated soil-test meters, containing a probe that is inserted into the ground to give a reading, are also available.

A

B

Bark chip mulches work well but can diminish nitrogen levels

Soil improvers

While we cannot completely change the basic soil type we have in the garden and must learn to live with it to a degree, we can temporarily alter its pH (by adding lime), feed it and improve its structure. The aim is to end up with soil rich in humus with a top layer of fine, crumbly tilth.

Even if your soil is naturally neutral and fertile it will need a certain amount of organic material in order to remain so. While plants may grow happily in this type of soil in the first year, they will suck the nutrients out of it. The soil must be constantly replenished if you want to carry on getting a good harvest.

The choice of manures and fertilizers available for improving and feeding your soil is enormous, and it can be perplexing working out which one is right for your plot and for what you want to grow.

The first thing to understand is that fertilizers fall into two groups. Organic fertilizers are made from animal or vegetable sources, while inorganic fertilizers are made up of minerals or chemicals. The organic fertilizers are bulky and quite slow-working, while inorganic, chemical fertilizers provide a fast pick-me-up for relatively little effort. However, chemical fertilizers will do nothing to improve the taste of your crops and long term they may actually make more work, as they will upset the balance of nature. As with all forms of gardening there is no such thing as a quick fix.

Compost and manure Compost made from organic household and garden waste (see pages 31–3 for instructions on making compost), horse, cattle and poultry manure, spent hops and mushroom compost are all invaluable sources of nutrients. Check that the manure is well rotted before you put it on the ground, as fresh manure will burn any plants it comes into contact with. Avoid peat-based composts, as the extraction of these for garden use is rapidly destroying irreplaceable wetland habitats for numerous plants and wildlife. Instead, look for some of the many substitutes on the market, such as coconut fibre. These will be just as effective in opening up the soil, improving its structure and helping to maintain moisture.

Concentrated organic fertilizers Extract of blood, fish, hoof, horn, bonemeal and seaweed are all concentrated organic fertilizers which will slowly release nutrients as they break down in the soil. They are easy to handle and apply but quite expensive and slow-working.

Green manures An attractive and equally efficient alternative to traditional compost is green compost or manure. This method uses living plants, such as alsike clover, comfrey and lupins, which are grown solely to be dug back into the soil to condition it. Green compost

TIP

Beware of incorporating unrotted organic materials, such as bark chippings, leaves and fresh straw. Although these will help to improve the structure of the soil they will also rob the soil of nitrogen as they decompose. This can be offset with regular feeds of a nitrogen-rich fertilizer.

A well-rotted compost heap is an essential item for any kitchen garden

Organic leaf mould is an invaluable source of nutrients for the soil

works especially well for light sandy or heavy clay soils, and has the bonus of demanding less effort than collecting, turning and spreading home-made compost. One disadvantage of this method is that the soil cannot be used for any other plants while the cover crop is growing.

Chemical fertilizers These types of fertilizers come in both solid and liquid form. They can be watered into the soil and will feed the trees and plants, providing an instant boost. The disadvantage of chemical fertilizers is that, unlike natural fertilizers, they will not improve the soil, and are generally washed away as soon as it rains. Foliar feeds are similar, although they are sprayed directly on to the plant rather than the soil, so are more suitable for greenhouse or container-grown plants.

Planning Your Garden

Once you have decided where to site your kitchen garden and have familiarised yourself with the growing conditions and the characteristics of the soil, the next step is to design a layout, decide what to grow and draw up a planting plan, taking into account crop rotation and planting progression (see page 22 for more details).

Designing Your Plot

Bed designs

It is always best to keep the design as simple as possible. The aim is for the kitchen garden to look attractive while making the best use of the available space (see illustration below).

A square plot, for example, works well when divided into either four smaller square beds dissected by a cross-shaped path, or four triangular beds with the paths running from corner to corner. A round plot with three or four wedge-shaped beds is a particularly efficient design, as the space around the edges can be used for fruit, although keep taller fruit trees where they cannot shade the other crops.

There are several reasons why it is a good idea to divide the kitchen garden up into smaller beds. Firstly, there is the question of accessibility. It is easy to damage the structure of the soil by walking on it too much, so keeping the beds to a reasonable size – a maximum of 1.5m (5ft) wide is ideal – ensures you stand on the soil as little as possible, thereby reducing the risk of compaction. Also, in practice, three or four smaller beds are easier to manage than one large one. Psychologically, the sense of achievement from having completely weeded one small bed, as opposed to partially weeded a large bed, should not be underestimated! And finally it is easier to keep track of a planting rotation plan if you have a number of beds, which you can match to the number of years' cycle your plan runs for (see page 22).

Red numbers refer to bed rotation (see also page 22)

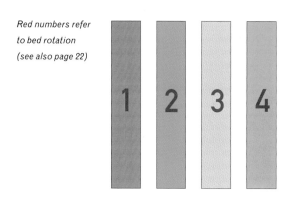

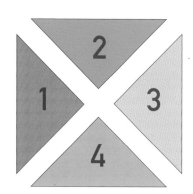

Vegetable Patch Bed Designs

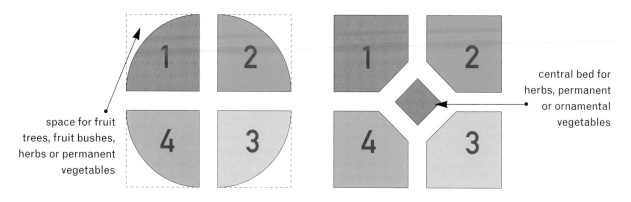

space for fruit trees, fruit bushes, herbs or permanent vegetables

central bed for herbs, permanent or ornamental vegetables

Permanent planting

When planning your design think carefully about where to site the movable and immovable plants. Only the annual vegetables are rotated, so the herbs and perennial vegetables, such as rhubarb, asparagus (which will yield more in its own bed) and globe artichokes, require permanent positions. Similarly, fruit trees and bushes will be permanent fixtures in the design.

When deciding where to plant these perennials, in particular you will need to consider their eventual height and whether they are very bushy, as this will determine the amount of shade they produce. For example, in a four-bed plan, three beds can be used for vegetables, while the fourth could be reserved for perennial vegetables and herbs; or it may be better to plant the perennial vegetables around the edge of the plot so that they do not cast shade on the annual beds.

Constructing the Plot

Once you have fixed upon the basic design of your kitchen garden, you must decide which specific practical elements will be required and how to construct them – namely, any fencing and wind breaks, paths and edging, and drainage and watering systems.

Raised beds

Planting beds can either be at ground level or raised up with edging constructed to hold back the earth. Raised beds can be any height or length but need to be sufficiently narrow so that the crops can be easily reached and tended to without the need to walk over the soil. This means there is no danger of compaction and the soil structure is not damaged. Similarly, as there is no need to leave space for access between rows, the crops can be planted closer than usual, increasing yield while reducing weed growth. Beds 1.3m (4ft 5in) in width are ideal.

To be successful the beds must be constructed correctly. Edging should be tough enough to hold back the weight of the earth in the beds, and the height needs to allow for an increase in the level of the soil as you add mulch and manure each year. Among the simplest of edging constructions are lengths of board held in place by wooden pegs hammered into the ground, or you can build longer lasting beds with bricks and mortar.

To raise the soil level, firstly skim the topsoil off the adjacent paths and place it on the beds, then work large amounts of organic matter into the soil – about 6kg (13lb) per square metre will really open up the structure. If the beds are prepared correctly they should need little more than light hoeing and a sprinkling of fertilizer for several years.

Wind breaks and fencing

When deciding upon a wind break, the key thing to remember is that hedges and loosely-woven fences are more effective than solid barriers, although not as long lasting. This is because permeable barriers, such as woven willow or hazel wattle hurdles, filter the wind, diminishing its ferocity, while solid barriers actually intensify the wind's force, sending it over the top of the barrier so that small but devastating eddies are created on the other side.

If you decide to plant a hedge keep it a good distance away from the beds to prevent it casting too much shadow and using up the nutrients in the soil. Rolls of plastic wind break sheets are very effective as temporary protection while the hedge is becoming established.

Paths and edging

Paths are important on the basic level of providing access to the beds. They should be a minimum of about 90cm (3ft) in width to allow access for a wheelbarrow, and tough enough to take the constant tread of heavy boots. Another vital element is a good all-weather material – closely-mown grass paths look wonderful yet quickly turn to a muddy mess at the first drop of rain. The

Example of a kitchen garden layout

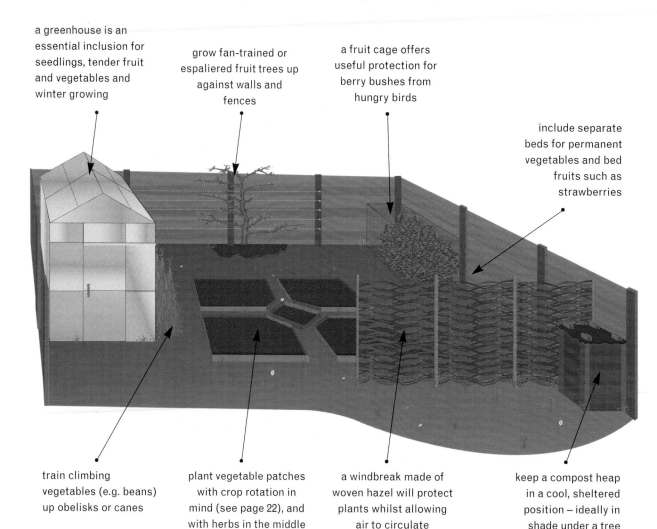

a greenhouse is an essential inclusion for seedlings, tender fruit and vegetables and winter growing

grow fan-trained or espaliered fruit trees up against walls and fences

a fruit cage offers useful protection for berry bushes from hungry birds

include separate beds for permanent vegetables and bed fruits such as strawberries

train climbing vegetables (e.g. beans) up obelisks or canes

plant vegetable patches with crop rotation in mind (see page 22), and with herbs in the middle

a windbreak made of woven hazel will protect plants whilst allowing air to circulate

keep a compost heap in a cool, sheltered position – ideally in shade under a tree

paths should also be fairly maintenance free, as you do not want to be weeding a path when you could spend the time weeding the kitchen garden.

It is best to avoid organic materials such as chipped bark or straw for paths and instead choose hard surfaces such as concrete slabs, brick pavers, gravel or stone. Concrete is perhaps the most practical surface, but it is also one of the ugliest. Laid in a bed of sand in a herring-bone pattern, pavers look especially decorative yet are extremely practical and hardwearing, provided they are frost proof. One of the easiest paths to lay is gravel. Laid over a sheet of plastic to deter weeds, gravel provides an instant effect. Lay it deep enough to hide the plastic yet not so deep that it makes pushing the wheelbarrow difficult.

Edging helps to contain the soil and provides a visual separation between the path and the bed. Bricks laid on edge to create a dog-tooth pattern is a popular and attractive form of edging. Other popular edging materials include box, grown as low hedges, which is very traditional and attractive but provides a haven for slugs and snails, and low woven hazel or willow hurdles.

Brick pavers make an attractive path to give access to your beds

Drainage

It is impossible to grow fruit and vegetables in waterlogged soil, so it is vital to get the drainage correct at the earliest stage of planning. Rectifying mistakes later will be very difficult and expensive.

In areas of heavy soil you may need to lay a drainage trench to remove excess water. This is an open ditch, 1m (3ft) deep with sloping sides and lined with gravel. However, the best means of ensuring adequate drainage in the first place is to avoid establishing the kitchen garden in an overly damp site. By simply observing your garden, avoiding dips and working out where the water drains away, you should be able to avoid trouble spots.

Watering systems

While drainage is a one-off problem, watering is an ongoing consideration, and one which will become a daily task at certain times of year. During hot, dry periods shallow-rooted plants, such as salad vegetables, will run to seed extremely fast unless kept well watered, so not having easy access to water can make a kitchen gardener's life impossible.

Water butts, which collect rain water run off from the roof of the house or the garden shed and greenhouse, are extremely useful, especially as rain water is better for the plants than mains water, and there is always the threat of water restrictions during periods of drought. Rain water also contains fewer chemicals than mains water and being at an ambient temperature is kinder on the plants. However, it is unlikely that you will be able to supply all your needs from collected rainwater alone. If you are serious about growing fruit and vegetables it is useful to have an automatic watering system.

There are many different systems on the market in all price ranges, the simplest being the trickle hose, which supplies a constant, small amount of water. Automatic sprinklers, set on a timer, will give plants more of a soaking, however the trickle hose is more flexible and is one of the most efficient ways of watering.

What to Grow

What you decide to grow in your kitchen garden will depend to an extent on the type of soil you have, as well as the amount of space at your disposal. But besides thinking about what will grow well, consider the plants that you are really keen to grow, as there is very little point in having a bumper crop of something you would not want to eat.

It is often worthwhile looking at what is expensive or difficult to get hold of in the shops and concentrating on that. And think about which things tend to be lacking in flavour in the shops. For example, shop-bought tomatoes cannot muster a fraction of the flavour of home-grown plants. Also consider which are the high performing fruit and vegetables in terms of yields, what looks pretty and also how much time you have to spend on care. If time is tight it would be best to avoid anything that requires constant attention.

There are certain things that every garden, however small, should try and find a place for. Freshly picked salad leaves and herbs, for example, have an unbeatable flavour, and new potatoes pulled from the soil just before cooking have an intensity of taste that shop-bought varieties cannot match.

Attractive planting

With a small garden especially, everything you plant must earn its place. There is no reason why fruit, vegetables and herbs cannot be highly decorative. All the different colours, shapes and textures can be combined to great effect. There is also no reason why they should be confined to the kitchen garden. Runner beans scrambling up an arbour or a trellis against the house wall may be unconventional, however they will look just as attractive as they would growing up a bamboo wigwam in the kitchen garden.

Similarly, soft fruit such as redcurrants and gooseberries need not exist solely as bushes grown in netting cages. It is easy to train them into standard

Pots and containers are ideal for growing herbs

shapes with careful pruning over a few seasons. These will look wonderful flanking a doorway or steps in the garden. Remember to net the bushes when the fruit ripens or the birds will strip your crop in minutes.

Fruit, herbs and vegetables can also be grown among your flowers and shrubs in the main garden. Many varieties are extremely attractive with fantastically architectural shapes – for example, beautifully shaped globe artichokes – or if it is spectacular coloured foliage you are after, fennel and kale are two of the many examples. Mixed in with a selection of edible flowers, such as nasturtium, there is no reason why every tree and plant in your garden shouldn't make a culinary contribution.

Growing against walls

Of the tree fruit the real heat lovers, such as the tender apricots, peaches, nectarines and figs, ideally need to be against a wall that can give them the most sun. While others, such as the hardy pears, apples, plums and gages, are happy facing in any but the coldest direction.

Among the soft fruit that will benefit from growing against a wall are blackberries and vines. In fact, if you are growing vines out of doors you will be unlikely to get any edible fruit unless it is trained against a very sun-drenched, sheltered wall.

TIP

Highly ornamental vegetables, fruit and herbs include: Globe artichokes, asparagus, beetroot, red 'rubin' Brussels sprouts, red cabbages, rainbow chard, chicory, endive, fennel, kale; highbush blueberries, cape gooseberries, strawberries; numerous herbs, including chives, cilantro (leaf coriander), dill, fennel, sweet cicely, thyme and parsley.

Space-saving fruit

There is no reason why fruit trees should be the preserve of large gardens. There are so many ways to train fruit that are hugely space-saving, and many apple tree varieties have been bred specifically with the small garden in mind.

Ballerina apple trees are very attractive and as they grow tall but with few sideshoots, rather like a column, they cast little shade. Minarettes are similar to Ballerinas, being column shaped and grown on dwarfing rootstock, and are also available as pears and plums.

The branches of apples and pears can be trained along horizontal support wires to create short 'stepovers', usually two wires in height, or 'espaliers' several wires high, as well as up a simple arch or arbour. Vines and kiwi also lend themselves to this treatment. Stepovers make perfect edging to paths, and look attractive as bed dividers.

Containers

If your garden is really small, even if it is little more than a courtyard or balcony, you can still enjoy fresh fruit,

Many fruit trees, such as this apple, can thrive in containers as a space-saving idea

herbs and vegetables. You just have to think hard about how best to use every bit of wall space, and buy a mass of containers.

Many fruit, vegetables and virtually all herbs will be more than happy in containers, given the right positioning and enough feeding and watering. Among the vegetables that are suited to containers are potatoes (there are specially designed tubs for potatoes), leeks, carrots, asparagus, courgettes, tomatoes (basil enjoys the same conditions so combine the two for an instant meal), lettuce, spinach, oriental vegetables and beans.

One of the advantages of growing fruit in containers is that they are portable. This is particularly useful with tender fruit (such as citrus and nectarine), as they can be taken into a sheltered place, such as a conservatory, for the winter.

Some fruit, such as figs, will actually fruit better if their roots are confined, so a fig tree growing in a large container against a sheltered, sunny wall will perform better than one planted out in a bed. Strawberries have traditionally been grown in terracotta pots and deep barrels, and dessert grapes fruit well trained as standards in pots.

Herbs are especially suited to containers, as many herbs come originally from hot, dry areas, so containers, that mimic those conditions perfectly, are ideal for them. A selection of herbs growing in pots outside the kitchen door or in a box outside the kitchen window will save space and time, and will ensure that the herbs are as fresh as possible.

Soil requirements

The type of soil in your garden will have a bearing on what grows well. It is possible to alter the acidity or alkalinity of the soil, and to lighten heavy soil or firm up light soil (see pages 10–11). You will reduce your workload considerably, however, if you stick to what will grow well naturally without numerous supplements.

Chalk and limestone soils are good for peas, beans, brassicas and fruit such as plums, which have stones. Problems arise with soft fruit and potatoes. Potatoes will need to be grown in trenches lined with peat substitute, and soft fruit need a good annual mulch of peat substitute or well-rotted manure. Sandy soil is good for early and overwintering crops, plus long varieties of root crops which cannot cope with clay. Clay is good for the majority of maincrop vegetables and for fruit, although they may take a while to become established.

Preparing the Site

After the survey, analysis and design comes the hard physical work – digging, clearing, soil preparation and any building. This is the back-breaking part of the whole process, but every ounce of effort expended here will be paid back many times over in healthy, bumper crops.

Clearing

Once you have decided upon the ideal site for your kitchen garden it is time to prepare the ground for planting. All preparation should take place over autumn, winter and early spring, so that everything is ready for the main cultivating period in late spring and summer.

If you are siting the kitchen garden in an area that has been previously uncultivated for a long time, where tenacious weeds and wild plants like brambles and nettles have taken hold, then the only way to clear it may be to spray with a heavy duty herbicide and cover over the area with black polythene and leave for a year.

Most areas, however, will not be so difficult. Simply pull up all the vegetation you can, remove any rubble, rocks or old tree stumps which could harbour honey fungus, then dig up every bit of root and weed.

Dealing with weeds

It is vital at the preparation stage to remove every trace of weeds, both annual and perennial weeds, especially the rampant growers such as bindweed, nettles, couch grass and ground elder.

There are three basic ways of destroying weeds – mechanical, manual and chemical. You can weed by mechanical means with the help of a rotavator and appropriate attachments. This is fine for removing annual weeds from a new site and can save a lot of time and effort. However, there is the risk of causing soil compaction and with perennial weeds you may just end up chopping all the roots and thereby distributing them more widely.

You should regularly remove perennial weeds from around crops

Manual weeding means removing the weeds and roots by hand, hoe and fork. Always do this during dry weather, when they will be easier to loosen and can be left on the surface to dry out and die. Annual weeds can be easily destroyed by repeated hoeing. It is particularly important to remove them before they set seed, otherwise you may have several hundred more to deal with.

Perennial weeds are much more difficult to deal with as they propagate themselves from their roots and stems as well as from seed, so can stay hidden underground. Any stray roots, or even bits of root, left undiscovered will soon gain a foothold and from there they can become unstoppable before you have even realised there is a problem.

Weedkillers

If you have a serious weed problem you may need to supplement the manual removal of weeds with chemical control. It is best to avoid chemicals wherever possible in the kitchen garden, but when clearing a difficult site it may be helpful to use them as a one-off. Apply the chemicals before digging, leave to work, then remove the dead foliage and roots.

TIP

Weeds can also be controlled effectively by means of light deprivation. Cover the chosen area with either a layer of black plastic or an old carpet and preferably leave for an entire season. Even when some perennial weeds are not killed off, they will be much weakened and easier to remove.

Weedkillers work in different ways. Foliage-acting or translocated weedkillers are sprayed on to the leaves and then either kill on contact, or are absorbed by the plant with the poison taken down to the roots. They can take anything up to a few weeks to work and may need several applications.

Soil-acting weedkillers are put on to the soil rather than the plant and are then taken in by the weeds' roots as they grow, thus killing them. These weedkillers may remain active for a long time, so you cannot sow in the treated ground until they have dispersed.

There are also selective weedkillers which either kill broad-leaved plants leaving narrow-leaved plants unharmed, or vice versa.

Digging

The intention behind digging over the soil is to open up the structure. This will improve drainage and loosen compacted soil – it is also the time to mix in organic material with the soil, and clear away any vegetation and weeds.

With very heavy clay soil, which is hard work to manage, nature can lend a hand. Dig the plot over at the beginning of winter, but do not bother to break down all the large clods. Then leave it open to the elements and if you live in a cold enough climate, the frost will magically break the clods down. If you have waterlogged clay soil, you may need to add sand or grit to open it up and improve drainage. Avoid adding fine sand as this may exacerbate the problem.

Lighter sandy soil is much easier to work, and it may be possible to do no more than fork it over, remove the weeds and cover with a thick layer of mulch. This is known as the no-dig method and is ideal for fragile, sandy soil, where over-digging may open it up so much that many of the nutrients get washed away over the winter and the soil ends up being poor and dry by spring.

Methods of digging

There are two main methods of digging: single spit and double digging. With both methods you need to do more than just mix in organic matter with the soil. Single spit digging involves turning over the soil to the depth of the spade blade (spit); double digging involves digging down to two spade blade depths then forking the ground beneath. Double digging is particularly useful in areas where the soil may be compacted or the drainage needs improving.

Digging techniques:

First mark out a square site and mentally divide it into two rows of oblong trenches about 30cm (1ft) wide.

Dig down to a spade's depth, approximately 25cm (10in). If you are double digging, then dig down to one spit and remove the soil, then dig down a second spit, remembering never to mix soil from the two spits and replacing them in the adjacent trench in the correct order.

Dig out the first trench, leaving the soil to one side. Then, working backwards to avoid compaction, dig out the next trench, filling in the first trench with the soil from this trench. Continue this process until you reach the final trench, the soil from which should be used to fill the first trench and vice versa.

With single spit digging, turn over the soil to the depth of the spade blade

Planting

For any plant or tree to do well they have to be planted correctly, in the right position and conditions. This is especially true for fruit trees as they are a long-term investment – a dead apple tree is rather more of a disaster than an unsuccessful batch of carrots.

Vegetables & Herbs

It is possible to buy vegetable and herb seedlings ready for planting out from nurseries and some garden centres, but these are expensive and are no substitute for seedlings that you have raised yourself. With your own seedlings you can be sure of the variety as well as their health.

Sowing outdoors

Many vegetables and herbs can be sown directly into the ground where they are to grow. However, to achieve success and to have as many seeds germinate as possible, you must first ensure that the timing and conditions are just right. So the temperature must be suitable – most vegetables simply will not grow unless the average temperature during the day is above 6°C (43°F) – the soil must be well prepared and you must follow the seed company's guidelines as to planting depth and distance.

In order for the seeds to germinate the earth must be warm enough and neither too dry nor too wet. If it is too wet the seeds will simply rot and if it is too dry they will shrivel up. The process of warming up the soil can be speeded along by placing cloches on the ground (tents made from glass or plastic, see pages 27–8) or spreading horticultural fleece over it.

To sow outdoors:

First of all, prepare your seedbed. This is a weed-free area which has been dressed with a general fertilizer

then raked until it is covered with a fine tilth. Next, using a taut piece of string with an old nail at the end or a plank as a guide, mark out a straight line [A]. With a dibber, make a drill along the piece of string to a uniform depth [B]. Check the seed packet to ensure the drill is the correct depth.

If the weather is dry then water the drill before sowing the seeds. Small seeds should be sprinkled sparingly and evenly [C], while larger seeds can be placed individually.

Finally, very lightly cover the seeds with soil [D], gently firm down and water.

As the seedlings emerge they will need to be thinned out, otherwise they will become overcrowded and cramped for space, to the detriment of their growth. Wait until they have a couple of leaves before gently pulling out and either transplanting or discarding the weaker seedlings in the drill.

Some vegetables, for example peas and 'cut-and-come-again' salad crops, are grown in wide rows, so will need to be sown in a wide drill of 23cm (10in).

Sowing indoors

There are various reasons for sowing plants indoors. Some plants are so tender that they need the extra heat and protection, and planting indoors helps you to get a head start. This will ensure that only the strongest and best make it into the kitchen garden, thereby reducing waste.

TIP

When planting crops it is best to sow in succession. For example, carrots can be planted outdoors every two weeks until late summer and lettuces can also be sown fortnightly outdoors between early spring and late summer. Thus you will have successive crops over a longer period, rather than too many all at once which will just go to waste.

Healthy young cauliflowers in a row

Some half hardy vegetables and tender herbs should be sown later, then protected from frost. Examples are French and runner beans, courgettes, squashes, cucumbers, peppers, sweetcorn and tomatoes.

To sow indoors:
Fill a clean seed tray to within 1cm (½in) of the top with a good multi-purpose or seed compost. Tap the tray to encourage the compost to settle, gently firm then lightly water. Sow the seeds thinly and evenly – large seeds can be placed individually with the use of a dibber [A] – and sprinkle a fine layer of sieved compost on top.

Water lightly and cover the tray with a sheet of glass or polythene. For extra protection from condensation or bright sunlight, spread a sheet of newspaper on top of the glass. Place the seed tray in a warm, well-lit, draught-free place. Wipe off excess condensation each day and check to see if the seeds have germinated. When the seedlings start to appear, remove the glass and place the seed tray on a bright window-sill.

As soon as the seedlings develop their first leaves, they are ready for pricking out. Fill a seed tray or modules with potting compost and water until moist.

A

Make a series of holes in the compost with a pencil 2.5–5cm (1–2in) apart. Carefully prise out the individual seedlings, taking care not to damage their tiny roots and holding them by their leaves not their stems.

B

C

Place the seedling in the holes, firm gently then water lightly. Put the seed tray on a bright window-sill, although not in direct sunlight as this will dry out the compost and burn the seedlings. Leave the tray there for a couple of days before moving to a sunnier position. Water daily to ensure the compost is kept moist.

When the seedlings outgrow the tray, and it is not yet time for them to be planted out, you will need to pot them on – move them into individual pots. Carefully remove them from the tray, taking care not to damage the root systems, and replant them in pots with compost [B]. Water daily to maintain the moisture.

Hardening off and transplanting

Before the seedlings are planted out they must become gradually acclimatised to their new conditions. After all they have been kept in quite luxurious conditions, with even temperatures, no wind and constant watering, and so if they were planted out without a hardening off period the shock could kill them.

Take the seed tray or pots outside to a sheltered spot on fine days, bringing them back in at nights. After about a week, depending on the weather, the seedlings can be left out, as long as you protect them if the weather turns harsh.

If you have a cold frame or cloches, then use these for hardening off, gradually opening the lids or removing the cloches for longer periods until the seedlings are strong enough to plant out (see pages 26–9).

As soon as the seedlings are hardened off it is time to plant them out. Dig a hole deep enough to allow the seedling to sit slightly deeper than it was in the seed tray or pot. As you prise it out of the compost be very careful not to damage its rootball [C]. Place it in the hole, firm in carefully and water well.

Crop Rotation

Crop rotation plans are not just schemes drawn up by professionals to complicate vegetable growing and alienate the amateur. There is scientific logic behind the method, and once you have gone to the trouble of drawing up a plan and actually applied it, you will find that your crops are healthier and less troubled by pests and diseases, and also that your yields are up.

Put simply, the theory is that each crop, or sometimes each family of plants, are prone to particular diseases and have particular pests that prey on them. By moving the crops from bed to bed you ensure that these do not get the chance to establish a strong foothold and also that the soil gets a chance to replenish itself. In addition, by dividing vegetables up into groups with similar needs, you will find it easier to satisfy these requirements. For example, some vegetables, such as cabbages, like rich ground while others, such as carrots, prefer poorer soil. It makes sense, therefore, to group these plants together in separate beds where their needs can best be catered for.

Vegetables can be divided into three or four main groups according to the design of your kitchen

garden. To keep matters simple, choose a plan which operates over the same number of years as you have beds. So if you have a four-bed kitchen garden, as on page 12, the plan should run for four years before it repeats itself, and so on.

Depending upon the type of crops you intend to grow and how much space you have, you may also want to keep one permanent bed for herbs or perennial vegetables.

A FOUR-YEAR CROP ROTATION PLAN

Year 1: Plant your four beds out in designated groups, as described below

| 1 | 2 | 3 | 4 |

Year 2: Rotate the contents of the four beds in the sequence shown

| 4 | 1 | 2 | 3 |

Year 3: Once again, rotate the contents of the four separate beds, as shown

| 3 | 4 | 1 | 2 |

Year 4: In the final year, rotate the positions of the plant groups one last time

| 2 | 3 | 4 | 1 |

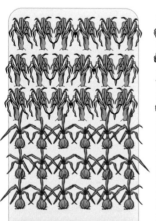

BED 1: ALLIUMS

Vegetables:
Bulb onion; shallot; garlic; spring onion; pickling onion; Welsh onion; leek; Japanese bunching onion

Care:
Double digging; mixing manure in soil; application of blood, fish and bonemeal

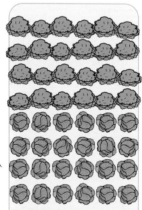

BED 2: BRASSICAS

Vegetables:
Cabbage; Chinese cabbage; Brussels sprout; cauliflower; kale; calabrese; broccoli

Care:
Single digging; mixing manure in soil; application of blood, fish and bonemeal

BED 3: LEGUMES

Vegetables:
Broad bean; French bean; Lima bean; pea; runner beans; yard long bean; asparagus pea

Care:
Single digging; mixing lime in soil; application of blood, fish and bonemeal

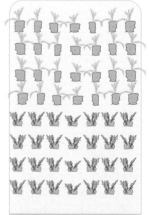

BED 4: ROOTS & TUBERONS

Vegetables:
Beetroot; carrot; parsnip; potatoes; salsify; scorzonera; swede; turnip; sweet potato

Care:
Double digging; liberal application of blood, fish and bonemeal before planting

Tree Fruit

There are quite a few different factors which have to be taken into consideration when deciding on which variety of fruit tree to choose. First, consider your local conditions in terms of weather, average temperature and soil type, and select a type and variety of fruit that will do well in these conditions. Then decide where you are going to grow the tree and how much space is available, as this will determine the ultimate size, the number of trees you can grow and whether the form of the tree should be bush, standard or something more decorative (see pages 36–8). Finally, there is the question of pollination, and it is vital to get this right or the tree simply will not bear any fruit.

Pollination groups

Although some fruit trees are self-fertile, most need to be cross-pollinated in order to bear fruit. With these trees it is pointless just buying one as it will never produce fruit, unless a neighbouring garden contains another specimen. It is therefore essential to buy at least two cultivars of the same tree.

For trees to be cross-pollinated there must be another tree in bloom at the same time nearby. This is why nurseries and growers divide up all fruit trees and their varieties into pollination groups, generally indicated by numbers. These lists tell you if a tree will flower early, in the middle or late on in the season, so you can buy another tree in the same group and be sure of cross-pollination.

Complications arise with some apples, called triploids, which need two pollinators, and some pears, which despite being in the same pollination group are incompatible.

Rootstocks

Most fruit trees on sale are grafted on to a variety of rootstocks which determine their ultimate size and speed of growth. Growing conditions also play a part in the rate of growth, so if the conditions are not ideal then choose a more vigorous rootstock to compensate for these. Use the table below to help select the correct commonly available rootstock for the type of growth you require.

The rootstock grafting point on an Apple 'Lord Lambourne' variety

CHOOSING THE CORRECT ROOTSTOCK

FRUIT	ROOTSTOCK
Very dwarf (up to 1.8m/6ft high approx.)	
Apple	M27
Cherry	Tabel
Dwarf (up to 2.5–3m/8–10ft approx)	
Apple	M9
Pear	Quince C
Cherry	Gisela 5
Plum	Pixy
Gage	Pixy
Damson	Pixy
Peaches	Pixy
Semi dwarf (up to 3–4.5m/10–15ft high approx)	
Apple	M26
Cherry	Damil
Semi vigorous (up to 3.5–4.8m/12–16ft approx)	
Apple	MM106
Pear	Quince A
Plum	St Julien A
Gage	St Julien A
Damson	St Julien A
Peach	St Julien A
Nectarine	St Julien A
Apricot	St Julien A
Cherry	Colt
Vigorous (up to 4.5–6m/15–20ft high approx)	
Apples	MM111
Peaches	Brompton
Nectarine	Brompton
Plum	Brompton
Cherry	Malling F12/1

Buying a tree

Once you have chosen what fruit you want to grow, and have selected a rootstock and variety – taking into account the pollination groups – then the next decision you will need to make is whether to buy container-grown or bare-rooted trees.

You can buy bare-rooted trees at a fraction of the cost of container-grown trees and they are often a better choice in that they are less likely to have been sitting in a nursery or garden centre getting pot-bound. However, bare-rooted trees should only be planted between late autumn and early spring when the roots are dormant, while container-grown trees can be planted all year round, as long as the soil is not waterlogged or frozen.

Trees are sold at differing levels of maturity, ranging from maiden whip trees with just one leader, and one-year-old feathered maidens with laterals (side shoots), to two- and three-year-old trees. Two-year-old trees are the best choice for most gardeners as they fruit faster and are more easily trained than the maiden trees. They have basically been given a good start at the nursery. Three-year-old trees may be hard to establish and are generally much more expensive, precisely because they will have received longer care at the nursery they come from.

Do not simply buy the first tree you see as it is vital to get a healthy specimen. There are various signs which will indicate whether the tree is a good choice. On a bare-rooted tree look for a straight, strong main stem, a well-developed root system growing in all directions, a good clean root graft and three to five evenly spaced branches.

Check container-grown trees over for any signs of pests and diseases; the tree should have a good clean root graft and there should not be any thick roots growing through the base of the containers. As with all container-grown trees and plants, the surface of the compost should be weed-free and the rootball should not move when you lift the tree.

Planting fruit trees

As with herbs and vegetables the ideal site for your fruit trees should be sunny and sheltered, with well drained, fertile soil, tending to be more acidic rather than alkaline. Remember there is always the option of training trees against walls or along wires – you don't just have to grow free-standing trees.

Before planting it is important to prevent the tree's roots from drying out and protect them from frost damage. So if there is a delay between buying and planting, then heel in the tree somewhere in the garden. This involves temporarily planting it in a trench, at an angle in order to protect the trunk, and covering it over with light soil which should be kept moist.

Water well before planting; if necessary soak the roots in a bucket for a couple of hours. With container-grown trees you may find the roots are growing in a spiral around the rootball. If this is the case then gently tease them out and cut back any damaged roots to about 30cm (1ft).

Planting a fruit tree:
Prepare the ground by digging it over thoroughly and incorporating plenty of well-rotted organic material and fertilizer, such as bonemeal, into the soil (see pages 18–9).

Dig a hole large enough to give the roots plenty of space and position the tree so that the graft point is 5–8cm (2–3in) above the soil level. Spread out the roots and check the hole is level and no deeper than the level it was planted in the nursery [A].

A

B

C

D

Fill immediately around the roots, first with compost and fertilizer then backfill with earth [B]. Firm in [C] and build the soil up to form a slight basin around the trunk, which will help to retain water. Secure the tree to a short stake with a collar-type tree tie [D].

Prune each branch of bush and half-standard trees back by a third of the previous season's growth (see pages 34–5).

Water thoroughly, and carry on watering during subsequent dry periods. Ensure the area around the tree is kept weed-free.

Apple trees can be trained into interesting – and useful – shapes

Soft Fruit

Soft fruit can be divided into two groups – bush or cane – with strawberries being the exception to this as they are herbaceous. The cane fruits include raspberries, blackberries and all the hybrid berries, such as loganberries and tayberries. The bush fruit consist of gooseberries and all the currants (black, red and white). The ideal site for all soft fruit is sheltered from strong winds, in full sunshine – although most will manage in light shade – with fertile, well drained, but not dry, soil.

Unlike tree fruit, virtually all soft fruit is self-fertile, so pollination need not be a worry. However, soft fruit does demand more attention in terms of feeding and pruning if you are to get a good harvest. If you look after your soft fruit bushes, however, they should last for a good ten years and provide as many harvests.

Planting soft fruit and canes

As with buying fruit trees it is important to go to a reputable nursery or garden centre and to look for healthy plants with a well developed root system. Check container-grown plants are not pot-bound and that they do not lift out of the container when you pick them up by the stem, which is a sure sign that they have been allowed to dry out.

Bush and cane soft fruit should be planted in the same way as fruit trees, but it is even more important to mulch around the base of the plants to minimize evaporation, as soft fruit need soil with a high moisture content. The mulch should be about 5cm (2in) deep and extend for 1m (3ft) from the stems. Make sure it does not actually touch the stem, as this can cause rotting.

Planting times vary between autumn and winter so check with each individual plant entry, although strawberries are again the exception, as they should be planted in the summer.

A good harvest of colourful berries is hard to beat

Growing Under Cover

Growing vegetables under cover, whether under glass or plastic, allows gardeners to extend both their repertoire of fruit and vegetables and the length of the season in which they can be grown. Yields are generally higher under cover and the quality better. Wind and storms need not be a worry and pests, such as rabbits, birds, cabbage root fly and carrot fly, can be easily excluded, while others such as whitefly and red spider mite can be more effectively controlled.

Where space is a problem, low mini polytunnels, cold frames, lantern lights and cloches – even upturned plastic bottles sliced in half – can perform part of the greenhouse's functions. Albeit on a much smaller scale, they will still be able to heat up the soil and offer light and warmth, plus protection from extremes of weather and many pests.

Lemon trees are excellent grown in a container under cover

Greenhouses

Choosing a greenhouse

There is a bewildering array of greenhouses on the market, and it can be quite difficult to decide which to choose. The starting point must be size. How much space do you have and how much do you want to grow?

Next decide upon the material for the frame. The two basic types are wood and aluminium, each with their advantages and disadvantages. Wood looks lovely, there will be fewer problems with condensation and it holds heat well; however, the frame will be bulkier than aluminium, therefore cutting down on the light, and, most important of all, it will require regular maintenance.

Aluminium is less attractive and gets quite cold, creating damp problems; however, it is relatively maintenance free, making it the popular choice of most amateur gardeners. Whatever material you decide upon, make sure the greenhouse has adequate ventilation to prevent it becoming damp, which is just the sort of environment that will encourage all sorts of pests and diseases to breed.

Heating the greenhouse

As far as heating is concerned, you could decide to simply rely on the sun's heat, which would be sufficient for basic crops, such as salad and carrots. Alternatively, you could maintain a hot greenhouse, which is classified as one where the temperature in winter stays above 16°C (61°F), although the cost of maintaining such heat could be prohibitive.

The best option is to go for a warm, rather than hot, greenhouse. In a warm greenhouse the temperature on a winter's night should not fall below 8°C (45°F), and this can be managed by installing electric or oil heaters. The portable paraffin type of oil heaters are the cheapest option. Insulating the greenhouse with rolls of bubble wrap will also help enormously.

Useful extras include blinds, automatic ventilators and a watering system.

> **TIP**
>
> You should think carefully about how to organize the contents of your greenhouse. Some crops will require more shade than others, and there will be those that need better ventilation. Many fruits and vegetables will also have different watering requirements. Much depends on the time of year, but a greenhouse will need consistent management.

Planning the space

The classic layout of a greenhouse consists of two beds and a concrete path running between them, with some 'staging' along one side in the form of benches. These should be at an appropriate height for working and be near the light to promote growth, making it ideal for trays of seedlings. Staging provides extra storage space and keeping it to one side allows you to grow taller crops on the other side. Staging that can be dismantled and moved provides even more flexibility.

What to grow

A huge variety of crops can be grown in a greenhouse, as the warmer conditions provide the opportunity to grow more tender genera of fruit, herbs and vegetables, such as melons and grapes, basil and aubergine and peppers. A greenhouse also allows you to grow a wide range of salad crops and vegetables throughout the winter. Good candidates include asparagus, beans, carrots, cauliflower, chicory, peas, potatoes, radishes, rhubarb and tomatoes.

Polytunnels

Plastic polytunnels provide many of the advantages of a greenhouse, are a fraction of the price and can be erected in a couple of hours and then taken down and stored when not required – although they can be a bit of an eyesore.

However, if you have the space in your garden then they will enable you to produce crops a good six weeks ahead of those grown in the open, which means you will be able to raise two crops a year instead of one. Low polytunnels are particularly useful as protection for crops prone to flying pests, birds and carrot flies. These can be homemade with a length of tough polythene, galvanised wire hoops and some twine and posts.

Cold Frames

The basic construction of a cold frame consists of a box with wooden or brick sides, covered over with a glass or plastic lid, often sloping. You can make a cold frame yourself quite easily by simply placing a sheet of plastic over a wooden box.

Cold frames are useful for hardening off greenhouse-grown plants and raising seedlings. They can also be used for growing tender plants, such as aubergines, peppers, melons and cucumbers, as well as protecting hardier crops.

To work to their full capacity, they should be put in a sheltered place where they get maximum exposure to the sun. On hot days prop the lid open to prevent overheating, while during cold, frosty spells spread old carpet, sacking or newspaper over the top as insulation.

Cloches & Lights

Cloches and lantern lights are simple plastic or glass tents, which are smaller than cold frames and portable, and as such are used to protect plants that are grown out. A glass cloche will hold the heat better than plastic, and being heavier it is less prone to being blown away. Glass is also less likely to become brittle and crack, although it is generally more delicate to handle.

Cold frames are ideal for hardening off young plants or raising seedlings

A modern cloche protects this young cauliflower plant

Conservatories

Conservatories have become very fashionable over the past couple of decades. However, the word 'conservatory' is slightly misleading. Modern conservatories bear little relationship to the ones that were attached to houses in the 19th and turn of the 20th century. They tend to be little more than an additional room, albeit a glass one, and have scarcely any ventilation, making them hot in the summer and cold in the winter, unless the householder has invested in blinds, heating and air conditioning.

Old-fashioned conservatories would have had a whole range of windows which could be opened in different combinations to bring air into every corner, as well as tiled floors with channels and drains, allowing the whole place to be sprayed and washed down.

However, with care it is possible to grow vines, figs and citrus fruit in modern conservatories. Vines should be grown with their roots planted outside the building in the cold, and their foliage trained inside. Citrus fruit are best grown in containers which can be moved outside in the summer, then back into the warmth in the winter.

Cloches and lights are useful for drying out and warming soil prior to planting, and will protect seedlings and hasten their growth. They will also harden off greenhouse-grown plants and, for older plants, they offer protection against pests, will speed up the ripening process and extend the growing season. They can even be used to protect some crops throughout winter.

One word of caution, however. Remember, when you start crops off under cloches they will be more delicate than their unprotected neighbours, so suddenly removing the cloche will be quite a shock. Instead, gradually acclimatise them to external conditions by only taking off the cloche during the daytime and replacing it at night.

Other Forms of Protection

Horticultural fleece and even a humble sheet of plastic film will also help out the kitchen gardener by warming and drying out soil, thereby protecting plants from extremes of cold and also pests.

Horticultural fleece operates differently from plastic as it allows light, air and water to pass through it, enabling plants to breathe. It is also lighter than plastic. Given all these characteristics it can be left on top of the crops as they mature, keeping off many pests and preventing wind damage.

Horticultural fleece should be wrapped around vulnerable plants to protect them from frost

Hotbeds

An ingenious method of providing warmth for tender plants, without the need for any elaborate electric heating cables, is to make a 'hotbed', which uses fresh horse manure to warm plant roots. As the manure rots down it gives off heat which is then trapped by the overhead frame.

In the 19th century, few large gardens would have been without a hotbed, which enabled the gardener to grow exotic fruit and vegetables which would otherwise not have survived one winter, let alone provided a crop.

> **TIP**
>
> Raised beds not only make it easier for the less able gardener, but they act in the same way as a hotbed, providing warmth and protection for plants. If you raise one side of the bed to be sloping towards the direction of the sun, this will warm the bed even more efficiently and promote early plant growth

To make your own hotbed:
Dig out a shallow hole in the ground then pile a large amount of fresh manure into it and leave it for about five days to allow heat to build up. You may need to turn the pile and sprinkle it with water if the weather is hot – if it dries out, the decomposition will slow down. The pile

Conservatories are ideal for growing all kinds of tender fruit and exotic vegetables

Raised beds can act like a hotbed as they warm up faster in spring

should not be too small or it will never be able to build up enough heat – four wheel-barrow loads should be sufficient to make a good-sized pile.

After about five days, when it should be really hot, flatten it as much as possible and cover it with a layer of loam to a minimum depth of 7.5cm (3in). This will ensure an even and regular rate of decomposition, and corresponding heat output.

Place a frame over the loam-topped manure to retain the heat. The frame should have a lid which can be opened if the temperature rises too high. Plants can be grown in the loam, while seeds should be sown in trays and placed on top.

Care & Maintenance

With all plants and trees the follow-on care is just as important as the initial effort. Like children, plants demand continuing attention, which they will then, hopefully, repay in the form of a bumper harvest.

All living things need food and water to stay alive, however herbs, vegetables and fruit need to do more than just survive. If we are to harvest crops from them they have to be in peak condition, and to be in peak condition they need just the right amount of water, food and ongoing maintenance.

If you have worked hard on the preparation of your kitchen garden – by digging in plenty of organic matter to improve the soil's structure, removed all traces of perennial weeds and ensured that your plants are sheltered from winds – then the job of looking after them once they are growing will be so much easier.

The plants will be healthy, well fed and ready to put down deep roots, and they will not be competing for water and nutrients with weeds. However, it is vital at this stage to monitor your plants continually for any signs of ill health or attacks by pests. Basic good husbandry, such as keeping weeds down and removing any debris which could harbour pests and diseases, is also important.

Herbs, however, are the exception which proves the rule, as once they have become established they thrive on neglect. Apart from a trim in the spring and summer to tidy them up and encourage new growth, they can be left alone until winter when the tender herbs need to be protected from frost.

Watering

The amount of water your plants require depends upon weather and soil conditions, as well as the health of the individual plant. Young plants and seedlings need frequent light watering. Try to ensure that they get a good soak every few days – once plants are mature, frequent light watering simply encourages their roots to stay near the surface rather than growing deep down into the ground.

Leafy salad crops will need extra water in dry periods to prevent them from running to seed, while the fruiting vegetables need more attention in terms of watering when their flowers appear and when the fruits and pods are growing.

TIP

To find out where to apply fertilizer to the ground around a fruit tree, tie a string to its trunk, extend the string to the full reach of the branches then rotate it around the tree marking out a circle. The roots of the tree will fall within this circle, so this is where you should apply the fertilizer.

Feeding

Good soil preparation will go a long way towards ensuring your plants have enough nutrients. Plants growing in soil that has had a large amount of organic manure dug into it for several years should not need extra feeding. However, the process of building up soil fertility can take a while to establish and in the meantime you may find it necessary to apply organic or chemical fertilizers to aid crop growth.

Most fruit, vegetables and herbs will benefit from an application of fertilizer feed at the beginning of the growing season, usually in late spring. Throughout the growing season look out for plants showing signs of a particular nutrient deficiency, such as a lack of potassium or nitrate (see pages 166–9), and feed with a fertilizer rich in that particular nutrient. With fruit trees, wait until they reach flowering age before feeding and take care not to overfeed or you will promote leaf growth at the expense of fruit yields.

Use liquid feeds to supplement organic manure

Mulching

To maintain soil fertility, it is vital to apply a nutrient-rich mulch every year. Mulch is the name given to various materials that are spread on top of the soil primarily to conserve moisture, keep down annual weeds and add nutrients. Mulching also protects the soil from heavy rain, which could wash it away or cause capping, and helps to prevent the soil from becoming too warm in summer and too cool in winter.

Mulching in early spring enables the soil to maintain moisture as well as keeping down annual weeds, and will provide a boost of nutrients. Suitable materials include garden and mushroom compost, seaweed, manure, grass cuttings and leafmould. Covering the ground with black polythene is an effective means of retaining moisture and keeping down weeds, but it obviously does not improve soil fertility so should be combined with digging in manure or compost. Avoid bark chippings or wood shavings, unless they are used to cover over polythene, as these have no nutritional value and, because they are unrotted, will use up nitrogen from the soil as they rot down.

> ## TIP
> Soft fruits particularly like a mulch of well-rotted farmyard manure, and all fruit requires a feed in winter in the form of top dressing. This operation simply involves replacing the top layer of compost (roughly 2.5cm/1in) with fresh compost. Your local riding stables will have an abundance of fresh manure!

The layer of mulch should be a minimum of 5–10cm (2–4in) thick to be an effective barrier against weeds and if the aim is to conserve moisture it should be spread when the soil is dry, ideally after it has had a good soak. Apply once a year in spring, although very free-draining soil will need another application in the autumn. The mulch will gradually disappear as it is dragged down by earth worms – this action releases the nutrients and also helps improve the soil structure.

Compost

Compost is a wonderfully dark, rich, sweet-smelling crumbly substance which you can easily make yourself from organic household and garden waste. When compost is dug into the soil or spread on top as a mulch, it adds water-retaining humus and nitrogen, which are vital for the well-being of plants.

Traditional compost heaps

Compost heaps work well in large gardens which produce a lot of waste. However, completely open heaps are untidy and not very efficient as the material at the edges does not compost at the same rate as the material in the middle, which means you need to turn the heap regularly. Cover the heap with a sheet of polythene or old carpet to keep off heavy rain, but do not allow it to dry out in the summer.

Ready-made compost bins

There are numerous ready-made plastic and metal bins on the market. These tend to be fully enclosed, which means that the composted material will heat up evenly and rot down quickly. The bins are also designed to make it easy to get at the composted material from the bottom. The disadvantage of such bins is that they may not be big enough to hold the amount of material a large garden can produce.

Making compost

To ensure there is enough material to heat up sufficiently, the heap or bin must be a minimum of 90cm (3ft) square by 1.2m (4ft) high. Start with a thick base of rough, bulky material, such as straw or shredded prunings, then sprinkle with either sulphate of ammonia (a dessertspoon per sq m/yd), a bought compost activator or fresh animal manure to speed up decomposition. Continue building up the heap in 15cm (6in) layers, adding a little lime to alternate layers if you wish in order to neutralize the acidity of the compost.

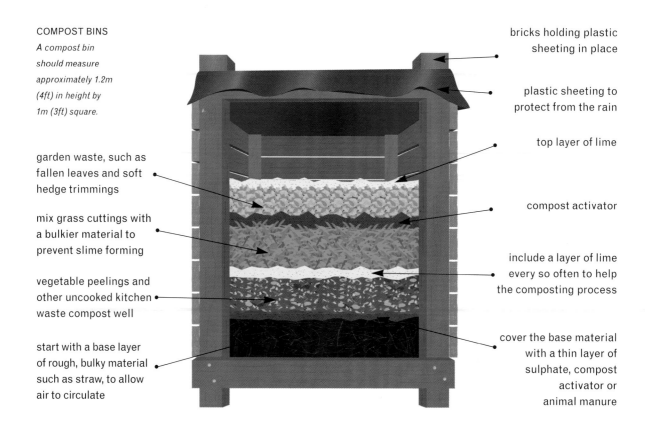

COMPOST BINS
A compost bin should measure approximately 1.2m (4ft) in height by 1m (3ft) square.

garden waste, such as fallen leaves and soft hedge trimmings

mix grass cuttings with a bulkier material to prevent slime forming

vegetable peelings and other uncooked kitchen waste compost well

start with a base layer of rough, bulky material such as straw, to allow air to circulate

bricks holding plastic sheeting in place

plastic sheeting to protect from the rain

top layer of lime

compost activator

include a layer of lime every so often to help the composting process

cover the base material with a thin layer of sulphate, compost activator or animal manure

Virtually any organic material can be composted. Suitable household waste includes teabags, peelings, eggshells, shredded newspaper, even old rags. Garden waste such as dead flowers and leaves, bolted vegetables and old bedding plants, grass clippings, soft prunings, hedge trimmings and weeds (before they have set seed) are ideal. For best results, avoid adding too much of any one thing at a time, for example too many grass clippings may result in a smelly, black slime.

Do not use cooked food or anything greasy as this will attract vermin, similarly destroy any parts of diseased plants, seed bearing annual weeds, or the roots of perennial weeds, such as ground elder and couch grass. These are so tough that they can survive

the composting process and you will end up spreading your problems. Anything too woody will not compost unless shredded.

Wormeries

These differ from ready-made compost bins in that they rely on a colony of worms (tiger or brandling worms) to produce the compost. The worms are put in a specially-designed worm bin on to a layer of material which has already rotted down, and then given fresh supplies of finely chopped household scraps every few days. The bins have a tray to collect liquid which can be drained off, watered down then used for plant food, and the compost which results is wonderfully rich.

Leaf mould

Leaf mould is a type of compost made from rotted down leaves, which has a crumbly texture and a high nutritional value, making it ideal for use as a soil conditioner or as a seed and potting compost.

Leaf mould is different from ordinary compost because the leaves rot down by means of cool fungal decay (a slower process), while compost heats up and

TIP

If space allows, it is a good idea to keep two compost heaps or bins on the go at the same time. This will ensure a constant supply of compost, as material can be rotting down in one bin while you are still filling up the other. It is highly likely, once you start composting, that you'll find you need two bins anyway!

the matter is then broken down by bacteria. This is because the different elements in a compost heap tend to contain a great deal of nitrogen, while leaves do not.

To make leaf mould, pile large amounts of fallen leaves in a leaf bin – a wire cage made from a roll of chicken wire and four wooden posts. Smaller amounts can be put in sealed, black plastic sacks with holes punched in them. The leaves may take up to a year to rot down. To speed things up, shred the leaves before gathering them and apply a leaf compost activator, then make regular checks to ensure the leaves do not dry out.

Well-rotted leaf mould is ideal as a soil conditioner

Protecting Plants

All herbs, vegetables and fruit will attract pests, but which particular pests will vary according to the plant. For example, the leafy herbs and vegetables are particularly attractive to slugs and snails, while birds will attack fruit, eating fruiting buds in winter and fruit in the summer and autumn.

Insects

If insects are the problem then you can avoid using chemical sprays by companion planting. This is a technique whereby plants are grown side by side, with one plant acting as either a deterrent or a lure. For example, if you grow onions with carrots, the strong smell of the onions swamps the delicate smell of the carrots, putting off carrot fly. Nasturtiums are used as a lure for aphids, while the roots of French marigold release an insecticidal material which will deter white fly on neighbouring plants.

Alternatively you could grow a plant that attracts beneficial insects which prey on particular pests, next to a plant which suffers badly from those same pests. Poached egg plant and pot marigold, for example, attract hover flies, which eat aphids.

Birds

Soft fruits are especially prone to attack by birds, who not only go for the ripe fruit but for the flower which will eventually form the fruit. The only real solution to this is to build a cage and grow the fruit inside it. This may seem like a lot of extra work, but a well-built, walk-in cage will last for years and, considering the time and effort that have to be put into soft fruit in order to get a harvest, it is well worth the extra effort.

Building a cage may be the only solution to protect your figs or other soft fruit from birds

Fruit cages can be constructed to fit the shape and area of your garden

Wind and frost

The dangers for plants are not confined to living creatures. Extremes of weather, such as high winds and frost, will kill tender plants and destroy fruit crops. Fast-growing weeds will also remove valuable nutrients from the soil and crowd out delicate herbs and vegetables.

The best protection against high winds is to erect a permeable barrier which will filter the wind, reducing its force. You can protect herbs, vegetables and fruit against frost with lightweight horticultural fleece, although if you have none to hand anything that will trap warm air around the plant, such as plastic bubble wrap or newspaper, will work just as well.

General Care for Fruit Trees

Thinning fruit

A branch laden with fruit may look good, however if you do not thin them out you will end up with a large amount of small, poor quality fruit, instead of a slightly smaller number of large, tasty fruit.

When thinning fruit, first remove any that are mis-shapen or unhealthy-looking, then thin so that the remainder have plenty of space to grow. This distance will vary according to the fruit, but for apples and pears about 5–8cm (2–3in) is ideal.

Supporting branches

If you have a bumper harvest you may need to support your tree's branches to prevent them being weighed down to the point were they may be damaged.

Large trees need supporting from below – old branches with a V-shaped crook at one end make excellent props – while the branches of smaller trees can be held up by string tied to a central stick lashed to the leader.

Pruning & Training Fruit: General

Both tree and soft fruit require an extra element of care that vegetables do not – they need to be pruned and trained on an ongoing basis. This pruning and training will help to produce high yields of quality fruit by encouraging an open structure and balanced growth, and also allows the gardener to produce numerous ornamental shapes, some more restricted and formal than others.

Pruning may seem daunting, but bear in mind it is almost impossible to do real harm to a tree by over-pruning. The tree will simply produce more strong, fresh growth. The worst that can happen is that the tree puts all its energy into growing wood rather than the buds which would eventually turn into fruit.

Pruning will help produce higher yields of fruit

Train fruit trees for screening, ornamental shapes and improved yields

numerous different forms, from the more common standards and half standards to the highly decorative espaliers and cordons.

As a rough guide, if the aim is to create a natural bush and half standard form, then these trees should be pruned by a third of the previous season's growth after planting. If you are intending to train your trees into fans or espaliers then you should cut them back by about half of the previous season's growth, depending on their size and the position of the supporting wires. By carrying out this formative pruning, you are encouraging the tree to produce fresh growth, while alleviating the planting stress and helping it to establish itself quickly.

Tying in and festooning

Stone fruit, such as plums, damsons, gages and peaches, respond better to tying in as a method of training, rather than pruning. In fact, for best results in terms of getting early crops of stone fruit, keep pruning to a minimum until they have fruited for several years.

Another method of encouraging early fruit production is to festoon trees, which means tying down each branch to pull it below the horizontal. Any shoots growing up from the tied down branches can either be tied down themselves or spur-pruned in mid-summer to 7.5–10cm (3–4in). This will encourage extra fruit buds to form.

General tips

Keep your tools sharp and clean as an uneven, jagged cut can encourage disease. Always cut above an outward-growing bud and leave a little space above the bud.

Spur pruning, which involves cutting all the season's growth back down to two or three buds, is best carried out for the first time in mid-summer. This will allow fruit buds to form and there will be no danger that the regrowth will shade any ripening fruit. After this the tree can be spur pruned again during the winter.

Summer and winter pruning

It is important to understand the basic differences between summer and winter pruning. Winter is the time to tidy up and keep the tree in shape by removing any excess growth, as well as cutting away and destroying dead or diseased parts. If you prune in the summer, this stimulates the growth of fruit buds for the next year and will open up the tree to sunlight, thereby helping the fruit to ripen.

Mid- and late summer is the best time to prune all fruit trained into formal shapes (such as cordons, fans and espaliers), because at that time the shoots are flexible and can be bent without danger of snapping.

Early pruning

To achieve productive, attractive trees it is important to pay particular attention to maintenance during their early years, when the branches are still very flexible. This is the time when you can prune and train them into

Staking in a newly planted tree is vital for the tree to get a good head start

Pruning To Create Specific Forms

The choice of form is very wide, ranging from the looser look of the bush, half standard and standard to the more formal style of the espalier, fan, cordon and double or multiple cordon. Use the table below as a guide to which style is suitable for which fruit.

Bushes, half standard and standard

Being closest to the natural shape of the trees these forms are quite easy to achieve and to maintain. They are especially suited to larger gardens, as they take up more space than all the other forms listed below. Following their initial pruning after planting, the trees

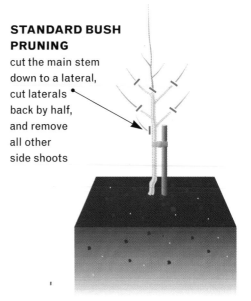

DIFFERENT FRUIT FORMS	
Form	**Suitable for**
Patio bush	Apples, peaches, nectarines and cherries
Dwarf bush	Apples, pears, cherries, gooseberries, figs and currants
Semi-dwarf bush	Apples, pears, plums, gages, gooseberries and damsons
Bush half-standard	Apples, pears, plums, gages, gooseberries, damsons and cherries
Standard	Apples, pears, plums, gages, damsons and cherries
Cordon	Apples, pears, red and white currents, vines and gooseberry
Double/multiple cordon	Apples, pears, red and white currents, vines and gooseberry
Mini cordon	Apples
Festooned bush	Apples, pears, plums, gages, damsons and cherries
Espalier	Apples and pears
Stepover	Apples and pears
Fan	Apples, pears, plums, gages, damsons, peaches, nectarines, apricots, figs, cherries and blackberries

should be left for a couple of seasons, then once they start to produce crops all the congested branches should be removed.

If you are aiming for an open-centred bush shape, then cut the leader (main stem) right down to a lateral (side shoot) as low as 75cm (2½ft) off the ground, making sure there are some well-spaced laterals beneath – ideally two on either side of the leader. These laterals should then be cut back by half, and all other shoots removed completely.

Cordons – single, double and multiple

A cordon is a single stem with numerous fruiting spurs, which can either be trained to grow at an angle or as a simple upright. Double and multiple cordons are similar to the single version apart from the fact that they have more stems, all of which are parallel.

This is a relatively easy form to achieve yet one that can be used to great effect. For example, you can create an apple tunnel by training cordons over a series of strong arches, and a series of cordons set side-by-side against a wall is extremely decorative, as well as being highly productive in a small space.

To train and prune a tree into a cordon, you will first need to tie the leader to a strong stake as soon as it is planted. The stake should be set at a 45° angle if you want the tree to grow on the diagonal. This is most easily achieved if the stake is itself tied to a series of horizontal, parallel wires. Alternatively, cordons can be trained against a wall or fence. After this initial training,

SINGLE CORDON
train the leader at a 45° angle and prune the laterals back close to the main stem

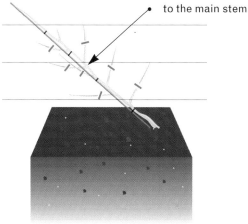

Fan

The fan form, the shape of which is exactly described by its name, is especially suited to stone fruit as it relies heavily on training rather than pruning, which they prefer.

Plant feathered maidens (a leader with some laterals) and cut back the previous season's growth by a half. At the same time remove all laterals apart from a couple on each side of the leader about 30cm (12in) above the ground and level with the lowest tier of supporting wire. These laterals should ideally be about 38cm (15in) long. Tie the laterals on to angled canes. The following summer allow four strong side shoots on each of these laterals to grow. The position of these shoots is vital to the final shape, so choose two shots pointing up from the lateral, one pointing down, and one at the tip. As they develop, tie them onto canes to keep them straight.

FAN
tie two main laterals on to angled canes, then the following summer select four strong shoots to produce the basic shape

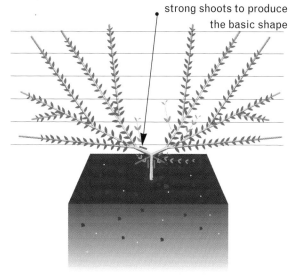

the aim is to prune the tree to produce a good number of spurs (little branches carrying fruit buds), rather than allowing it to develop strong laterals.

A double cordon is produced by cutting back the leader in winter to two strong buds a short distance of no more than 30cm (12in) above the ground. Two new main shoots are then produced the following year, which are first tied on to angled canes and then, as they grow, tied on to further vertical canes to produce the distinctive double cordon shape of two parallel branches.

DOUBLE CORDON
prune the leader back to two main buds, then tie in the stems with angled and vertical canes

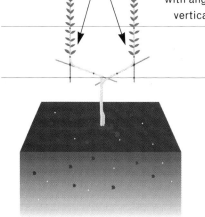

The aim now is to allow the new sideshoots to develop four sideshoots of their own, so forming the fan shape. Once you have developed the fan shape, all you need to do is pinch out any new shoots to prevent the space becoming over-crowded.

With soft fruit, such as blackberries, the newly planted canes should be kept in a bunch until the first autumn, when you should cut out all the fruited canes and then tie the new growth to the horizontal wires in a fan shape.

Espaliers

Espaliers consist of a single vertical main stem with pairs of evenly-spaced branches growing out from it at right angles, forming horizontal tiers. To form an espalier, plant a maiden tree then prune it back to a strong bud about 5cm (2in) above the lowest training wire. As the leader grows keep it tied against a vertical cane, and as the laterals develop tie them onto angled canes. Cut back any other side shoots. In late autumn tie the two angled laterals to the lowest wire, making the first tier of the espalier. The next summer repeat the process with the next tier of laterals until the tree is as tall as required.

ESPALIER

tie the angled laterals to the lowest wire, to form the first tier

Hardwood cuttings from a goosebery bush

Propagation

Many plants can be propagated by means of collecting and planting their seeds (for further details, see pages 20–1). To propagate a great many of the perennials, bushes and trees, however, you will need to master a few other techniques – dividing, layering and taking cuttings.

Different fruit, herbs and vegetables require different techniques. Soft fruit bushes, such as gooseberries and blackcurrants, are propagated through cuttings, while herbs, strawberries and cane fruit, such as blackberries, loganberries and the hybrid berries, are more suited to layering. Perennials need to be divided, while fruit trees are usually propagated by grafting.

Dividing

This is the simplest method. Dig up the plant as soon as the foliage has died back in the autumn and divide it in two or as many divisions to give fair sized plants. Some plants produce smaller bulbs or baby plants around the parent plant, which can be removed and planted elsewhere.

Cuttings: hard and soft

To propagate fruit, such as gooseberries, currants, vines and figs, take hardwood cuttings. Cut off a section of new stem in mid-autumn, generally about 30cm (1ft) long, pinch off the lower buds and remove the tip and any foliage. Place the cutting in a pot of light compost or directly into a 15cm (6in) narrow slit in the ground. Leave for at least one year, or two for figs, before transplanting. For softwood cuttings, cut off the growing tips of stems at the start of the summer, roughly 10–20cm (4–8in) long. Remove all but the top leaves and pot up in a light compost.

Layering: tip, mound, runners, suckers

Blackberries, loganberries and the hybrid berries are ideal candidates for tip layering. Place the tip of a stem, face downwards, in a shallow hole then pin it in place and cover with soil. Leave it in situ until the autumn, then you can shear it off from the main plant and replant.

Mound layering is suitable for woody herbs such as rosemary and thyme. Pile up a mound of free-draining soil around the plant in spring and top it up during the summer. New roots will grow on the covered stems, which can then be cut off in the late summer and replanted.

Certain plants spread themselves by sending out runners which take root when the tip touches the ground, such as the strawberry. Propagating these plants involves waiting until the runners are well established then cutting them off the parent plant and replanting them. Other plants, such as raspberries, rely on suckers to spread, and these can be used for propagation in the same way as runners.

Harvesting, Storing & Freezing

While freshly picked fruit, vegetables and herbs have an unequalled flavour, with careful preparation and storage there is no reason why you shouldn't be able to enjoy the results of your labours out of season. The key to success is to select the best of your crop – the younger and more tender the better. Never keep anything that is damaged, and always freeze or prepare for storage immediately after picking as any delay allows decay to set in.

Freezing

While our forebears would have relied mainly on bottling to preserve their produce, we have the advantage of the deep freezer, which has made the whole process relatively painless – we need only collect, bag and freeze.

The success of your freezing will depend on the varieties you grow. Certain cultivars have been specially bred for this purpose, so bear this in mind when buying seed. Pick your crop at a young age when the crops are still tender and bursting with flavour. There is no point in putting effort into preserving crops that are past their best and have become tasteless and tough.

Vegetables can be tray dried – that is, cut out and spread on a tray so that they do not touch, then frozen – before being packed in bags for longer term freezing. However, most vegetables need to be blanched before

Many fruits can be frozen successfully for out of season usage

---

VEGETABLES FOR FREEZING

Sweet corn: choose young, tender cobs. Remove husks and tassels then blanch.
Jerusalem artichokes: scrub, chop and purée.
Broccoli and calabrese: divide into even-sized florets, wash, steam blanch and bag up.
French beans: choose young, small beans, blanch and freeze whole.
Kohl rabi: choose small roots, scrub and freeze whole or purée.
Cabbage: remove the outer leaves and stems, wash and shred, then blanch before sealing in polythene bags.
Turnips: best frozen as a purée.
Asparagus: sort into similar-sized bundles, remove any imperfections, steam blanch then seal in polythene bags.
Carrots: choose small carrots, wash and remove tops, blanch, then seal in polythene bags, can also purée.
Brussels sprouts: select tight, small sprouts and remove the outer leaves, blanch.
Cauliflower: divide into even-sized florets, wash, steam blanch and bag up.
Spinach: trim the stems, wash, steam blanch before freezing.
Peppers: wash, remove stem and seeds, slice then bag.
Aubergines: after washing, slice, sautée, then sort and seal in polythene bags.
Courgettes: wash, slice, sautée then freeze.
Broad beans: choose small beans, shell, blanch and sort into bags of similar size.
Runner beans: after washing, slice into 25mm (1in) lengths, blanch and seal in polythene bags.
Leeks: remove the outer leaves and tops. Wash and bag up.
Swedes: choose small swedes, peel, trim, blanch and bag.
Parsnips: best frozen as a purée.
Tomatoes: freeze whole, with their skins left on. They will retain their flavour well and are ideal for cooking, although not salads.
Peas: choose young, sweet peas, shell, then bag.
Onions: peel and slice.
Squash: slice and lightly sautée before freezing.

---

freezing, as they are low in acid and contain high numbers of enzymes, which the blanching kills off and would otherwise cause them to deteriorate.

For delicate vegetables, blanching involves being lightly steamed. For tougher vegetables, place them in cold, unsalted water, bring to the boil, then skim the top, leave to simmer for a few minutes and drain. Plunge the vegetables into cold water before drying off, and they will seem even fresher when defrosted.

Vegetables also freeze well when boiled and puréed. Those with a high water content, such as courgette and marrow, benefit from being lightly sautéed before freezing.

Root vegetables can be frozen, although they will store for a while left in the ground or in a cool, dry, dark place. While some, such as young, small carrots, can be frozen whole, most benefit from being puréed before freezing.

Soft fruits freeze whole particularly well and hold their flavour, while tree fruits are better puréed before freezing.

Certain herbs, such as mint and basil, will freeze well. Simply pick the leaves and freeze in the quantities you will require in small polythene bags.

Drying

This is one of the most traditional methods of preserving food, possibly practised by our distant ancestors with nuts and roots. Drying fruit and vegetables correctly is something of a balancing act – if you dry them too fast at too high a temperature the fruit will lose nutrients and flavour as well as becoming tough and chewy. But if you dry them too slowly at too low a temperature, you run the risk of allowing micro-organisms to start to breed.

There are three basic methods of drying fruit and vegetables: sun-drying, which requires bright sunshine and a really hot, dry day and so is not suitable for the

FRUITS FOR FREEZING

Apples and pears: peel and cook into a purée then freeze in containers.

Apricots, nectarines, peaches and plums: slice in half, stone, then freeze in a syrup.

Blackberries, hybrid berries and raspberries: spread the berries out on trays and freeze for a couple of hours before packing into bags.

Cranberries, all types of currant, gooseberries, figs and rhubarb: these can be tray frozen, however it is quicker to dry pack them in blocks and freeze. Be sure to strip the currants from their bunches and to top and tail the gooseberries.

Strawberries: these easily disintegrate, so to preserve their shape spread them out on a tray, sprinkle with sugar and freeze for a couple of hours before packing into bags.

climate in some countries; oven-drying, which simply requires a reliable oven, preferably a convection oven; and air drying, which requires an airy, insect-free area.

Oven-drying

Certain fruit and vegetables make better candidates for oven drying than others. For example, any fruit with a high water content, such as melon and citrus, will lose much of their flavour. Similarly, small soft fruits containing lots of pips end up as all hard pips and no fruit when dried.

The time you need depends on what you are drying and how thick the slices or chunks are. As a rough guide, allow two hours for slices of 6mm (¼in), and four times that for 12.5mm (½in) slices. If you are planning to do this on a regular basis then it would be worth buying a commercial dehydrator. If it is only likely to be an occasional event then a regular convection oven is sufficient. It is vital to keep the temperature between 49°–60°C (120°–140°F).

Arrange the fruit and vegetables on trays, making sure that there is enough space on either side of the tray for air to circulate. There must be at least 7.5cm (3in) between the trays. These trays should be rotated and moved around the oven occasionally, so that the fruit and vegetables are evenly exposed to the heat. As soon as the juices have dried up, turn over the fruit and vegetables every now and again to ensure they dry at an even rate.

Air drying

This method is most suited to herbs. Harvest the herbs in the early morning, then discard all but the best and arrange these in bundles tied with string. Hang the bundles upside down in a dark, dry place – an airing cupboard is ideal – until dry. Once dry, strip the leaves from the stalks and store in airtight glass containers. Herbs will retain their taste for longer if kept out of the light.

Preserving in Oil

Infused oils can add a totally unique and unexpected element to dressings and marinades, and are so simple to make that anyone growing herbs could throw one together.

Use a lightly flavoured oil as the base for the more delicate herbs, such as basil, marjoram and thyme. Stronger oils, like olive oil, will fight against the subtle flavours. Olive oil does, however, make a good base for the more robust flavours of garlic, fennel, mint and rosemary.

Fill half a bottle with oil then add whatever ingredients you wish to infuse, adding herbs as sprigs rather than leaves. Cover and leave for at least a couple of weeks.

Olive oil infused with the flavours of garlic, chillies and bay leaves

and remove any imperfections, along with stalks, stones and cores. Fruit with thick or furry skin should be peeled.

You can use plain water for bottling, however a little sugar (or lemon juice, in the case of pears) will improve the fruit's flavour while also helping to preserve its texture and colour. Make sure the fruit is completely covered. The amount of time the water needs to boil varies. Tomatoes need the longest time, 45 minutes, while delicate fruit, such as the currants and berries, only need 15 minutes.

Once the fruit is packed in the sterilized jar, the jar should be placed in a saucepan and covered by at least 25mm (1in) of water and brought to the boil. Bottled fruit will last up to a year if kept in a cool, dark place.

Storing Fruit and Vegetables

Tree fruit

Apples and pears will last for many weeks, depending on the variety, if laid out in wooden boxes stored in a cool place – though not so cool that they are in danger of freezing. Wrapping apples individually in newspaper helps prevent the spread of disease, but pears need such frequent inspection that this would be very time consuming.

Choose a storage area away from anything strong smelling, such as paraffin or creosote, which could spoil their flavour, and keep apples and pears separate. Inspect the fruit regularly, picking out and discarding any that are starting to decay before they ruin the rest of the box.

Root vegetables

Root vegetables will keep for a few months if stored correctly. Beetroot, carrots, parsnips, salsify, scorzonera, swedes, winter radishes and turnips can all be left in the ground until frost threatens, then lifted and placed in boxes of damp sand and put in a cool place. Potatoes can be stored in thick paper sacks, well sealed to exclude all light.

Saving Seed

While many gardeners collect and save flower seed, vegetable seeds often get ignored. However, collecting from plants that produce larger seeds, such as runner beans, is very easy. Simply leave a few beans on the plants as long as possible, removing them when frosts threaten, then pod and choose the healthiest looking seeds to keep.

After this time if you want a clear oil then strain it, otherwise leave the flavourings in the oil – they will not decay and look very attractive.

Preserving in Alcohol

Alcohol is a wonderful agent for preservation, being especially suited to fruit. As the fruit absorbs the alcohol it produces sugar, which gradually causes the surrounding alcohol to turn into a rich, strong, sweet syrup that can be spooned over the fruit when it is served.

As with infused oils, the method could not be easier. Pack a wide-necked jar with layers of different fruit, or just one type, then pour in the alcohol. Sherry, brandy and rum are ideal. Seal and leave for at least three weeks, turning the jar upside down occasionally to ensure the fruit receives equal coverage.

Bottling Fruit

Before the arrival of the deep freezer, every household would have bottled their excess fruit. This method preserves food by heating it to a high temperature while it is sealed inside a sterilized bottling jar. It is vital to use the correct jars, which can be hermetically sealed. Any others will allow harmful bacteria to develop.

Fruit can be bottled in its raw or cooked state and, as with every other form of preservation, it is important to choose only the best of the crop. Thoroughly wash the fruit

Vegetables

Salad Vegetables

It is worth all the effort of designing and preparing a kitchen garden to grow salad vegetables and nothing else. They are fast growers, which provides instant satisfaction, and are undemanding, only requiring watering and the occasional weeding. Salad vegetables can even be protected from pests and diseases without too much difficulty.

Another advantage of salad vegetables is that they are generally hardy, and so with a little thought you can time your sowings to give a year-round harvest.

On top of all of these attributes, salad vegetables are extremely decorative. You can choose from a variety of colours – from the palest yellow through deepest green to the richest red – as well as numerous shapes. For example, compare the tight, pointed tips of chicory with the pretty, soft frills of a loose-leaf lettuce.

Salad vegetables will grow happily among flowers in the main garden or in containers. So even if you only have a windowbox, you can still enjoy the unbeatable taste that comes from home-grown salad – a taste which supermarket salads can only dream of rivalling.

Lettuce

Lactuca sativa

There are four distinct types of lettuce: Loose-leaf; Butterhead (Bib); Iceberg (Crispheads); and Cos (Romaine). They all look quite different and their leaves vary markedly in texture and taste.

Lettuce take anything from between six and 14 weeks to mature, according to the variety. With careful planning, it is possible to harvest lettuce for nine months if you select the right varieties and have the opportunity to grow some under glass.

Lettuce needs a sunny position with rich, free draining but moisture retentive soil. Summer lettuce can be sown sparingly in situ from early spring to mid-summer into finely raked soil. Check that it is warm and moist, and if necessary lightly water the drills before sowing the seeds. If you live in a very warm climate, partial sun would be preferable. Perhaps giving lettuce shade by using strategically placed taller vegetables, such as runner beans or tomatoes, is a good way of providing protection from the hot sun.

The exact spacing between plants will vary according to the variety, but as a rough

soil	Rich, moisture retentive but free draining soil is best for lettuce. Ideal pH of 6.5–7.5
site	A sunny, sheltered site, well protected from strong winds and pollution
watering	Ensure that the soil is thoroughly moist when sowing lettuce. Water frequently during dry spells
feeding	If soil is poor, add nitrogen fertilizer. Otherwise, lettuce will flourish without feeding
general care	Hoe around lettuce to keep weeds down. Otherwise, lettuce are very resilient and require little care
pests and diseases	Aphids, sparrows, slugs and snails can cause problems for lettuce. Keep a close eye out for downy mildew

Lettuce 'Lollo Rossa'

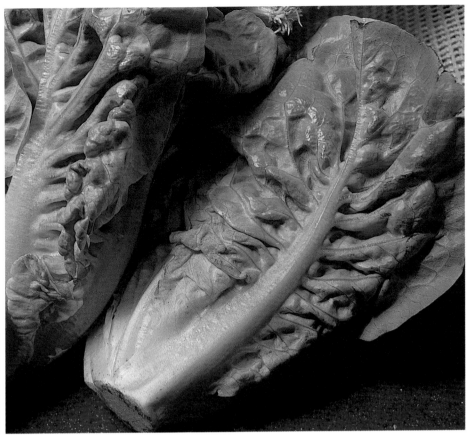

Lettuce Cos 'Little Gem'

guide sow seed 1cm (½in) deep, and space rows for small varieties 15cm (6in) apart, while larger lettuces should be spaced at double that distance. The same figures apply when it comes to thinning.

To ensure a steady supply of lettuce, sow little and often – about every two weeks from early spring to mid-summer should provide a good amount. Some lettuce, such as the hearted varieties, will not last in the ground, so do not sow too many of these at once.

In early autumn sow the spring-maturing varieties. These stay in the soil all winter, ready to grow in spring. Good varieties for autumn sowing are 'Winter Density', 'Valdor' and 'Arctic King'. Sow 'Little Gem' in early autumn for winter use under glass. Some of these spring-maturing varieties cannot cope with summer heat, so may bolt immediately if sown earlier in the year.

Loose-leaf varieties are best for growing as cut and come again as they do not form solid heads. With cut and come again, this method allows you either to cut individual leaves or the whole plant right down, only for it to grow back again to create another crop. Two or three harvests can easily be produced from each sowing.

Sow the seed sparingly in tight rows about 15cm (6in) apart, and start to cut leaves once the plant has reached 5–8cm (2½–4in) high. You can cut the plant down to about 4cm (2in). 'Saladini' is an especially tasty cut and come again variety.

As the weather becomes warmer and the days longer, lettuce begin to mature faster and there is a risk that they will bolt and run to seed. Once this happens, the plants develop a bitter flavour and should be discarded.

All lettuce can be eaten while still small, but some varieties are especially suitable. 'Blush': attractive mini lettuce with pretty, tinged leaves. 'Mini Green': baby Iceberg which grows tight, crunchy heads. 'Crispino': Iceberg lettuce with pale green heart and delicate flavour. 'Spiky': compact Iceberg, with pale green, frilled leaves. Harvest whole or as individual leaves.

To prevent bolting, give the plants plenty of water during dry spells, and if you live in a drought-prone area, look for varieties which are slow to bolt, such as 'Tom Thumb' or 'Oakleaf'.

If your kitchen garden is fairly small and limited for space, a good idea is to grow fast maturing crops such as lettuces, radishes or spinach, before or between other longer term crops such as sweetcorn, tomatoes and brassicas. This will enable you to harvest before the slow crops fill out the plot. This is known as catch cropping and is a very efficient use of space in the garden.

Lettuces can be grown alongside Brussels sprouts and cauliflowers, which enjoy similar high-nitrogen soil conditions. If you have space in an ornamental bed, you could try planting a catch crop of lettuce to fill the space there as well. Don't be afraid to experiment in the garden!

Lettuce, with their succulent leaves, are tempting to many creatures. The main problem for young plants is sparrows, although the plants can be protected with horticultural fleece or chicken wire. The crop can also be protected with cloches and cold frames, which may bring on the harvest by up to three weeks.

Slugs and snails will also attack plants, so set out snail traps (jam jars filled with beer and sunk into the ground up to their necks), between rows. Do not be tempted to use slug pellets, as birds will pick up the corpses and feed them to their young. Slug pellets can also be harmful to household pets, so this is another reason to avoid using them if you own a dog or a cat. Grapefruit skins placed open end down around your crop are more attractive traps; collect the victims in the morning and dispose of them.

The different types of lettuce require different sowing and harvesting times (see also the variety table on the opposite page for further details).

Lettuce Butterhead 'Tom Thumb'

Loose-leaf: Sow outdoors from early spring to mid-summer. Harvest from early summer to mid-autumn. This type is ideal for cut and come again (see page 45).

Cos (Romaine) and semi-cos: For summer crops, sow outdoors from early spring to mid-summer. Harvest from late spring to mid-autumn. Cos lettuce are slower maturing than butterheads, with elongated, sweet leaves.

Butterhead (Bib): Sow from early spring onwards to late summer. Harvest during late spring to mid-autumn. Butterheads are

Lettuce 'Iceberg'

a loose-hearted, fast-maturing lettuce, with soft, delicate leaves.

Iceberg (Crispheads): Sow these from early spring up until mid-summer. Harvest the crop from early summer to mid-autumn. Icebergs are slow-maturing lettuces with good heat resistance and crisp, tasty leaves.

Lettuce mini: All lettuce can be eaten while still small, however some varieties are especially suited to this purpose (for details, see 'Miniature Lettuce' box on previous page).

Lettuce 'Mini Blush'

Type	Variety	Season (Spring–Winter)	Description
[LOOSE-LEAF]	'Salad Bowl'	planting spring; harvest summer–autumn	Abundant, tender fresh green leaves. Copes well with dry periods
	'Oak Leaf'	planting spring; harvest summer–autumn	Tasty, dark red leaves. Slow to bolt and resistant to downy mildew
	'Lollo Bionda'	planting spring; harvest summer–autumn	Pale green, frilly, tasty leaves. Copes well with dry periods
	'Lollo Rossa'	planting spring; harvest summer–autumn	Frilled, red-tinged, leaves. Crisp and delicious
	'Saladini'	planting spring; harvest summer–autumn	Combination of endive, lettuce and chicory. Great as cut and come again
[COS/SEMI-COS]	'Little Gem'	planting spring; harvest summer–autumn	Compact with good resistance to root aphid. Fast maturing, sweet and crispy
	'Lobjoit's Green Cos'	planting spring; harvest summer–autumn	Crisp, dark green leaves. Full of flavour. Excellent winter variety
	'Winter Density'	planting spring; harvest summer–autumn	Crisp semi-cos variety, with lovely flavour. Harvest from spring
[BUTTERHEAD]	'All the Year Round'	planting spring; harvest summer–autumn	Traditional variety with medium-sized heads and good flavour. Long season
	'Tom Thumb'	planting spring; harvest summer	Quick-growing, early variety with a solid, crisp heart. Grows well under cover
	'Sangria'	planting spring; harvest summer–autumn	Decorative variety with pale green leaves tinged with red
	'Valdor'	planting/harvest spring–autumn	Hardy variety with large, tight hearts. Ideal for outdoor sowing under cloches
	'Artic King'	planting/harvest spring–autumn	Hardy variety bred to be sown outdoors in the autumn. Very compact form
[ICEBERG]	'Webb's Wonderful'	planting spring; harvest summer–autumn	Popular variety with large, crisp leaves and succulent flavour
	'Saladin'	planting spring; harvest summer–autumn	Large-headed, crisp variety. Full of flavour
	'Lakeland'	planting spring; harvest summer–autumn	Tight heads with large, dark green leaves. Few outer leaves

planting   harvest

Peppery salads

A common complaint is that salads too often taste bland and uninteresting. However, with the judicious use of this group of strongly flavoured, peppery salad plants, you can ensure that this suggestion is never made at your dining table.

Endive
Cichorium endivia

There are two distinct types of endive – curled and plain leaved – both of which have a succulent, slightly bitter taste. These robust vegetables are excellent grown as autumn and winter salads. Use as cut and come again (see page 45), either harvesting individual leaves or cutting the whole plant down to about 2.5cm (1in) from the ground. Endive requires fertile, well drained soil, preferably sandy, and full sun. Sow: mid-spring to mid-summer. Harvest: early summer to mid-autumn.

Endive 'Palla Rossa'

Mustard & Cress

Mustard (*Brassica hirta*)

Mustard is eaten while still at the seedling stage. Sow: outdoors in spring and autumn every seven to ten days and under cover between autumn and spring. You can also sow all year round in containers lined with damp tissue. Harvest: when 4cm (1⅝in) tall. Will only last two to three cuts.

Garden Cress/Peppercress (*Lepidium sativum*)

Garden cress is similar to mustard in that it is eaten as seedlings and their flavours complement each other so well that they are generally eaten together.

Sow: Outdoors, broadcast the seed then allow four weeks before harvesting. Like mustard, it can also be grown indoors in containers lined with damp tissue.

Watercress (*Rorippa Nasturtium-aquaticum*)

Dark green leaves with a delicious, spicy flavour. Watercress is hardy, so can be grown as a winter salad vegetable. Keep watercress in a shady area. If you have access to running water you will achieve a more succulent crop.

Use rooted cuttings rather than seed. Place a stem in a jar of water and wait until it sprouts roots, then plant cuttings in a 5cm (2in) deep water-saturated soil slit with sand in the bottom. Water well.

soil	Rich, moisture retentive but free draining – apart from watercress, which requires lots of moisture
site	A sunny, sheltered spot, well away from strong winds. Watercress prefers slight shade
watering	Ensure that the soil is moist when sowing these plants. Water frequently during dry spells. Watercress must be kept moist
feeding	Feed well with organic matter before planting. A subsequent feed may help if growth is slow
general care	Hoe all around these plants to keep weeds down. Otherwise, these vegetables are very resilient and require little care
pests and diseases	Slugs and snails can be a problem for all these plants. Rocket is prone to attack from flea beetle

Watercress has a wonderful, tangy flavour

Rocket
Eruca vesicaria

Rocket has a delicious tangy, peppery taste without being bitter. It is a very hardy, vigorous plant which will thrive in most soils, although it prefers a moist, fertile soil. It can be cultivated under cover.

Sow: spring to summer fortnightly in rows 30cm (12in) apart. Cover with a sprinkling of fine soil. Gently firm. Thin to 10cm (4in) apart. Harvest: approx four to five weeks after sowing.

Rocket

Chicory and Radicchio
Cichorium intybus

Among the most decorative salad vegetables, chicory and radicchio, (sometimes called red chicor), have pleasantly crunchy leaves with a very distinctive bitter flavour. They are easy to grow and very hardy. Radicchio is especially useful as a winter salad vegetable.

The best time to harvest is eight to ten weeks after sowing (see table below).

Radicchio 'Palla Rossa'

Corn Salad/Lamb's Lettuce/Mache
Valerianella locusta

Attractive, dark green, shiny leaves with a delicate flavour. Corn salad is very easy to grow and can be grown as a summer or winter crop. Grows well under cover and in containers. Good grown as cut and come again crop.

Sow: late winter to mid-autumn in succession (outdoors mid- to late summer). Harvest: mid-spring to mid-winter.

Corn salad

	SPRING	SUMMER	AUTUMN	WINTER	
Endive 'Chicorées Frisées'	planting	harvest			Very attractive frilled leaves. Also known as 'Moss Curled'
Endive 'Palla Rossa'	planting	harvest			Popular variety with a good, strong flavour
Endive 'Green Curled'	planting	harvest			Succulent, green leaves. Hardy
Garden Cress 'Fine Curled'	planting/harvest		planting/harvest		Tiny, tender leaves. Excellent as an all-year-round crop
Garden Cress 'Extra Double Curled'	planting/harvest		planting/harvest		Delicious garnish. Quick and easy to grow. Good as all-year-round crop
Chicory 'Pain de Sucre/Sugar Loaf'	planting	harvest	harvest		Crisp, green leaves – less bitter than other varieties. Resists drought well
Chicory 'Winter Fare'	planting	harvest	harvest		Very hardy variety and excellent for winter cropping
Radicchio 'Palla Rossa'	harvest/planting		harvest		Leaves start off green then turn red in winter. Excellent variety to overwinter
Radicchio 'Augusto'	planting	planting	harvest		Rich red, round heads with wide white veins. Grows vigorously, slow to bolt
Radicchio 'Cesare'	planting	planting	harvest	harvest	Early variety with a delicious strong flavour
Radicchio 'Alouette'	planting	planting	harvest	harvest	Early variety with attractive white-veined red leaves
Corn Salad 'Vit'	planting	harvest	harvest	planting	Delicate taste, like a young lettuce. Sow outdoors late summer/early autumn
Corn Salad 'Large Leaved'	planting	harvest	harvest	planting	Excellent variety for winter salads. Sow outdoors late summer/early autumn
Corn Salad 'Jade'	planting	harvest	harvest	planting	Superb variety with tender leaves. Sow outdoors late summer/early autumn

planting   harvest

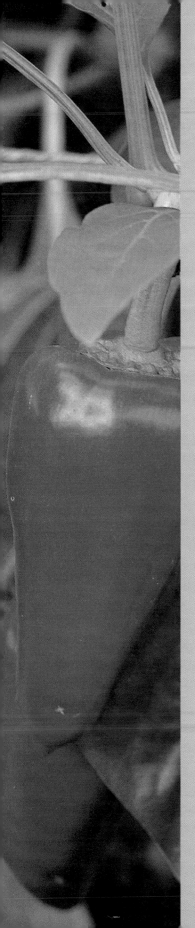

Fruiting Vegetables

The fruiting vegetables are a tender group, happiest growing under cover but able to brave the great outdoors if given a very sunny, warm, sheltered spot.

Among this group, tomatoes are the most commonly grown. Home grown tomatoes have so much flavour compared with bland-tasting shop bought ones, that growing them rapidly becomes addictive. Once you have started growing your own it is very difficult to go back to buying them.

Aubergines and peppers, both sweet and hot, are relatively simple plants to grow once you have mastered their temperature requirements. They have many of the same needs as tomatoes, so the technique for nurturing them is virtually identical. This means that if you are able to grow tomatoes, you will be able to grow peppers and aubergines as well.

These vegetables are excellent roasted or stuffed and baked and, combined, conveniently form the key ingredients of some marvellous dishes, such as the classic French Provençal recipe ratatouille. Cooked with lashings of olive oil, their sunshine flavours have the ability to transport us to Mediterranean warmth, whatever the weather.

Tomatoes

Lycopersicon esculentum

There are numerous types of tomatoes – ranging from the tiny cherry varieties, through the elongated plums, to the huge beefsteaks. The bite sized cherry tomatoes are generally supersweet and unbeatable eaten straight off the vine, and the large beefsteaks are perfect for slicing and stuffing. Plum tomatoes are especially suited to cooking, bottling or making tomato sauce and purée. Even if you only have a windowsill or hanging basket you can still enjoy a good crop of tomatoes.

It is worth growing even one plant, for the taste of home grown tomatoes is so superior to that of shop bought ones. While most supermarkets only stock mid-red tomatoes, they actually come in a wide range of colours, from the brightest golden yellow to the deepest red, almost purple. There are even varieties which are striped, most notably 'Tigerella'. Some of the most interesting tomatoes are actually very old traditional varieties – heirloom or heritage varieties as they are known. Many have been on the verge of being lost, and there is now a strong movement to rediscover and preserve them.

The different forms of tomato include bush and dwarf, cordons and the more recent tumbling varieties, which are specially bred for tubs and hanging baskets. Of these, the bush and tumbling types – sometimes called 'determinate' – require

soil	Rich, fertile and well drained. Ideal pH of 5.5–7. High phosphorous but low nitrogen levels
site	Situate tomatoes either under cover or in a sunny and sheltered spot, preferably against a wall
watering	Keep tomatoes well watered – especially those growing in containers or hanging baskets, which will dry out more quickly
feeding	Indoor plants need fortnightly feeds with a liquid tomato fertilizer
general care	Pinch out the shoots and tips of cordon types. Support the plants as necessary. Mulch heavily to retain moisture
pests and diseases	Slugs, whitefly, stem rot, tomato mosaic virus and botrytis can all cause problems for tomatoes

Tomato 'Tumbler' in a hanging basket

the least attention. Cordon tomatoes (indeterminate), must be supported as they grow and have their sideshoots (any small shoots that appear in the angles between the main stem and any of the leafy stems) pinched out regularly and their top pinched out in mid- to late summer. The pinching out helps the plants keep their shape and, in the case of the tops, stops more flowers from forming once they approach the end of their season. Preventing extra flowers from forming helps to channel the plant's energy into the fruits already developing, rather than making extra height.

Tomatoes can be grown out of doors in a warm, sheltered spot. However, to be sure of a successful harvest, it is best to grow them under cover. They have a large root system and thus need sizeable containers, filled with a rich compost, such as John Innes No. 3. Another method is to plant them in growbags, a couple of plants per bag. These are filled with just the right mixture of soil-based compost to satisfy their hunger.

If you are after an exceptionally heavy harvest, then split open one growbag and place another on top of it with its base cut open. The tomatoes planted in the top growbag will then have greater depth and goodness for their roots to enjoy.

If you wish to grow tomatoes out of doors, then prepare the soil thoroughly, digging in large amounts of compost or

Tomato Standard 'Ailsa Craig'

Tomato Standard 'Shirley F1'

well-rotted manure to a depth of at least 30cm (12in). The plants will do best grown against a sunny, protected wall, as they will be able to bask in the heat that the wall soaks up and then reflects.

As they grow, make sure that the main stem is well supported. As the plant produces its crop, then some of the side stems may also need extra support or tying up, as the weight of the crop can cause the whole plant to tilt over. Bamboo canes or lattice supports are ideal for this. As the plant grows, tie the stems – not too tightly – to the canes.

Tomatoes grown under cover need regular feeding and watering; however, it is important to get the balance right. Too much water or feed can adversely affect the fruit's flavour, while too little will hinder fruiting. Plants grown out of doors should not need extra feeding, provided the ground has been well prepared prior to planting.

Tomatoes are readily available as plants, but sadly the choice of varieties is often strictly limited. Consequently, if you want anything other than the most common varieties, you should raise your tomatoes from seed, using the following method.

Spread the seed sparingly on the surface of the compost in the seedtray, then cover with a light sprinkling of compost. Water and spread a sheet of clingfilm over the top of the tray to hold in the heat and moisture, so aiding germination. As soon as the seedlings have developed a couple of leaves, prick them out into individual 7.5cm (3in) pots.

They can be transplanted, either out of doors or under cover, depending upon the variety, once all danger of frost has passed.

Tomato Plum 'Roma'

Tomato Beefsteak 'Marmande'

If planting outside, be sure to harden the plants off first (see page 21), or the change in temperature will be too much of a shock for them.

Allow fruits to ripen on the vine and pick when they have developed their full colour. At the season's end, the remaining green fruits can be picked and left in a warm place indoors to ripen.

Sow indoor tomato types from mid-winter to mid- to late spring. Outdoor types should be sown mid-spring under cloches. Leave 45–60cm (18–24in) space between plants. Harvesting is normally in late summer.

	SPRING	SUMMER	AUTUMN	WINTER	
Standard 'Shirley F1'	planting	harvest	harvest	planting	Popular, heavy cropping, early variety. Indoors
Standard 'Blizzard'	planting	harvest	harvest	planting	Early variety, providing high yields over a long season. Indoors
Standard 'Ailsa Craig'	planting	harvest	harvest	planting	Traditional variety bearing medium sized fruits. Indoors/outdoors
Standard 'Alicante'	planting	harvest	harvest	planting	Reliable, early variety producing 5cm (2in) fruit. Indoors/outdoors
Beefsteak 'Marmande'	planting	harvest	harvest		Early variety with exceptional flavour. Outdoors
Beefsteak 'Buffalo F1'	planting	harvest	harvest	planting	Heavy cropping variety with fantastic flavour. Indoors/outdoors
Beefsteak 'Big Boy'	planting	harvest	harvest	planting	Reliable cropper. Delicious fruits can reach 10cm (4in) across. Indoors
Plum 'Roma'	planting	harvest	harvest		High yielding and versatile producing tasty, almost seedless fruit. Outdoors
Plum 'San Marzano'	planting	harvest	harvest		Reliable and heavy cropping Italian tomato. Indoors/outdoors
Plum 'Incas F1'	planting	harvest	harvest		Early, bush tomato. Excellent for cooking. Some disease resistance. Outdoors
Cherry 'Gardener's Delight'	planting	harvest	harvest		High yields of sweet tasting, deep red fruit. Indoors/outdoors
Cherry 'Tumbler'	planting	harvest	harvest		Plants bear cascades of trusses groaning with fruit. Indoors/outdoors
Cherry 'Sungold'	planting	harvest	harvest		New variety with sensational taste. Bright orange fruit. Indoors/outdoors

 planting   harvest

Sweet peppers/ Capsicum

Capsicum annuum Grossum Group

Hot/chilli peppers

Capsicum annuum Longum Group

There is often confusion over peppers. Green peppers are exactly the same vegetables as red, orange and yellow ones – they are simply not fully ripened. As chilli peppers ripen they become hotter, yet as Capiscum, or sweet peppers, ripen they taste sweeter and their flavour becomes milder.

Some varieties of peppers have been bred to be eaten when the fruits are still green, while others are best left to ripen fully. One advantage of harvesting the peppers while they are still green is that you will encourage the plant to set more fruit.

Capsicum are delicious raw in salads or cooked. Chilli peppers are generally cooked. Their fiery heat is produced by the pith and seeds rather than by the 'walls' of the fruit.

Peppers are tropical plants and so are generally thought of as a crop for growing under cover. However, they can be grown outside so long as the site is sunny and warm. Growing up against a sheltered, sun-drenched wall would be ideal, although they may still need a covering of lightweight agricultural fleece as protection at night, particularly when temperatures dip.

Sow peppers under cover in trays from late winter to mid-spring. The seeds need a temperature of 21°C (70°F) to germinate. Once the seedlings appear, reduce the temperature to about 18°C (65°F). Prick out to a 7.5cm (3in) pot once the first two sets of leaves appear. Finally, transplant them to their final site once they begin to flower, leaving a gap of about 50cm (20in) between plants. Harvesting is normally around mid-summer to early autumn.

soil	These plants prefer fertile, well drained soil with moderate nitrogen levels
site	Grow these plants under cover or against a sheltered, sun-drenched wall
watering	Keep all peppers and chillies thoroughly watered, especially as the fruits are forming
feeding	Container grown plants may need an occasional application of tomato feed
general care	Regularly pinch out growing tips to encourage healthy growth. Otherwise, little care is needed
pests and diseases	Red spider mite, whitefly and tomato mosaic virus can all cause problems for chillies and peppers

		SPRING	SUMMER	AUTUMN	WINTER		
[SWEET]	Peppers 'Redskin F1'	🪴🪴✎	⊘⊘⊘				Heavy cropping, early, dwarf variety. Excellent choice for containers
	Peppers 'Bell Boy F1'	🪴🪴✎	⊘⊘⊘				Deep green, sweet fruit. Strong, disease resistant, very productive variety
	Peppers 'Purple'	🪴🪴✎	⊘⊘⊘				Unusual variety with dark red stems and fruit – verge on black when ripe
	Peppers 'Figaro F1'	🪴🪴✎	⊘⊘⊘				Stumpy fruit which become strong red when ripe. Good disease resistance
[HOT/CHILLI]	Peppers 'Cayenne'	🪴🪴✎	⊘⊘⊘				Suitable for use when green or red and fresh or dried
	Peppers 'Hungarian Wax'	🪴🪴✎	⊘⊘⊘				Yellow fruits, long and pointed. Sweet when immature, hot when mature
	Peppers 'Habenero'	🪴🪴✎	⊘⊘⊘				Popular, very hot peppers. Small fruits are light orange when mature
	Peppers 'Jalapeno'	🪴🪴✎	⊘⊘⊘				Extremely hot, larger chilli peppers. Sometimes known as 'pizza' peppers

✎ transplanting   ⊘ harvest   🪴 sowing

Aubergines

Solanum melongena

Aubergines, otherwise known as egg plants, came originally from India and are, therefore, tender. This means they are happiest growing under cover, although they can generally cope outside in a sheltered, sunny position.

Aubergines are related to tomatoes and peppers, and should be cared for in the same way. However, they are always eaten cooked and have a longer growing season, taking a full five months to reach fruition.

The small aubergine bushes bear glossy, waxy, pendulous fruits. These come in a rich array of colours. There are the well known purple-black varieties, but also white fruit streaked with maroon and, most unusual of all, pure white varieties. These white varieties, such as 'Mohican', no doubt explain how the aubergine got its alternative name of egg plant.

Being bushy plants with such ornamental fruit, aubergines look very decorative grown in containers. Container grown plants are also easy to move if the weather turns cold.

To ensure each aubergine reaches its full potential size, limit the number of fruits on each plant by pinching out any excess flowers. Generally four or five fruits per plant is sufficient, although this will vary according to the variety. It is also necessary to pinch out the growing tips when the plants are 30–38cm (12–15in) high to promote bushy growth.

Sow: under cover mid-winter to early spring. Soak seed in warm water to speed up germination and keep a temperature of 21°C (70°F), until after they have germinated, when they should be kept at about 18–20°C (65–68°F). Prick out to a 7.5cm (3in) pot,

Aubergine 'F1 Moneymaker'

then transplant once they reach 8–10cm (3–4in), allowing about 60cm (24in) between plants. Harvest: mid-summer onwards, sixteen to twenty four weeks after sowing.

soil	Aubergines prefer fertile, deep, well drained soil, with moderate nitrogen levels
site	Grow under cover or up against a sheltered, sun-drenched wall
watering	Keep aubergines well watered, especially as the fruits are forming, as this will encourage growth
feeding	Aubergines benefit from a fortnightly application of liquid feed during the growing season
general care	Mulch to preserve moisture. Dampen down the greenhouse to increase humidity. Support as necessary
pests and diseases	Red spider mite, aphids, powdery and downy mildew can all cause problems for aubergines

Aubergine 'Black Beauty'

	SPRING	SUMMER	AUTUMN	WINTER	
Aubergine 'Black Beauty'	🪴 ✋ 🥄	🫘 🫘 🫘		🪴 🪴	Prolific, early variety. Glossy, purple-black fruits shaped like pears
Aubergine 'F1 Moneymaker'	🪴 ✋ 🥄	🫘 🫘 🫘		🪴 🪴	Productive, early variety. Outstanding taste and quality
Aubergine 'Long Purple'	🪴 ✋ 🥄	🫘 🫘 🫘		🪴 🪴	Dating from start of 20th century, bears delicious deep violet fruits

 transplanting   *harvest*   🪴 *sowing*

Squash Vegetables

For a real taste of summer, the frost-hating squash vegetables cannot be beaten. Tender plants with pretty, colourful fruit and delicate, wide open flowers, they have an attractive trailing habit, and their fresh, delicate flavours encapsulate summer sunshine.

Pumpkins and squashes occupy an especially prominent place in this group. For many they are inextricably linked with New England, USA and the festival of Hallowe'en. In New England roadside stalls groan under the weight of monstrous fruits in every shape and hue imaginable, while at Hallowe'en pumpkins are hollowed out and carved into ghoulish lanterns.

Courgettes have more European associations, and are a staple of many Mediterranean dishes. Marrows, however, have more links with northern Europe, being somewhat heartier vegetables.

Cucumbers are actually native to Africa and Asia and have a long history, being cultivated in India as far back as 3,000 years ago. Today they are the focus of much attention in Japan, where growers are expending a great deal of effort in attempts to improve them.

Squash vegetables can be greedy, but generally they are easy to grow and not especially prone to disease. They like to spread – particularly the pumpkins and squashes – but being so horizontal they make excellent companions for more vertical vegetables. And if space is really tight, with the exception of cucumbers, they will even be happy growing on top of your compost heap.

Cucumbers
Cucumis sativus

As the most tender plant in the squash family, cucumbers are often considered to be solely an indoor crop, so they are often dismissed by those without a greenhouse. However, there are varieties suitable for growing out of doors, so there is no reason why everyone cannot enjoy the subtle, fresh flavour of these plants.

Cucumbers can be divided into three categories: the outdoor 'ridge' type; the indoor types; and the gherkin/pickling types.

The outdoor 'ridge' cucumbers are the traditional varieties, while indoor cucumbers have been bred to have smoother, thinner skins. Outdoor varieties are less fussy than the indoor types; they grow at lower temperatures and humidity and are generally easier to deal with. However, indoor cucumbers tend to bear fruit earlier.

Gherkin/pickling cucumbers are a shorter type of outdoor cucumber, which are picked when about 2.5–7.5cm (1–3in) long for preserving.

soil	Well manured, well drained but water retentive. Cucumbers prefer a low nitrogen level
site	Grow cucumbers in any sheltered sunny spot outdoors; can cope with light shade
watering	Do not allow these vegetables to dry out, especially during flowering and fruiting stages when they need moisture
feeding	Sow in well manured soil. Plants benefit from an organic liquid feed during fruiting
general care	Keep weeds down around these plants and mulch to retain moisture. Support as necessary
pests and diseases	Red spider mite, aphids and cucumber mosaic virus can all cause problems for cucumbers if not kept in check

Sliced cucumber is a staple of summer salads

The main thing all cucumbers have in common is that if you keep picking, they will keep producing. Sow indoor types from mid-winter to late spring and transplant in early summer. Sow outdoor types in mid-spring to early summer, initially protecting with cloches. Seed should be sown on its side at a depth of 2.5cm (1in). Raise the soil into a small mound to ensure good drainage. Harvest indoor types from early summer to mid-autumn, and outdoor types from late summer to mid-autumn.

Pickling Cucumbers

'Venlo Pickling': prolific, trouble-free variety, producing a mass of fruit. Suitable for outdoors.
'Conda F1': Outdoor variety bearing little tender fruit.
'Alvin F1': Almost seedless little fruit, which can be eaten raw as well as pickled. Suitable for greenhouse as well as outdoor, sheltered, sunny spot.

Outdoor Cucumber 'Burpless Tasty Green F1'

	SPRING	SUMMER	AUTUMN	WINTER	
Cucumber 'Kalunga F1'	🪣🪣🪣	✍🌀🌀🌀	🌀🌀	🪣	Indoors. Relatively tolerant of cold. Excellent disease resistance
Cucumber 'Telegraph Improved'	🪣🪣🪣	✍🌀🌀🌀	🌀🌀	🪣	Indoors. Popular, traditional variety. Reliable cropper
Cucumber 'Pepinex 69 F1'	🪣🪣🪣	✍🌀🌀🌀	🌀🌀	🪣	Indoors. Long, straight, deep green fruit. Thin, smooth skin. Subtle flavour
Cucumber 'Bush Champion'	🪣🪣🪣	🌀	🌀🌀		Outdoors. Excellent variety where space is tight. Good disease resistance
Cucumber 'Burpless Tasty Green F1'	🪣🪣🪣	🌀	🌀🌀		Outdoors. Dark green skin, good disease resistance. Prolific and tasty
Cucumber 'Long Green'	🪣🪣🪣	🌀	🌀🌀		Outdoors. Reliable, heavy cropper. Medium-length fruit with good flavour

 transplanting   harvest   🪣 sowing

Courgettes & Marrows

Cucurbita pepo

Courgettes, sometimes known as zucchini and classified in the USA as summer squash, are really immature marrows. Over the years growers have been working to improve them – making sure their flesh tastes sweet and their skin is especially thin. However, forget to pick them and your tender little courgettes will soon grow into large, tough marrows.

Courgettes are generally tastier than marrows and have a better texture, making them delicious raw, sautéed or lightly steamed. Marrows can become very large and heavy, and are of less culinary use the larger they become, as their skin turns leathery and their seeds grow too large. However, marrows have an unbeatable flavour when stuffed and baked, so they really should not be dismissed.

Pick courgettes once they have reached about 10cm (4in) long and still have their flower. Pick the fruit regularly to encourage more to grow.

The pretty, yellow-orange flowers these plants produce are also edible, and are excellent battered then fried, or stuffed

soil	Well manured, well drained but water retentive. These plants prefer a low nitrogen level
site	Grow these plants in any sheltered sunny spot outdoors; can cope with light shade
watering	Do not allow these vegetables to dry out, especially during flowering and fruiting stages when they need plenty of moisture
feeding	Sow in well manured soil. Plants benefit from an organic liquid feed during fruiting
general care	Keep weeds down around these plants and mulch to retain moisture. Support climbing varieties as necessary
pests and diseases	Slugs may be a problem when plants are young. Cucumber mosaic virus and mildew can also cause problems

Miniature Courgettes

'Ambassador F1': popular variety, producing bumper crops of dark green fruit. Excellent flavour. Pick when 7.5cm (3in) long. 'Leprechaun': decorative variety, producing little round fruit with a fantastic flavour. Very heavy cropper. 'Bambino F1': prolific variety, producing tasty, little dark green fruit. Long season.

with rice, peppers, onions, garlic and meat and then baked. Pour a tomato and basil or oregano sauce over them for extra interest and colour.

While the plants are generally trouble-free and easy to grow, they require large amounts of water – especially at the critical periods when the flowers and fruit are forming. To stop water running off the surface of the soil, shape the soil around each plant into a saucer shape. This will hold the water, allowing it to slowly soak down to the roots. Also be sure to apply a thick layer of mulch in order to retain as much moisture as possible.

Courgettes tend to be bush plants, while marrows have a more lax, trailing habit. Either way, they take up a great deal of space, so be careful to leave ample room around them or they will crowd out their neighbours. Bush plants need about

Courgettes are best picked no larger than 10cm (4in) long

Marrow 'Long Green Bush 2'

90cm (3ft) of space in all directions, while trailing varieties may need as much as double that.

This climbing or trailing habit will mean that some form of support is needed to prevent the fruits from resting on the ground, leaving them susceptible to soiling or rotting, as well as inviting slugs and snails. This is easily done by placing a piece of wood or a brick underneath the ripening fruits, thus raising them off the soil.

The spreading shoots and large leaves of the maturing courgette or marrow will suppress weeds by themselves and tend to eliminate the need for weed control. At the start of its growth, however, an organic mulch will smother any weeds until the plant's leaves mature and take over the job.

Courgettes should be sown from mid-spring to early summer. If they are sown indoors, they should be transplanted outdoors after the last frosts. Alternatively, sow courgettes outdoors in situ after the last frosts.

Marrows can be sown in late spring. Place individual seeds on their sides 2.5cm (1in) deep.

Courgettes and marrows are both harvested from mid-summer to mid-autumn (or the first frosts). For courgettes with the best flavour, pick the young fruits when they are roughly 10cm (4in) long. If they are left any longer, the flavour and texture of the fruit diminishes – in addition, they will divert the plant's energy from forming any new fruits.

	SPRING	SUMMER	AUTUMN	WINTER	
Courgette 'Defender'	🪴🪴🪴	🌿🌿🌿	🌿🌿🌿		Early cropper with long season. Open habit, good disease resistance
Courgette 'Afrodite F1'	🪴🪴🪴	🌿🌿🌿	🌿🌿🌿		Quite hardy, disease resistant variety. Easy to pick
Courgette 'Gold Rush F1'	🪴🪴🪴	🌿🌿🌿	🌿🌿🌿		Unusual golden-yellow fruits, borne over a long period. Early
Courgette 'Zucchini F1'	🪴🪴🪴	🌿🌿🌿	🌿🌿🌿		Produces early, heavy crops of mid-green fruit. Good flavour
Marrow 'Long Green Bush 2'	🪴	🌿🌿🌿	🌿🌿🌿		Either pick fruit young as courgettes or leave to develop. Compact
Marrow 'Tiger Cross F1'	🪴	🌿🌿🌿	🌿🌿🌿		Award-winning, early, bush variety. Good disease resistance
Marrow 'Zebra Cross F1'	🪴	🌿🌿🌿	🌿🌿		Attractive, evenly striped fruit. Good disease resistance. Reliable
Marrow 'Long Green Trailing'	🪴	🌿🌿🌿	🌿🌿		Pale stripes on deep green fruit. Spreads itself widely

 transplanting   🌿 harvest   🪴 sowing

Pumpkins & Squash

Cucurbita maxima,
Cucurbita
moschata and
Cucurbita pepo

These must be among the easiest group of vegetables to grow, in fact once they start to develop they are unstoppable. This makes pumpkins and squash perfect for children; they cannot fail to awaken a love of gardening, as the children have the joy of watching the plants develop and then, in the case of pumpkins, the added bonus of carving them into Hallowe'en lanterns.

For the grown-ups, much of the pleasure comes from the fruit's wonderful array of bright colours and range of diverse forms – from round and flat to strange, elongated bottle shapes.

As if their looks were not enough, pumpkins and squash taste delicious. The young leaves, shoots and flowers can all be eaten, but it is the flesh which is the main event. This tastes fantastic made into pies, soups and roasted. On top of that, many varieties have edible seeds, which make a delicious snack lightly roasted, with a pinch of salt.

Summer squash are part of the same family as courgettes and marrows, and are grown to be eaten as soon as they are harvested, while pumpkins and winter squash keep extremely well. Some varieties, such as 'Atlantic Giant', can be stored for up to four months as long as they are 'cured', which means being left

soil	Rich, well drained and medium to high nitrogen content. Ideal pH5.5–7.5
site	Relatively unfussy but prefer a sunny and open position in the garden
watering	Pumkins and squashes will thrive as long as they are given plenty of water, very frequently
feeding	The ground should be well manured before sowing
general care	Build earth up into a saucer shape around each plant to retain water. Mulching also helps
pests and diseases	Apart from slugs attacking young plants, fairly trouble-free from pests and diseases

Pumpkin 'Mammoth'

Pumpkin 'Sunny (Hallowe'en) F1'

out in the sun until their skins become hard and dry.

Pumpkins and squash are extremely vigorous plants once they get going; however, they do require a little protection at their first stage. They should be sown under cover, then planted out of doors once all danger of frost has passed. They are very greedy plants, so they need extremely rich soil and plenty of water to grow to their full potential.

Pumpkins and squash are not generally troubled by pests and diseases, but slugs may attack the soft new foliage during their most vulnerable time, just after they have been transplanted.

Sow: early to late spring under cover (soaking the seeds in water speeds up germination). Place the seeds on their sides about 2.5cm (1in) deep in a propagator or cover with plastic until they have germinated. Transplant the young plants in early summer, allowing a minimum of 1.2m (4ft) space around them.

Harvest pumpkins from early autumn, Winter squashes from mid-summer and Summer squash from late summer. Summer squash are generally ready within seven to eight weeks.

Winter squash 'Butternut'

Summer squash 'Acorn'

Winter squash 'Sweet Dumpling'

	SPRING			SUMMER			AUTUMN			WINTER			
Pumpkin 'Atlantic Giant Prizewinner'	sowing	sowing	sowing	transplanting			harvest	harvest	harvest				Break all records with this pumpkin, which can grow to 320kg (700lb)
Pumpkin 'Mammoth'	sowing	sowing	sowing	transplanting			harvest	harvest	harvest				Another giant show stopper. Firm flesh and good flavour
Pumpkin 'Sunny (Hallowe'en) F1'	sowing	sowing	sowing	transplanting			harvest	harvest	harvest				Bright orange fruit. Perfect for pies and lanterns
Summer squash 'Acorn'	sowing	sowing	sowing	transplanting	harvest	harvest	harvest	harvest					Pretty, acorn-like shape and appetizing flavour
Summer squash 'Sunburst F1'	sowing	sowing	sowing	transplanting	harvest	harvest	harvest	harvest					Colourful variety with glossy, tender skin and fantastic flavour. Easy to grow
Summer squash 'Spaghetti Squash'	sowing	sowing	sowing	transplanting	harvest	harvest	harvest	harvest					Stringy tendrils of flesh give it its name. Boil whole then scoop out flesh
Winter squash 'Butternut F1'		sowing	sowing	sowing	harvest	harvest	harvest	harvest					Delicious orange flesh. Sweet and nutty. Stores well
Winter squash 'Sweet Dumpling'		sowing	sowing	sowing	harvest	harvest	harvest	harvest					Very decorative, creamy white mottled green skin
Winter squash 'Butternut'		sowing	sowing	sowing	harvest	harvest	harvest	harvest					Pale-grey skin enclosing sweet flesh with an appealing firm texture

 transplanting   harvest   sowing

Shooting Vegetables

The shooting vegetables are an attractive bunch. They range from the very architectural – the artichokes and cardoons, which provide spiky height – to the very decorative asparagus, fennel and celery, which have frilled, feathery foliage. Add a touch of drama, provided by the immense girth of rhubarb, and you have a fine selection.

This group also contains some of the greatest delicacies in the vegetable world. Asparagus is prized for its fleeting, yet memorable, season, and while the other vegetables may not have such a short season, they do offer equally fantastic flavours and textures.

The other argument for growing these vegetables is that most of them are extremely expensive in the shops, and some are not even readily available. Unfortunately, even those that are easily obtainable have lost much of their flavour, as these subtle flavours – so sublime when ultra-fresh – start to deteriorate the instant that the plant is harvested.

This group also includes some vegetables which, once established, provide crops for years to come – sometimes as many as twenty. This longevity makes them extremely good value and well worth any initial effort expended on getting them going.

Asparagus
Asparagus officinalis

Asparagus is a luxury vegetable. One that is here for a brief period – unusual in these days of international trade – and one which has such a sublime taste that it defies all description.

A perennial, that once established will carry on providing mouth-watering, tender spears for at least fifteen years with very little maintenance, asparagus takes at least two years to crop. It has a very short season (only six to eight weeks) and needs carefully prepared beds, set aside so that it can be left undisturbed. Asparagus might seem a daunting vegetable to grow, but if you can find the space for an asparagus bed, all your effort will be repaid a hundredfold.

Asparagus can be raised from seed, but it is usually bought as one- to three-year old crowns. You will need at least thirty crowns.

The time and effort you put into conditioning the soil will determine the success of your crop. Asparagus needs soil that is rich, well drained, sandy and completely free of weeds. Therefore, you will need to incorporate a good amount of well rotted manure before planting.

To prepare a bed, dig a trench 20cm (8in) deep and 30cm (12in) wide. Shape the soil along the bottom of the trench into a ridge 10cm (4in) high running its entire length and place the crowns, 60cm (24in) apart, upon this ridge, spreading their roots down on either side. Gently fill the trench with soil, leaving 8–10cm (3–4in) of stem exposed. Add more soil to the trench as the plant grows, making sure that there is always the same amount of stem uncovered.

Asparagus is ready to be harvested once the spears have reached about 15cm (6in).

soil	Well fed, free draining and sandy. pH level of between 6.5 and 7.5. Low nitrogen levels
site	Asparagus prefers a situation that is open but not exposed to the elements
watering	Prefers a good amount of moisture but at all costs must not become waterlogged
feeding	The ground should be well manured before asparagus is planted in it
general care	Lightly hoe to keep weeds down. Mulch with manure in late winter. Cut dying foliage back when it is yellow
pests and diseases	Slugs, asparagus beetle and violet root rot can all cause problems for asparagus. Keep a watchful eye

Asparagus 'Connover's Colossal'

Asparagus tips

	SPRING	SUMMER	AUTUMN	WINTER	
Asparagus 'Giant Mammoth'					Copes well with heavy soil; transplant early summer if sown
Asparagus 'Andreas F1'					Very productive, high quality hybrid; transplant early summer if sown
Asparagus 'Martha Washington'					Popular, traditional American variety; transplant early summer if sown

 planting   harvest   sowing

Globe Artichokes
Cynara scolymus

&

Cardoons
Cynara cardunculus

Often grown purely for their dramatic, tall stature, globe artichokes are perennial plants resembling huge thistles with giant flower buds. They may reach 120–180cm (48–72in). Cardoons, also perennials, are related to and look similar to globe artichokes, although their flowerheads are slightly smaller and their foliage grey blue. However, they are just as statuesque in form.

Globe artichoke 'Green Globe'

The main difference between the two plants is that it is the flowerheads of the globe artichoke which are edible, while you eat the leaf bases of the cardoon, which when harvested resemble sticks of celery.

Both globe artichokes and cardoons are easy to grow plants, which can either be raised from seed or, in the case of globe artichokes, more easily from rooted offsets or suckers.

Globe artichokes should not be harvested during their first season, but left for a second year. However, once they start to crop, they will continue for about five years. Their flower buds have a wonderful smokey flavour, and the fleshy scales and succulent heart are delicious eaten hot with melted butter or cold in a vinaigrette. They are a popular part of people's diets in many parts of the world.

Cardoons should be blanched to improve flavour and reduce any bitterness. The process should be started in early autumn and will take a few weeks. The simplest method of blanching is to tie up all the plants' leaves and earth up; alternatively, the plant could be covered by a cardboard tube or even sacking. The main thing is to ensure that light is excluded.

Sow: For artichokes sow seeds in late winter indoors or in spring outdoors, transplanting in the following spring. Space plants at least 60cm (24in) apart in rows 120cm (48in) wide. For cardoons, sow seeds in early spring indoors and plant out mid-spring onwards. Artichokes and cardoons: plant rooted offsets between early and late spring 75cm (30in) apart, with 120cm (48in) space between rows.

Harvest: Artichokes are ready from early summer to mid-autumn, when the flower buds have reached the size of tennis balls. Harvest cardoons in mid- to late autumn.

soil	Light, well drained and manured. Cardoons prefer moist soil. Low nitrogen levels.
site	Both artichokes and cardoons prefer a sheltered, sunny site if grown outdoors
watering	Globe artichokes: no special needs. Cardoons must be kept moist throughout the summer months
feeding	Top dress with well rotted manure in winter and organic fertilizer in spring
general care	Keep weeds down and mulch heavily. Cut down foliage in late autumn and protect over-wintering plants with straw
pests and diseases	Lettuce root aphids can cause problems for both these plants. Eradicate these if found (see page 154)

	SPRING	SUMMER	AUTUMN	WINTER	
Globe artichoke 'Green Globe'	sowing, sowing, transplanting	harvest, harvest	harvest, harvest	sowing	Traditional variety with excellent flavour
Globe artichoke 'Vert de Laon'	sowing, sowing, transplanting	harvest, harvest	harvest, harvest	sowing	Reliable. Heavy crops from second year
Cardoon 'Gigante di Romagna'	sowing, transplanting, transplanting		harvest, harvest	sowing	Italian. Tall and tasty
Cardoon 'Plein Blanc Enorme'	sowing, transplanting, transplanting		harvest, harvest	sowing	French. Reliable and easy

transplanting   harvest   sowing

Florence Fennel

Foeniculum vulgare var. *dulce*

A firm favourite of kitchen and flower gardeners alike, Florence fennel is a close cousin of the herb common fennel, and shares many of its characteristics.

It has the same feathery foliage and mild aniseed flavour, however the big difference between the two is that Florence fennel is cultivated for its crisp, white fleshy bulb, not for its foliage. It is the bulb which holds most of the flavour and makes Florence fennel worth growing, although the pretty foliage can be chopped up and used in the same way as common fennel.

The bulb has a mild aniseed flavour and can either be eaten raw or cooked. It can be grated on to salads, steamed or braised and is famous as an accompaniment for fish dishes, the mild flavours of which it complements perfectly.

soil	Moisture retentive, light and sandy. Ideal pH of between 6 and 7
site	Florence fennel prefers to be situated in a protected position in full sun
watering	Do not allow Florence fennel to dry out or it will bolt. However, the plant should not be waterlogged
feeding	The planting ground should be thoroughly manured before sowing
general care	Hoe regularly to keep this plant weed free. Mulch to conserve moisture. Earth up for support
pests and diseases	Florence fennel does not suffer from any specific pests and diseases and is generally free of problems

Florence fennel

Florence fennel is an easy vegetable to grow. Its main requirement is that it must not be allowed to dry out. If it does not get enough water, it will simply run to seed immediately.

The only other thing to remember is that it should be earthed up once the bulbs begin to swell. Excluding the light will blanch the stems, making them whiter and sweeter.

Sow: mid-spring indoors in modules, early summer outdoors in situ. Delay sowing if the weather is particularly cold, otherwise the plants will bolt. Sow seed sparingly along drills 1cm (½in) deep, with the drills spaced 30cm (12in) apart.

Harvest: early autumn onwards, once bulbs reach the size of a tennis ball. This usually takes about fifteen weeks.

	SPRING	SUMMER	AUTUMN	WINTER	
Florence fennel 'Zefa Fino'	🪣🪣	🪣	🌱🌱🌱		Fast to mature, yet slow to run to seed
Florence fennel 'Rudy F1'	🪣🪣	🪣	🌱🌱🌱		Fast maturing, high quality, delicious flavour
Florence fennel 'Sirio'	🪣🪣	🪣🪣	🌱🌱🌱		Sweet tasting, aromatic Italian variety. Matures quickly

 harvest   sowing

Celery

*Apium
graveolens*

In cultivation for about 2,000 years, originally for its medicinal qualities, the biennial celery is a popular vegetable, yet one which can be quite tricky to grow. Celery is generally divided into two main types, the trench type and the self-blanching varieties. As the name implies, trench varieties require a greater expenditure of effort – in that their cultivation requires a fair amount of digging – but their flavour is so superior to self blanching that it is worth putting in the extra work.

The other type of celery which is becoming more popular is American Green celery. American Green celery varieties have green stems and are in demand because they do not need to be grown in a trench or earthed up and yet still produce tasty, crunchy stalks. They are best grown in a block, with a 28cm (11in) space between plants.

Trench celery is best grown in trenches 38cm (15in) wide and 45–60cm (12–18in) deep. Allow 30cm (12in) space between plants. In late summer, wrap newspaper or corrugated paper around the stalks to stop earth from falling between them. Next fill the trench with about 15cm (6in) of earth, leave it for about five days

soil	Prefers humus-rich, deep, water retentive soil. Ideal pH of between 6.6 and 6.8
site	Celery prefers a sunny, warm and sheltered situation
watering	Frequent watering is essential for celery. It will not mature properly without a regular supply of water
feeding	The planting ground should be well manured a few months before sowing
general care	Hoe around celery to keep weeds down and mulch to retain moisture. Earth up or wrap up to blanch
pests and diseases	Slugs, celery fly, fungal leaf spot and violet root rot can all cause problems for celery

Celery (self-blanching)

before adding another 15cm (6in), and carry on this way until the trench is filled to the top.

To blanch trench celery grown in normal beds, wrap the stalks up in the same way, making certain no light can get to them.

Sow: Indoors mid-spring. Celery needs a temperature of about 15°C (60°F) to germinate. Transplant out of doors after the last frosts. Harvest: Self-blanching and American Green, late summer to mid-autumn. Trench celery from late autumn.

		SPRING	SUMMER	AUTUMN	WINTER	
[TRENCH]	Celery 'Giant White'	🪣🪣 ✿	✿		🌰🌰🌰	Well flavoured. Long, crisp, succulent stems
	Celery 'Giant Pink'	🪣🪣 ✿	✿		🌰🌰🌰	Old fashioned, late, hardy variety. Easy to blanch. Lovely pink tinge
[SELF-BLANCHING]	Celery 'Celebrity'	🪣🪣 ✿	✿	🌰🌰🌰		Popular variety, full of flavour. Slow to bolt
	Celery 'Pink Champagne'	🪣🪣 ✿	✿	🌰🌰🌰		Unusual variety with tall, crisp stems tinged with pink
[AMERICAN GREEN]	Celery 'Tall Utah'	🪣🪣 ✿	✿	🌰🌰🌰		Long stalks with fine flavour
	Celery 'Victoria'	🪣🪣 ✿	✿	🌰🌰🌰		Early variety with good bite

 transplanting   *harvest*   🪣 *sowing*

Rhubarb

Rheum x cultorum

Rhubarb is another easy to grow, perennial plant which deserves its own permanent place in the kitchen garden. It is generally bought as crowns or sets, rather than seed, and once established can carry on cropping for as many as twenty years.

Growing so large – up to 60cm (24in) tall and 2m (6ft) wide – rhubarb needs a fair amount of space. Its leaves are spectacular, reaching 45cm (18in) wide, and the elongated, fleshy stalks of this plant range in colour from a pretty pale pink or green to red.

It is these stalks which are eaten, while still young and tender (the leaves are very poisonous), cooked and used in the same way as fruit, although rhubarb is technically a vegetable.

Rhubarb is often forced, to provide early crops of tender sticks. Traditionally this was done using specially made terracotta pots; however, these are now difficult to come by and expensive, so light proof boxes or bins can be used instead. The technique is simple: first, cover the crowns with straw and place the forcing pot, or substitute, over the top; as warmth builds up under the pot early growth is stimulated, while the lack of light makes the stalks grow longer and thinner.

Rhubarb must be kept as free from weeds as possible. Apply a mulch to hold in the moisture and water regularly to keep it actively growing until the autumn.

Sow: plant crowns between autumn and spring, leaving 90–100cm (35–39in) between plants. Place the crown so that the dormant buds just break the surface of the soil.

Harvest: spring and early summer. Pull and twist to remove stalks – do not cut – and leave some stalks to keep the plant active.

Rhubarb 'Champagne Early'

soil	Deeply dug, well manured and well drained. Prefers a medium nitrogen level while young
site	Rhubarb likes a sunny, sheltered situation, although it does need ever-present moisture
watering	Rhubarb should be moist and kept well watered especially during dry periods
feeding	Top dress with compost or well rotted manure in the autumn or spring
general care	Keep the weeds down around the rhubarb and mulch heavily. Divide every five or six years
pests and diseases	Apart from general viral problems and honey fungus, rhubarb is fairly tolerant of pests and diseases

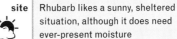

	SPRING	SUMMER	AUTUMN	WINTER	
Rhubarb 'Victoria'	🌱🌱🌱🌱			🌿🌿🌿🌿	Reliable variety with fine flavour. Mid- to late season
Rhubarb 'Champagne Early'	🌱🌱🌱🌱			🌿🌿🌿🌿	Tender and tasty, early variety. Excellent for forcing
Rhubarb 'Glaskin's Perpetual'	🌱🌱🌱🌱			🌿🌿🌿🌿	Quick growing, early variety. Very productive

 planting   *harvest*

Leafy Vegetables

The leafy vegetables rightly deserve their place at the top of nutritionists' lists of superfoods. Packed full of vitamins and minerals – including the vital folic acid – they also look decorative, making them among the must-haves of the kitchen gardener.

This is a large group, with a range of very different plants in all shapes and sizes – from the sturdy, stubby, tight, round cabbages to the frilly, loose, upright chard and kale. However, all of these vegetables come in a range of quite vivid colours.

Leafy vegetables are also extremely versatile, as they are all delicious cooked and just as delicious, but very different in taste, when eaten raw. In fact, there are so many potential candidates for salad among this group, that you could dispense with lettuce altogether and make exotic, tasty salads from these vegetables alone.

Leading the field in terms of versatility come cabbages. These unassuming vegetables can be made into some of winter's most warming recipes, yet also make up the main ingredient of that most quintessential of summer dishes, coleslaw.

Relative newcomers, the Oriental vegetables, have proved their worth to such a degree that now even the most unadventurous kitchen gardener is making space for them beside the more traditional spinach and kale.

Cauliflowers

Brassica oleracea
Botrytis Group

Originally from the Mediterranean, cauliflowers have become popular throughout Europe for their tight creamy-white heads, or curds, surrounded by contrasting dark green leaves. Cauliflowers can be divided into two groups, those which over-winter to mature in spring, and the summer and autumn-maturing varieties.

These are hungry, thirsty plants which demand plenty of water and well dug soil, packed full of compost or manure. If nitrogen levels are still low, mix more nitrogen into the soil just before transplanting then apply a top dressing of nitrogen after about six weeks. Unlike other brassicas, cauliflowers do not like acid soil.

Cauliflowers cannot cope with drought and should be given a thorough soaking every week. Frost and sunshine, especially the early morning sun, can also harm their delicate curds.

Cauliflowers will not stand for even a few days, so must be cut as soon as they ripen. Any delay and they will 'blow', which means the curds will quickly start to discolour, separate and decay.

Take great care when harvesting not to knock the curds as bacteria will set in immediately. Cut through the stem carefully,

soil	Prefers extremely rich soil, deeply dug and firm, tending towards the alkaline
site	Cauliflowers need to be sheltered from strong winds and frosts
watering	Cauliflowers are thirsty plants and should be kept well watered throughout the growing season
feeding	Your plants may need an application of nitrogen fertilizer from time to time
general care	Keep weeds down and mulch around plants to preserve moisture. Net cauliflowers to deter birds
pests and diseases	Cabbage rootfly, clubroot and pigeons can all cause problems for cauliflowers. Keep a watchful eye

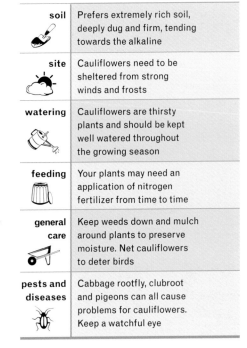

and place in a refrigerator as soon as possible after harvesting.

Sow: Summer varieties should be sown under cover from mid-winter or out of doors from spring in a seedbed 1cm (½in) deep. Transplant after six to eight weeks, allowing a minimum of 60cm (24in) space between plants – 15cm (6in) spacing each way for mini cauliflowers. Spring-maturing varieties should be sown a few weeks later.

Harvest: Summer and autumn varieties from mid-summer to mid-autumn; spring varieties from early spring to early summer.

Cauliflower 'Castlegrant F1'

	SPRING	SUMMER	AUTUMN	WINTER	
Cauliflower 'Castlegrant F1'	sowing	harvest	harvest	sowing	Summer/autumn. Delicious white curds. Uniform quality
Cauliflower 'Nautilus F1'	sowing	harvest	harvest	sowing	Summer/autumn. Reliable cropper. Freezes well
Cauliflower 'Lateman'	sowing	harvest	harvest	sowing	Summer/autumn. Long sowing/harvesting season, plus outstanding flavour
Cauliflower 'Walcheren Winter 3'	harvest / sowing				Frost resistant, hardy variety. Excellent choice for a spring crop
Cauliflower 'Snowbred'	sowing / harvest				Very early variety, matures late winter to early spring
Cauliflower Mini 'Idol'	sowing	harvest	harvest	sowing	Compact habit and tight curds. Fast maturing. Good for containers

transplanting   *harvest*   *sowing*

Broccoli & Calabrese

Brassica oleracea
Italica Group

Calabrese and broccoli are often thought of as one vegetable. In fact they are quite different. The main difference is that calabrese has non-hardy, green shoots, which mature in late summer to early autumn, while broccoli has hardy, white or purple shoots, which mature in mid-winter to spring.

The shoots of calabrese are far larger than those of broccoli – calabrese tends to produce one large head, occasionally with some sideshoots, while broccoli produces numerous, far smaller sprouts. Calabrese shoots are generally more tender and have a slightly sweeter flavour than broccoli.

Sprouting broccoli is extremely hardy and the purple and white shooting varieties are very useful, as they are ready to harvest early in the year when there are not many other fresh vegetables available. The strong-tasting shoots can also be picked over a long period.

Broccoli and calabrese are useful crops for gardens with poor soils, for although they will grow best in very fertile soil, they are quite tolerant of less rich ground. However, they do require a warm position, and the summer sown crops will benefit from light shade. They can also grow quite

soil	Well drained and fertile. In acid areas dust soil with lime before planting. Ideal pH 5.5–7
site	Both broccoli and calabrese thrive in warm sites, sheltered from strong winds
watering	The basic instruction for watering is simply to ensure the plants never dry out
feeding	Depending on soil levels, plants may need a nitrogen top dressing
general care	Generally easy to care for. Earth up broccoli to support it as it matures and net to protect both from birds
pests and diseases	Both prone to clubroot and cabbage rootfly. Broccoli is sometimes attacked by pigeons in the winter

Broccoli 'White Sprouting'

tall and have a spread of a couple of feet, so are not the best crop for a small garden. Broccoli also has the disadvantage that it is very slow to mature. It is not ready to pick until almost a year after sowing, which means that a lot of space is tied up for all that time.

Calabrese can be sown in situ. This is preferable to sowing in seed trays then transplanting outdoors, as calabrese does not cope with having its roots disturbed and may run to seed. The crop should be ready to harvest from summer to autumn.

Calabrese 'Corvet'

As with so many vegetables, sow little and often to ensure a good progression of crops.

Broccoli should be sown earlier than calabrese, and can either be sown in seed trays or out of doors.

When harvesting broccoli, cut the central head first to encourage side shoots to grow. The shoots are ready when they are about 15cm (6in) long. Regular cropping will encourage more shoots to form, and one plant will carry on resprouting for several weeks.

The one disadvantage of broccoli is that it is so slow to mature that it can take up a

lot of space in the kitchen garden, at the expense of faster, more versatile crops.

Sow broccoli mid- to late spring either in modules or out of doors, sowing seed thinly 1cm (½in) deep in drills. Thin to 60cm (24in) in all directions. If the seed has been sown in modules, transplant in from early to mid-summer keeping to the same spacing. Harvest the crop from late winter to spring.

Sow calabrese from early spring to mid-summer, in succession. Sow in situ 1cm (½in) deep and 15cm (6in) apart, with 30cm (12in) gaps between rows. The crop will be ready to harvest just 11–16 weeks after sowing.

	SPRING	SUMMER	AUTUMN	WINTER	
Broccoli 'Nine Star Perennial'	🪴🪴🪴🪴	✂ ✂		🥬	Pretty, white flowered plant. Packed full of nutrition
Broccoli 'Extra Early Purple Sprouting Rudolph'	🪴🪴🪴🪴	✂ ✂			Hardy, reliable, purple-flowered variety
Broccoli 'White Sprouting'	🪴🪴🪴🪴	✂ ✂			Attractive white shoots ready to harvest in early to mid-spring
Calabrese 'Flash F1'	🪣🪣🪣	🪣🪣🪣🥬	🥬🥬		One of the fast-growing varieties, producing succulent shoots
Calabrese 'Corvet'	🪣🪣🪣	🪣🪣🪣🥬	🥬🥬		Delicious light green heads and numerous sideshoots
Calabrese 'Shogun'	🪣🪣🪣	🪣🪣🪣🥬	🥬🥬		Produces tender, tasty, large, greeny-blue heads

✂ transplanting   🥬 harvest   🪣 sowing

Cabbages

Brassica oleracea
Capitata Group

There is a cabbage for every occasion and every time of year. They are a very versatile vegetable, and can be eaten raw, cooked and even pickled. Cabbages are also extremely nutritious, especially the varieties with dark green leaves. They contain calcium, iron and vitamins A, B and C.

Surprisingly for a vegetable which is so associated with northern and eastern Europe, cabbages originate from the Mediterranean, where they grow wild to this day.

Cabbages can be divided into various groups, either according to the season they mature in (spring, summer, autumn, winter) or their types (savoy, looseleaf and pointed, ballheads, red and white).

It is worth sitting down and working out a planting plan to get a year-round crop. Sow spring-maturing cabbages in

soil	Spring-maturing varieties like light soil; others like plenty of organic matter
site	This group enjoys a sunny position, sheltered from strong winds
watering	No special watering requirements except to keep them moist during dry spells
feeding	Plants need extra nitrogen; late varieties benefit from potash and extra phosphate
general care	Hoe to keep weeds down. Inspect for any signs of pest or disease attack. May need to net to keep birds off
pests and diseases	Cabbages are particularly prone to clubroot, cabbage rootfly and damage from pigeons

Miniature Cabbages

'Primero F1': red variety. Delicious, deep red heads. Very compact. Good for successive sowing.
'Protovy F1': a Savoy variety. Pretty leaves and tight habit. 'Castello': ballhead variety. Very tasty, dense heads. 'Minicole F1': a compact, white Dutch variety. Long lasting.

Cabbage savoy 'January King 3'

mid- to late summer and transplant in early to mid-autumn. Place in rows 45cm (18in) apart and allow 22–30cm (9–12in) between the seedlings. Spring-maturing cabbages have a much looser habit than other varieties, rarely forming heads. They are often referred to as spring greens.

Sow summer and autumn-maturing crops from late winter under

cover, or straight out of doors from early spring. Like other leafy vegetables, sow little and often to ensure a succession of crops.

Red and white cabbages should be sown in early to mid-spring, then transplanted when large enough to move to roughly 45cm (18in) apart. They can be cut in early winter and are the best varieties for storing.

Varieties that are intended to mature during winter should be sown between mid- and late spring, then planted out as seedlings in moist soil. Thin to around 5cm (2in) between plants.

The stars among the winter cabbages are the savoys, which are extremely hardy, even improving after a touch of frost. They should be planted out in mid-summer,

Red cabbage is a good variety for storing

then they can be left in the ground throughout the winter and cut from as early as autumn to as late as the end of winter.

Prepare the ground well for cabbages. They like soil containing a great deal of humus, so dig in a good amount of compost, leaf mould or manure the autumn prior to planting. They also benefit from a top dressing of lime, especially if the soil is at all acid. These requirements mean that they make an ideal follow-on crop to peas and beans.

When transplanting seedlings be very careful not to disturb the rootballs, then water the plants in well and make sure that the soil is firm around them. Mulch to conserve moisture.

White cabbage should be sown early to mid-spring

		SPRING	SUMMER	AUTUMN	WINTER	
[SAVOY]	Cabbage 'Tundra'	sow		harvest	harvest	Autumn/winter, white ballhead cross. Tasty, bright green heads. Hardy
	Cabbage 'January King 3'	sow		harvest	harvest	Autumn/winter. Lovely, dark green hearts with a touch of purple
	Cabbage 'Savoy King F1'	sow		harvest	harvest / sow	Autumn/winter. Classic variety with beautifully frilled leaves
[RED]	Cabbage 'Ruby Ball'	sow / harvest	harvest	harvest		Summer. Attractive variety with tightly-packed leaves
	Cabbage 'Marner Large Red'	sow		harvest		Large ballhead. Stores well
	Cabbage 'Red Drumhead'	sow		harvest	sow	Fine textured head. Good all year round variety
[WHITE]	Cabbage 'Derby Day'					Summer ballhead. Light green heads with delicious fresh flavour
	Cabbage 'Spring Hero F1'	sow / harvest	sow / harvest	harvest		Spring ballhead, Can be sown as a summer cabbage
	Cabbage 'Freshma'	sow		harvest		Reliable with lovely fresh flavour. Long cropping period

 harvest   🪣 sowing

Spinach

Spinacia oleracea

&

New Zealand Spinach

Tetragonia tetragonioides, syn *T. expansa*

With its tasty, soft, green leaves packed full of calcium and iron, spinach is rightly extremely popular. Its baby leaves have the most delicate flavour eaten raw, while mature leaves are delicious lightly steamed.

Spinach is extremely fast growing, which makes it a very useful catch crop (see page 46); however, it will bolt at the first sign of hot, dry weather, so it must be kept very well watered at all times.

New Zealand spinach (*Tetragonia tetragonioides*, syn *T. expansa*), which has smaller, triangular leaves, is much more tolerant of high temperatures and dry conditions. It also requires less nitrogen in the soil than ordinary spinach. However, it cannot cope with frost, so it is only really suitable grown as a summer crop.

Pick individual leaves often to encourage resprouting and thin crops to ensure good air circulation and so prevent the development of downy mildew.

Puréed, spinach freezes very well and can be cooked straight from frozen.

Sowing: in succession, little and often, outdoors from early to late spring for

soil	Needs a moisture retentive soil with medium nitrogen. New Zealand spinach needs less nitrogen
site	An open site is suitable, but spinach can cope perfectly well with light shade
watering	Ensure that the soil is moist when sowing spinach. Water spinach frequently during dry spells
feeding	When preparing the site for planting spinach, add nitrogen fertilizer to the soil
general care	Keep the planting site for spinach weed free and thoroughly moist at all times
pests and diseases	Downy mildew can be a problem, but otherwise spinach does not suffer from pests and diseases and is trouble-free

Spinach is a good vegetable to freeze

summer use. Set seed no more than 1.5cm (¾in) deep, in rows 30cm (12in) apart. New Zealand spinach should be sown 1cm (½in) deep and 38cm (15in) distant. For winter use, sow mid-summer to mid-autumn (under cover in exposed areas). It is possible to harvest all year round if grown under cover in the winter.

	SPRING	SUMMER	AUTUMN	WINTER	
New Zealand spinach					Variety most able to cope with dry soil and heat. Stands well
Spinach 'Bloomsdale'					Delicious, dark green leaves. Easy to grow
Spinach 'Matador'					Large, medium green leaves. Slow to bolt with a long growing season

harvest   sowing

Chard & Leaf beet

Beta vulgaris
Cicla Group

Chard 'Bright Lights'

Chard, sometimes known as Swiss chard or seakale, and leaf beet, also known as spinach beet or perpetual spinach, are virtually identical. They are both undemanding vegetables, coping with drought and bad weather with ease.

They are happiest in cool weather yet also cope well with hot summers. This makes them an excellent alternative to spinach, as while they are very similar to it – in looks and taste – they are far slower to bolt.

These are very hardy vegetables, so useful as a winter crop. Use the leaves young in salads, or leave to mature and steam.

Sow: Spring to summer in succession for summer crops, later for winter harvests. Sow seed in situ 1.5cm (¾in) deep in rows 38–45cm (15–18in) distant. Thin to 30cm (12in) apart. Harvest: possible all year round.

soil	Chard and leaf beet prefer nitrogen rich soil. Can cope with quite dry soils
site	Both these vegetables are ideal to grow on a site recently vacated by beans or peas
watering	Keep the young plants of both these vegetables well watered at all times, although they will cope with drought
feeding	Young chard and leaf beet plants may need some liquid feeds from time to time
general care	Prepare site by digging in plenty of compost or manure. Mulch to conserve moisture and keep down weeds
pests and diseases	Chard and leaf beet both have good resistance to pests and diseases, although birds may eat seedlings

	SPRING	SUMMER	AUTUMN	WINTER	
Chard/Leaf Beet 'Bright Lights'					Colourful stems (white, red, yellow and pink) – most decorative variety
Chard/Leaf Beet 'Rhubarb Chard'					Extremely ornamental, with dark leaves and bright red stems
Chard/Leaf Beet 'White Silver 2/Swiss Chard'					Thick white stems, delicious lightly cooked. Eat leaves raw while young

Kale/Borecole

Brassica oleracea
Acephala Group

Kale 'Dwarf Green Curled'

Hardy plants related to cabbages, kale have foliage which is so decorative that it looks good grown in the flower border or alone in containers.

Kale makes an excellent winter crop and is hugely nutritious, the leaves being full of iron as well as vitamins A, C and E. If picked

soil	Prefers fertile, well drained soil with a medium level of nitrogen
site	Tolerant, but prefers sun and shelter from strong winds
watering	Keep seedlings well watered for the best results. Water frequently during dry spells
feeding	Over-wintering plants benefit from a spring top dressing of nitrogen
general care	Hoe around kale/borecole plants to keep weeds down and soil moisture content up
pests and diseases	Kale/borecole do not suffer from any specific pests and diseases and are generally trouble-free

 harvest   sowing

young, the leaves can be eaten raw, and harvested as a cut and come again vegetable. Older leaves are better cooked.

Kale stands being left in the ground for a long time and also freezes well. It has strong resistance to disease and is not troubled by pests. All in all it is very undemanding.

Sow: early spring to mid-summer out of doors in situ or in a nursery bed 1cm (½in) deep. Water well. Transplant mid-summer, allowing 30–45cm (12–18in) space in all directions for dwarf plants and 75cm (30in) for the larger varieties. Harvest: early autumn to early spring.

	SPRING	SUMMER	AUTUMN	WINTER	
Kale/Borecole 'Darkbor F1'	🪴🪴🪴	🪴🪴	🌱🌱🌱🌱🌱🌱		Distinctively shaped leaves with a good texture
Kale/Borecole 'Redbor F1'	🪴🪴🪴	🪴🪴	🌱🌱🌱🌱🌱🌱		Very hardy variety with attractive red leaves
Kale/Borecole 'Pentland Brig'	🪴🪴🪴	🪴🪴	🌱🌱🌱🌱🌱		Tall plant with delicious texture and flavour

Miniature Kale/Brussels

Kale 'Starbor F1': a very compact, prolific and hardy variety. Grows all year round. Kale 'Showbor F1': a dwarf habit that makes this an excellent choice for a tight space. Brussels sprouts 'Energy F1': fast-growing variety which lives up to its name. Freezes well.

Brussels Sprouts

Brassica oleracea Gemmifera Group

Brussels sprouts are extremely hardy and tolerant plants. They are also very space saving, growing vertically rather than spreading horizontally.

If you choose your varieties carefully you can harvest sprouts from early autumn to early spring. Always pick the sprouts from the bottom of the plant up.

To store plants once the weather turns cold, dig them up whole, then hang upside down in a cool, dry place and pick as required. Choose F1 varieties if you plan on freezing part of your crop.

Brussels sprouts 'Braveheart'

soil	Medium to heavy, firm, well drained and fertile. Ideal pH of 6.5
site	Brussels sprouts prefer an open and sunny, sheltered spot away from strong winds
watering	Water Brussels sprouts frequently during very dry spells and keep moist at all other times
feeding	Apply general base dressing, but not manure, before planting. May need mid-summer feed
general care	Mulch to deter weeds. Remove diseased leaves immediately. Earth up and support with stakes
pests and diseases	Pigeons, mealybugs, aphids and downy mildew can all cause problems for Brussels sprouts

Sow: under glass in mid- to late winter, or out of doors in succession from early spring (depending on the variety). Sow in a nursery bed 1cm (½in) deep and transplant from late spring, replanting 60cm (24in) apart. When it comes to harvesting, pick from the base upwards.

	SPRING	SUMMER	AUTUMN	WINTER	
Brussels sprouts 'Bridge F1'	🪴🪴✂	✂		🌱🌱🪴🪴	Disease tolerant, vigorous variety
Brussels sprouts 'Cascade F1'	🪴🪴🪴	✂		🌱🌱🌱🪴	Mid-season variety with sweet taste. Good disease resistance
Brussels sprouts 'Rubine'	🪴🪴🪴	✂		🌱🌱🌱🪴	Decorative variety with red sprouts. Good flavour

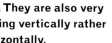

✂ transplanting	🌱 harvest	🪴 sowing

Oriental vegetables

Oriental vegetables are relatively new arrivals in the kitchen gardens. They are dual-purpose vegetables, in that they can either be harvested young and used in salads, or can be left to grow a little longer then cooked. They are especially good in stir fries and the leaves are packed with nutrition. Cut young Oriental vegetables will regrow, so are ideal as cut and come again crops. Alternatively, grow them for winter salads, sowing seeds in the late summer and autumn.

Pak Choi (*Brassica rapa* var. *chinensis*)

One of the most popular of the Oriental vegetables, Pak Choi is easy to grow, and its round leaves are mild and succulent. Treat as a cut and come again vegetable. Cut down to about 2.5cm (1in) above the ground and the plant will resprout. Sow: in succession from spring through to mid-summer. Harvest: for salad use after five weeks.

Chinese Cabbage (*Brassica rapa* var. *pekinensis*)

Although it resembles a rather tight, upright lettuce, the leaves of Chinese cabbage are far firmer, with quite solid stems and thick veins. They have a mild flavour, and are delicious served raw in salads, stir fried or steamed. Chinese cabbages also keep well in the refrigerator. Sow: early to mid-summer. Harvest: ready to be cut after six to seven weeks, earlier for salad.

Oriental Mustard (*Brassica juncea*)

Strong-growing, robust plant which can be eaten raw when young. Disease-resistant and relatively pest free, therefore very low maintenance. Sow: mid- to late summer. Harvest: anything between six and twelve weeks. Cut individual leaves as required.

Mizuna Greens (*B. rapa* var. *nipposinica*)

A decorative vegetable with serrated pale green, very delicate-looking leaves, Mizuna can be harvested as seedlings after two weeks, or mature plants at ten weeks. Very hardy. Sow: Spring to summer. Harvest: late spring to autumn. Take individual leaves.

soil	Oriental vegetables prefer fertile, moisture retentive, but free draining soil
site	Oriental vegetables should be situated in a sunny spot and sheltered from strong winds
watering	It is vital to keep Oriental vegetables well watered in order to encourage fresh, healthy growth
feeding	If soil is poor, add nitrogen fertilizer to enrich it, ideally prior to planting the vegetables
general care	Keep weeds down by regularly hoeing around the plants and mulch in order to retain moisture
pests and diseases	Oriental vegetables are prone to attack from cabbage root fly but otherwise free from problems with pests and diseases

Pak Choi 'Joi Choi'

Chinese cabbage 'Kasumi F1'

	SPRING	SUMMER	AUTUMN	WINTER	
Pak Choi 'Joi Choi'	sow	sow/harvest	harvest		Attractive variety with white stems/veins contrasting with dark green leaves
Pak Choi 'Shanghai'	sow	sow/harvest	harvest		Nicely-shaped, rounded green leaves
Pak Choi 'Mei Quing Choi'	sow	sow/harvest	harvest		Tasty leaves with a lovely texture
Pak Choi 'Pueblo'	sow	sow/harvest	harvest	harvest	Good variety to grow under cover for winter leaves
Chinese cabbage 'Kasumi F1'		sow/harvest	harvest		Attractive, barrel-shaped variety. Grows up to 25cm (10in) high
Chinese cabbage 'Nagaoka' (Pe Tai)		sow/harvest	harvest		Fast-growing with a good crunch to the leaves
Oriental mustard 'Mustard Red Giant'		sow/harvest	harvest		Large, red-tinged-leaves
Oriental mustard 'Miike Giant'		sow/harvest	harvest		Greeny-purple leaves. Will survive temperatures as low as -10°C (14°F)
Oriental mustard 'Green in Snow' (Gai Choy)		sow/harvest	harvest		Piquant flavoured leaves
Mizuna Greens 'Tokyo Belle'	sow	sow/harvest	harvest		Very attractive, tasty variety
Mizuna Greens 'Tokyo Beau'	sow	sow/harvest	harvest		Long growing season

 harvest 　🪣 sowing

Pod & Seed Vegetables

Pretty enough to be grown for their decorative qualities, yet also full of vital vitamins and minerals, the pod and seed vegetables are an essential part of any kitchen garden.

Podded vegetables can be roughly divided into those which produce edible seeds and those which are grown for their pods. The range of colours among them, not only of their flowers but of the pods, is breathtaking, and their delicate tendrils, constantly reaching out to find something to twine around, are sweetly pretty. All in all, this group provides a happy combination of beauty combined with productivity.

The generally more prosaic-looking sweetcorn and okra may seem the odd ones out among these showy neighbours, yet they are just as decorative in their own way. Sweetcorn, in particular, comes in numerous vivid colours – some varieties even have multi-coloured cobs – and their stiff, upright habit mean that they contrast wonderfully with their more frivolous-looking companions.

Planted in blocks, these vegetables can be colour coded, and they provide welcome vertical interest in the kitchen garden, where so many plants are low growing. Being very sturdy they can also provide shelter for other more tender plants, although be careful to place them where they will not shade sun lovers.

Peas, Mangetout, & Sugar snaps

Pisum sativum

With their attractive twining habit, peas, mangetout and sugar snaps all look as good as they taste. Peas picked straight from the pod are so sweet that they can be eaten as a snack, and sugar snaps and mangetout are also delicious raw in a salad.

Mangetout and sugar snap varieties are bred to be eaten whole, pod and all. Mangetout are ready when the pods are flat, before the peas have developed, while sugar snaps should be eaten once the peas are fully developed and the pods have rounded out. The pods of mangetout are quite tender with a delicate, sweet flavour, while sugar snap pods are crunchier.

Peas are often described as round or wrinkled. This is not a precise description of the shape of the peas, rather it is a way of classifying them as hardy or tender, but suitable for sowing in succession. Round peas are hardy and suitable for winter sowing from mid-winter or early spring, while wrinkled peas should be sown at three or four weekly intervals from early spring to early summer.

Sow: see above and table below. Sow 4–5cm (1½–2in) deep, 5–7cm (2–3in) apart.

Harvest: early varieties 11 to 12 weeks after spring sowing. Second early varieties are ready 13 to 14 weeks after sowing. Harvest maincrop 14 to 16 weeks after sowing.

Mangetout 'Oregon Sugar Pod'

Sugar snap 'Sugar Snap'

Dwarf pea 'Feltham First'

soil		These plants prefer well dug, fertile and moist soil. Apply lime to soil if acid
site		This group of plants prefers a damp and cool spot in the garden, with light shade.
watering		Water thoroughly during dry periods and keep the plants at least moist at all other times
feeding		The planting ground should be well manured before these plants are sown
general care		Keep weeds down and mulch when the plants are 15cm (6in) tall. Support with twigs and net against birds
pests and diseases		Mice, birds and fusarium wilt can all cause problems for these vegetables. Keep a watchful eye

	SPRING	SUMMER	AUTUMN	WINTER	
Pea 'Kelvedon Wonder'	sowing	sowing/harvest	harvest		Second early. Sow in succession for a heavy crop of wrinkled peas
Pea 'Hurst Green Shaft'	sowing	sowing/harvest	harvest		Second early. Reliable, fast grower with delicious sweet wrinkled peas
Pea 'Ambassador'	sowing	sowing/harvest	harvest		Maincrop, wrinkled pea. Long cropping period. Very tasty; disease resistant
Mangetout 'Oregon Sugar Pod'	sowing	sowing/harvest			Delicious sweet pods. Rightly very popular
Mangetout 'Delikata'	sowing	sowing/harvest			Tasty dark green pods. Good disease resistance
Sugar snap 'Sugar Bon'	sowing	sowing/harvest			Prolific dwarf variety. Grow under cover for extra early crops
Sugar snap 'Sugar Snap'	sowing	sowing/harvest			Sweet, fresh flavour. Resistant to fusarium wilt
Sugar snap 'Sugar Snap Delikett'	sowing	sowing/harvest			Dark green pods with a delicious sweet flavour
Dwarf pea 'Little Marvel'	sowing	harvest			Early variety wrinkled pea, excellent for growing under cover
Dwarf pea 'Feltham First'	sowing	sowing/harvest		sowing	Early variety with round peas. Very hardy

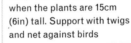 harvest   sowing

French beans/Snap beans

Phaseolus vulgaris

French beans are a very versatile vegetable. They can be grown for their pods and eaten whole, for their seeds, or cultivated simply because they are very decorative.

The taller climbing beans are especially useful for smaller gardens, as they can be grown to scramble up an arch, over a path, or up an obelisk set in the flower border.

The other huge benefit is that French beans are so prolific. In fact, the more you pick them, the more they will grow. Climbing French beans have a longer cropping period than the dwarf varieties.

Flageolets, the tender, delicately flavoured beans so popular in France, are actually the half-ripe, shelled bean seeds, while haricots are the dried, mature bean seeds.

To produce haricots, simply leave the pods unpicked until they have turned brown, then pull up the whole plant and hang it upside down until it has dried out. The beans will then be ready to be shelled and stored.

Sow: under glass in mid-spring or from mid-spring to mid-summer in situ. Make a few successional sowings. Harvest: early summer onwards. These plants generally last for six to eight weeks.

French bean 'Hunter'

Dwarf snap bean 'Masterpiece'

Dwarf snap bean 'Purple Queen'

soil	These plants prefer their soil deeply dug, rich and light. Neutral to low acid
site	All species of these plants ideally need a sheltered site in order to flourish
watering	Keep these vegetables moist when their flowers are setting and throughout the growing season
feeding	The soil for these plants should be well prepared before planting
general care	Keep weeds down and support with pea sticks or canes. Dwarf varieties may need earthing up. Net to deter birds
pests and diseases	Pollen beetles and bean mosaic virus are the two most troublesome pests and diseases for these plants

	SPRING	SUMMER	AUTUMN	WINTER	
French/Snap bean (Climbing) 'Blue Lake'	🌱🌱	🌱🌱🌱🍃🍃	🍃		Wonderful flavour. White-seeded beans excellent dried as haricots
French/Snap bean (Climbing) 'Hunter'	🌱🌱	🌱🌱🌱🍃🍃	🍃		Heavy cropping, white-seeded beans in stringless pods
French/Snap bean (Bush) 'Royalty'	🌱	🌱🌱🍃🍃	🍃		Eat while young. Lovely, fresh taste
French/Snap bean (Bush) 'Rocquencourt'	🌱	🌱🌱🍃🍃	🍃		Striking yellow pods and green foliage – extremely decorative variety
French/Snap bean (Dwarf) 'Purple Queen'	🌱🌱	🌱🍃🌱🍃	🍃		Delicious, stringless pods in a striking deep purple. Pick young
French/Snap bean (Dwarf) 'Masterpiece'	🌱🌱	🌱🍃🍃	🍃		Prolific, early variety. Delicious straight, flat pods
French/Snap bean (Dwarf) 'Montano'	🌱🌱	🌱🍃🍃	🍃		Compact plant with dark green, stringless pods. Excellent taste

🍃 harvest   🌱 sowing

Runner beans

Phaseolus coccineus

Runner beans are the most ornamental bean of all, with their twining habit and bright blooms. They are also extremely prolific, in fact runner beans are among those wonderful plants which positively thrive on being picked.

Runner bean 'Polestar' (stringless)

Runner bean 'Desirée' (stringless)

Dwarf varieties are especially suited to exposed gardens as they are less affected by wind than the taller climbers. They are also quite compact, which makes them an excellent choice for a very small garden.

Planning ahead is key to getting a good crop of runner beans, as the soil should be prepared about six months before. Dig in masses of well-rotted manure or compost and dig deep, as runner bean roots go down a long way.

Runner beans are very tender, so cover them with lightweight horticultural fleece if a late frost is forecast. It is also important that runner bean roots never dry out and stay cool, so the soil must be moisture retentive and the plants constantly watered throughout the growing period – especially when the beans are setting flowers.

Runner beans freeze well, so plant extra to take advantage of this. Sow: mid-spring under glass; late spring to early summer out of doors. Sow 15cm (6in) apart. Harvest: mid-summer to early autumn. Generally mature within twelve to sixteen weeks.

soil	Runner beans prefer fertile, well dug soil with good moisture retention
site	Grow these plants in sheltered light shade, away from strong winds and frosts
watering	Water runner beans copiously throughout the growing season. Do not allow to dry out
feeding	The soil should be rich in manure or compost before planting runner beans
general care	Mulch thoroughly to preserve moisture and keep down weeds. Protect from late frost
pests and diseases	Pollen beetles are the only pest or disease that really troubles runner beans. Eradicate them if found

	SPRING	SUMMER	AUTUMN	WINTER	
Runner bean 'Painted Lady'	sow sow	sow harvest harvest	harvest		Old variety. Very colourful with red and white flowers
Runner bean 'Enorma'	sow sow	sow harvest harvest	harvest		Consistent prizewinner yielding heavy crops of long, narrow beans
Runner bean 'Scarlet Emperor'	sow sow	sow harvest harvest	harvest		Traditional early variety. Top quality taste
Runner bean 'Crusader'	sow sow	sow harvest harvest	harvest		Good flavour and long season
Runner bean 'Gulliver'	sow sow	sow harvest harvest	harvest		Dwarf variety. Attractive, tight habit and excellent flavour
Runner bean 'Hammond's Dwarf Scarlet'	sow sow	sow harvest harvest	harvest		Very decorative, compact dwarf variety bearing tender beans
Runner bean 'Pickwick'	sow sow	sow harvest harvest	harvest		Dwarf. Bushy plant producing plenty of stringless beans. Red flowers
Runner bean 'Desirée'	sow sow	sow harvest harvest	harvest		Prolific, stringless with a fine flavour – a popular choice. Freezes well
Runner bean 'Polestar'	sow sow	sow harvest harvest	harvest		Early, with a long season. High yields of tasty beans. Stringless
Runner bean 'Red Knight'	sow sow	harvest harvest harvest	sow sow sow sow sow		Stringless variety. Top quality, heavy cropper. Pretty red blossom

 transplanting   *harvest*   *sowing*

Broad beans/Fava beans
Vicia faba

Broad beans are so easy to grow that they will even germinate on a piece of damp blotting paper, as generations of school children will testify.

These plants are hardy, extremely prolific and top of the list as nutrition providers. They also contain very high levels of protein.

Broad beans can be eaten like French beans, pod and all. Pick them while they are young and still tender. The beans can be red, white or green.

One of the great bonuses of broad beans is that they fix nitrogen into the soil, so grow them in ground earmarked for a nitrogen-loving crop or sow them as a green manure.

Sow: mid-winter to mid-spring, 3cm (1½in) deep, 23cm (9in) apart. Harvest: early summer onwards.

Butter/Lima beans
Phaseolus lunatus

Butter beans

Butter, or Lima, beans are very tender, as one would expect from a plant which originated in the tropics. In fact, seeds will not germinate unless the temperature reaches 18°C (64°F).

Like broad beans, there are climbing and dwarf varieties, so there should be one suitable for you whatever the size of your garden. The climbers can grow as tall as 4m (12ft), while the dwarfs stay at 90cm (3ft) and spread to about 45cm (18in).

As butter beans require so much heat, they do very well grown in a greenhouse.

Sow: spring under cover at a depth of 2.5cm (1in). Transplant outside when about 10–15cm (4–6in) tall, having first hardened them off. Allow 30–45cm (12–18in) gaps for climbers and 30–40cm (12–16in) for dwarfs, and 60–100cm (24in–36in) between rows. Harvest: approximately twelve to sixteen weeks after sowing.

Broad bean 'Aquadulce Claudia'

soil	The soil for these plants should be heavy, well dug and fertilized. Ideal pH of 5.5–6.5
site	All these beans prefer a site sheltered from strong winds. Cool shade for later varieties
watering	Water these plants thoroughly once the flowers begin to form and the beans start to swell
feeding	Manure the planting ground thoroughly before sowing these vegetables
general care	Keep weeds down, mulch in order to retain moisture and support the plants as necessary as they grow
pests and diseases	Aphids are only real source of concern. These vegetables are generally trouble-free and do not need close attention

	SPRING	SUMMER	AUTUMN	WINTER	
Broad/Fava beans 'Aquadulce Claudia'		harvest	sowing	sowing	Vigorous, old variety producing white beans. Autumn/early spring sowing
Broad/Fava beans 'Imperial Green Longpod'	sowing	harvest		sowing	Reliable, prolific cropper. Excellent for freezing
Broad/Fava beans 'The Sutton'	sowing	harvest	sowing	sowing	Bushy, high yielding plant – grows to 60cm (2ft). Sow under cover in autumn
Broad/Fava beans 'Bonny Lad'	sowing	harvest		sowing	High yields of tender pods and beans make this a popular variety
Butter/Lima beans 'Challenge'	sowing	sowing/transplanting/harvest	harvest		Prolific and reliable climbing variety
Butter/Lima beans 'Florida Butter'	sowing	sowing/transplanting/harvest	harvest		Popular climbing variety with excellent flavour
Butter/Lima beans 'Wilber'	sowing	sowing/transplanting/harvest	harvest		Climbing variety. Delicious flavour and good texture
Butter/Lima beans 'Fordhook 242'	sowing	sowing/transplanting/harvest	harvest		Bushy, dwarf plant bearing very white beans
Butter/Lima beans 'Henderson'	sowing	sowing/transplanting/harvest	harvest		Excellent dwarf variety for smaller gardens

 transplanting   *harvest*   *sowing*

Sweetcorn

Zea mays

Sweetcorn cobs

Ripe ears of sweetcorn swaying in the breeze are very evocative of long, hot, late summer days.

Sweetcorn can be classified according to the sweetness of its cobs. There are three levels of sweetness. 'Normal', 'sugar-enhanced' and 'supersweet'. 'Supersweet' plants have more than double the sugar levels of other varieties yet are also the most tender and need more heat than other varieties. They also need to be kept separate from other types of sweetcorn, as any cross-pollination will reduce their sweetness. Cook as soon as possible after picking to enjoy fully the sweet flavour, as the sugar will turn to starch if the cobs are left.

Sow: under cover in spring or outdoors in blocks in late spring. Transplant spring-sown plants one month later. Harvest: summer to autumn. Take fourteen to sixteen weeks to mature.

soil	Sweetcorn prefers fertile, well drained and slightly acid soil
site	This plant needs a sheltered and warm situation in order to thrive
watering	Water thoroughly once the ears begin to swell. Do not allow the plants to dry out
feeding	Sweetcorn has no special requirements in terms of feeding
general care	May need to protect seed with upturned jam jars and earth up plants if exposed. Net if birds are a problem
pests and diseases	Slugs, mice and birds are all keen on the sugary taste of sweetcorn and will ravage plants if given a chance

	SPRING	SUMMER	AUTUMN	WINTER	
Sweetcorn 'Sundance F1'	🪣🪣	🌾🌾🌾	🌾		Early maturing variety, creamy-yellow kernels. Copes well with short summers
Sweetcorn 'Champ F1'	🪣🪣	🌾🌾🌾	🌾		Reliable variety with even, sweet cobs
Sweetcorn 'Candle'	🪣🪣	🌾🌾	🌾🌾		'Supersweet' variety. Fantastic flavour

Okra

Abelmoschus esculentus

Okra's dried pods can be used as a flavouring

Sometimes known as ladies' fingers, okra is a fast growing and prolific vegetable, yet one which is strangely neglected.

Okra can grow to about 1m (3ft) and produces long red, white or green pods which are delicious eaten whole while still immature. It will crop best if grown under cover, in a greenhouse or polytunnel. The seeds also require a minimum soil temperature of 16°C (61°F) to germinate. Soak the seeds.

Sow: Spring under cover, in situ. Harvest: eight to eleven weeks after sowing.

soil	Okra prefers well drained soil with low to medium nitrogen levels
site	Best grown under cover, or outside if the site is warm and sheltered
watering	Keep okra well watered throughout the growing season and do not allow the plants to dry out
feeding	Feed okra plants with a general-purpose fertilizer every fortnight
general care	Keep weeds down and mulch around plants to preserve moisture. Support as necessary
pests and diseases	Aphids, red spider mites and powdery mildew can all cause okra problems. Keep a watchful eye

 transplanting   *harvest*   *sowing*

Bulb
Vegetables

Leeks, onions and garlic are all closely related, being members of the Allium family. They are all quite hardy and really very easy to grow, requiring little attention other than being kept free from competition from weeds and, in the case of leeks, having any flower stems removed.

The pungent flavours and aromas of the alliums are very distinctive. Garlic and onions, in particular, can lift a dish, totally transforming it from bland to vibrant.

Besides their culinary attributes, these plants have another talent. They are decorative. Leeks have foliage in a wonderful eye-catching grey blue, a really unique colour. On top of that, if left to go to seed, leeks produce beautiful flowers which look like a series of explosions of small lilac stars.

Onion and garlic have narrow, ribbon-like upright leaves, which contrast well with some of the more squat, spreading vegetables. The spring onions, with their fresh green foliage, are particularly attractive, while the evergreen varieties of Oriental bunching onions look good throughout the winter, when the kitchen garden can look a little drab.

Leeks
Allium porrum

Extremely hardy vegetables, leeks are undemanding and easy to grow and are especially useful for small gardens as they can be grown quite close together. They have the added advantage of shapely foliage which can be quite beautiful.

Different varieties of leek are suitable for different seasons. They make particularly good winter vegetables, but may be grown to mature at any time from early autumn to early spring. They can be roughly divided into early to mid-season and late types, and can be bought as plants or sown as seed.

Leeks are extremely accommodating vegetables and will grow in most soils, although for a really good crop you will need to dig plenty of well rotted manure or compost into the ground. Make sure you dig deeply and that the ground is moisture retentive while draining well.

Leeks need little attention while they are growing, apart from the need for the periodic removal of any flower stems that might appear. Thinned seedlings can be eaten raw like spring onions.

Sow: seeds in early to mid-spring in a seedbed 1cm (½in) deep. Transplant early to mid-summer into holes 15cm (6in) deep, and the same distance apart in every direction (half that for miniature leeks), then fill the holes with water, not soil. Bought plants should be planted in the same way in the summer. Harvest: late summer to late spring the following year. Leeks will stand for many months.

Leek 'Musselburgh' (early)

soil	Leeks will grow in most soils, but prefer a deeply dug, rich soil with a pH of 6.5–7.5
site	Leeks prefer a sunny, sheltered site if grown outdoors
watering	Water the plants well during the early stages of growth, and then only water when very dry spells occur
feeding	The ground should be well manured before leeks are planted
general care	Lightly hoe around leeks to keep weeds down. Mulch if necessary. Pick off flower stalks
pests and diseases	Onion flies, onion white rot and rust can all cause leeks problems. See pages 164–9 for how to deal with these

Miniature Leeks

Here are a couple of miniature leek varieties to grow. They are ideal to try if you are short on space in your kitchen garden, as well as looking extremely decorative. 'Varna': delicious raw in salads or lightly steamed. 'Jolant': a variety mild enough to eat raw, as well as being an early cropper.

	SPRING	SUMMER	AUTUMN	WINTER	
Leek 'Prizetaker'	sowing	transplanting	harvest		Prize winning, early hardy variety with fine flavoured stems
Leek 'King Richard'	sowing	transplanting / sowing / harvest			Long, thin tasty stems. Excellent early variety grown as a mini veg
Leek 'Musselburgh'	sowing	transplanting	harvest	harvest	Early, hardy and reliable. Long, thick, fine flavoured stems
Leek 'Malabar'	sowing / transplanting		harvest / sowing	harvest	Fast maturing, late and heavy cropping variety. Fine taste
Leek 'Giant Winter 3 – Vernal'	sowing	transplanting		harvest	Popular reliable late variety. Superb flavour
Leek 'North Pole'	sowing	transplanting		harvest	Late variety, extremely hardy. Stands well

 transplanting harvest sowing

Onions

Allium cepa

&

Shallots

Allium cepa
Aggregatum
Group

Just how vital onions are to our cooking should never be underestimated. They have formed the basic ingredient to countless dishes for more than 5,000 years and the culinary world would be a far duller place without the flavours they offer.

Onions come in numerous different guises, from the mild thin salad onions to the strong bulbous globes. There are also white onions, red onions, shallots, pickling and Oriental bunching onions.

All onions are usually sold as sets, except for pickling and bunching onions, which are immature. Seeds are also available. Sets are more expensive than seed, yet usually more reliable and less demanding. The sets are often heat treated to kill the flower embryo, so preventing bolting. The main physical differences between treated and untreated sets are that the treated sets have a lower moisture content and their skin tends to be darker. They also often take longer to get established, however once settled their growth quickly takes off.

Seed is cheap, yet can be harder to get going. However, the choice of varieties available as seed is far wider than those available as sets.

Onions can be raised under cover or sown in situ. There are varieties suitable for sowing at different times of year. Their season can be extended by planting in spring and autumn. Spring sets should be planted as early as possible, as soon as the soil is workable, to be ready in mid-summer, while autumn planting sets should be planted in early autumn for a summer crop.

Onion 'Ailsa Craig Prizewinner' (bulb)

When sowing and planting, it is important to remember that the amount of space you leave between plants will affect their ultimate size and yield. So, for a small yield of large bulb onions, leave a wide gap, and for smaller onions but a high yield, leave less space.

The optimum spacing to achieve the highest number of medium sized onions is about 5cm (2in) between plants and 25cm (10in) between rows. For the small pickling onions 1cm (½in) gaps between plants and 30cm (12in) between rows is about right.

Bulb onions store very well. In fact, onions tied up in ropes and left hanging in a cold, dry place will last for many months. It is important, however, to select only the very best of the crop to keep. Any with thick necks or any damage will not last.

soil	Onions prefer well drained and manured soil. Firm, light to medium. Lime if at all acid
site	Plant onions in full sun, in an open position with some protection from wind
watering	Watering is only necessary while plants are becoming established or if the weather is very dry
feeding	The ground should be well manured in the autumn before onions are planted
general care	It is vital to keep weeds down by hoeing around plants and using an organic mulch for protection
pests and diseases	Onion fly, onion white rot and downy mildew can all cause onions problems and should be treated if necessary

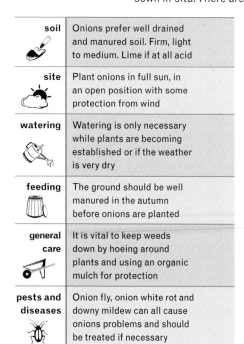

Onion 'Paris Silver Skin' (pickling/mini)

Onion 'Ambition F1' (mini)

After the onions are lifted, allow them to sit in full sun until they are completely dry before making into ropes.

Sow: seed; out of doors, late summer/early autumn for early varieties and salad onions. Early to mid-spring for maincrop. If not sown in situ, then transplant in spring. Indoors, from midwinter, transplanting outdoors in spring. Harvest: possible nearly all year round with careful planning.

Onion 'White Lisbon' (salad/spring)

	SPRING	SUMMER	AUTUMN	WINTER	
Onion 'Bedfordshire Champion'	🪣🪣🖐️ 🖐️	🌰🌰	🌰🌰🌰🌰	🪣🪣	Bulb. Long-lasting, large yellow/light brown bulbs
Onion 'Red Baron'	🪣🪣🖐️	🌰🌰	🌰🌰🌰🌰	🪣	Bulb. Deservedly the most popular red onion. Lovely flavour
Onion 'Ailsa Craig Prizewinner'	🖐️🖐️	🌰🌰	🌰🌰🌰🌰	🪣🪣🪣	Bulb. Large, yellow brown bulbs. Excellent quality
Onion 'Paris Silver Skin'	🪣🪣🪣🪣🌰🪣🌰🌰	🌰🌰	🌰🌰		Famous pickling/mini variety producing crunchy, tight, white bulbs
Onion 'Pompeii'	🪣🪣🪣🌰🌰🌰	🌰🌰			New pickling/mini variety. Very fast maturing. Excellent flavour
Onion 'Vera Prima'	🪣🪣🪣🌰🌰🌰	🌰🌰			Very early maturing and tasty pickling/mini variety. If left will mature
Onion 'White Lisbon'	🪣🪣🪣🪣🌰🪣🌰🌰	🌰🌰			Traditional salad/spring variety with crunchy white bulbs
Onion 'White Lisbon Winter Hardy'	🪣🌰🌰🌰	🪣🪣🪣			Salad/spring. Bred to provide 'White Lisbon' throughout spring
Onion 'North Holland Blood Red Redmate'	🪣🪣🪣🪣🌰🪣🌰🌰	🌰🌰	🌰		Mild and crisp salad/spring. Lovely red colour
Onion 'Ishikuro'	🪣🪣🪣🌰🪣🌰🌰	🌰🌰	🌰		Japanese, oriental bunching variety, long white stalks and virtually no bulb
Onion 'White Evergreen'	🪣🪣🪣🌰🪣🌰🌰	🌰🌰	🌰		Extremely hardy oriental bunching variety, will overwinter for spring use
Onion 'Ambition F1'	🪣🪣🖐️	🌰🌰	🌰		Shallots/mini. Red brown skin and white flesh. Bolt resistant
Onion Shallot/mini 'Purplette'	🪣🪣🪣🖐️	🌰🌰	🌰		Shallots/mini. Attractive reddish-purple onion
Onion Shallot/mini 'Santé'	🪣🪣	▯🌰🌰	🌰		Shallots/mini. Fine flavoured, high yielding variety

Garlic
Allium sativum

Garlic has an instantly recognizable flavour

Garlic's unique flavour and distinctive aroma are popular all over the world.

Garlic plants can grow to 60cm (24in) tall and reach 15cm (6in) wide. They are also very tolerant, withstanding most conditions.

Garlic will keep for many months if thoroughly dried out and stored in a dry, airy place. Simply lift the bulbs once the first six leaves turn yellow, allow them to dry out in the sunshine, and then plait them into ropes.

Garlic is not grown from seed but from cloves. Before buying these, check that they are certified virus free. Break the bulb into cloves and plant these upright, with their tips just covered with soil.

Sow: plant from the autumn through to early spring, depending upon the type, 15–20cm (6–8in) apart in rows 30cm (12in) distant. Harvest: mid-summer. Takes sixteen to thirty six weeks to mature depending upon type.

soil	Garlic prefers light, free draining and fertile soil. Low nitrogen levels
site	Cultivate garlic in open, full sunshine, yet sheltered from strong winds
watering	Watering is only necessary for garlic during very dry periods. The bulbs require dry conditions to thrive
feeding	Garlic is an unfussy vegetable with no special feeding requirements
general care	Keep weeds down by hoeing around plants and using an organic mulch for protection
pests and diseases	Onion fly, onion white rot and downy mildew will all occasionally afflict garlic plants and should be treated

 transplanting   harvest   sowing

Root Vegetables

This group includes some of the most popular vegetables in cultivation today, and yet these plants are the Cinderellas of the vegetable world.

They do not have the glamour of asparagus or artichokes, the beauty of the peas and bean family, or the novelty value of the squashes. However, they are loved because they are undemanding vegetables and ones which provide a high comfort factor. They are associated with warming, filling meals – soups and casseroles. Good winter fare.

Yet there are vegetables among this group which also provide a real taste of the warmer months. New potatoes, for example, epitomize summer. Their early varieties are ready at the start of that season, and no barbecue would be complete without a potato salad. Carrots, grated raw in coleslaw, are also a summer staple, as is beetroot and radishes.

Root vegetables provide some of the most satisfying moments of kitchen gardening. There is something almost magical about plunging a spade into the ground, turning it over and uncovering a hidden cache of potatoes and carrots. This never fails to delight, even after the hundredth time.

Carrots
Daucus carota

With their fluffy fern like foliage and delicious roots, carrots are a feature of nearly every kitchen garden, as they look extremely decorative and produce a flavour far superior to that of many shop-bought vegetables.

Sow at regular intervals – for a repeat crop, every two to three weeks. Choose an overcast day, as there is less risk of the carrot fly moving in on the crop.

Carrot fly can be such a problem that it is worth considering setting up a low barrier of fine mesh around the crop or, alternatively confusing the carrot fly by interplanting the carrots with onions. This works as the carrot fly is guided by the smell of the carrots, which is masked by the strong smell of the onions. The low barrier works because carrot flies move close to the ground, so the barrier prevents them from reaching the crop. Another method is to delay sowing the carrots until summer, when the carrot fly is less active.

Store maincrop roots in boxes of sand or else leave in the ground until frost is threatened. Carrots freeze very well.

Sow: late winter for the earliest varieties, early spring to mid-summer for later ones. Sow in situ very sparingly 1cm (⅓in) deep, in drills 15cm (6in) apart. Harvest from late spring onwards. With careful planning it is possible to get a crop through most of the year.

soil	Carrots prefer any light, deep and well drained soil as long as it is not stony
site	Fairly unfussy. Enjoys an open position but not too exposed to wind
watering	There are no special watering needs. The only thing to watch out for is not to over water
feeding	Feed (but not with fresh manure), before sowing your crop
general care	Aside from keeping the weeds down, carrots can generally take care of themselves
pests and diseases	Apart from carrot flies, carrots are practically free from other pests and diseases

Carrot 'St Valery' (maincrop)

Mini carrots – sweet and tender

Miniature Carrots

'Amini': these are cylinder-shaped baby carrots with very little core. An early cropper. 'Pariska': these have tender, cherry sized roots. Excellent for the smaller garden. It is a maincrop. 'Parmex': really full-flavoured mini roots. Good for shallow soil. An early cropper.

	SPRING	SUMMER	AUTUMN	WINTER	
Carrot 'Amsterdam' (any varieties)	✎ ✎ 🥔🥔🥔			✎	Early variety. Delicious, sweet, small roots. Freeze well
Carrot 'Nantes' (any varieties)	✎ ✎ 🥔🥔	🥔🥔🥔		✎	Early variety. Fast maturing, tender with fantastic flavour
Carrot 'Chanteney Red Cored'	✎ ✎ ✎ 🥔🥔	🥔🥔	🥔🥔		Maincrop. Excellent texture and taste. Long cropping period
Carrot 'St Valery'	✎ ✎ ✎ 🥔🥔🥔	🥔🥔	🥔🥔		Maincrop. Award winning variety with long roots. Reliable and stores well

✎ *planting*   🥔 *harvest*

Root Vegetables

Parsnips
Pastinaca sativa

Parsnips are an unglamourous vegetable. This reputation is quite unfair, as they have an understated, sweet flavour, fully brought out by being roasted and made into soups.

They are easy to grow and hardy. In fact they are one of those vegetables which benefit from the cold, as a drop in temperature only serves to make them sweeter – turning part of their starch to sugar.

Parsnips freeze well and can, conveniently, be left in the ground to over winter with no ill effects. If left to run to seed, parsnips muster a surprising display of beauty, producing in their second season extremely tall stems, up to 1.8m (6ft) high, with wonderful golden seedheads.

soil	A light, stone-free and deep soil is preferable, with an ideal pH of about 6.5
site	Parsnips are fairly unfussy about their position but do thrive in a more open site
watering	No special requirements, as long as they are kept watered regularly and not allowed to become dry
feeding	Very easy to maintain. There are no special feeding requirements
general care	Aside from keeping the weeds down around the vegetables, parsnips are easy to care for
pests and diseases	Apart from canker, celery fly and carrot fly, parsnips are relatively free from pests and diseases

Parsnip 'Gladiator F1'

In fact the only bad characteristic of the parsnip is that they can be slow to germinate – a problem easily got around by sowing the seed as early as possible.

A good method of ensuring a progression of crops is to sow the seed closer together than usual. Then, instead of leaving them all to mature and be harvested at the same time, lift every other parsnip while still relatively small, leaving their neighbours to grow larger.

Sow: out of doors from late winter to late spring, 1cm (½in) deep in rows 30cm (12in) distant. Thin to 20–30cm (8–12in) apart. Distances slightly vary according to variety. Harvest: mid-autumn to early spring. Harvest as required.

Miniature Parsnips

Miniature parsnips are a delicious crop to grow, producing delicate vegetables.
'Lancer': a smooth skinned, bayonet type which has the added bonus of having good disease resistance.
'Arrow': a delicious, narrow shouldered variety. Good for high density sowing.

	SPRING	SUMMER	AUTUMN	WINTER	
Parsnip 'Avonresister'	🌱🌱		🥒🥒🥒🥒		Early variety with delicious taste and good disease resistance
Parsnip 'Gladiator F1'	🌱		🥒🥒🥒🥒		First F1 hybrid. Disease resistant with outstanding flavour
Parsnip 'Tender and True'	🌱🌱		🥒🥒🥒🥒		Prize winner, reliable, with fantastic flavour

🌱 *planting*   🥒 *harvest*

Turnips
Brassica rapa

&

Swedes
Brassica napus

Once dismissed as only fit for cattle fodder, turnips and swedes now rate as two of the most popular vegetables in the kitchen garden. This is hardly surprising as they are among the easiest to grow, plus they contain large amounts of nutrients and minerals.

Turnips came originally from southern Europe and are an extremely fast growing vegetable – some varieties are mature within six to ten weeks. Generally grown for their roots, the leaves of turnips can also be eaten.

Swedes, sometimes known as the Swedish turnip, are actually a hybrid mix of a turnip and wild cabbage. They are larger and more hardy than ordinary turnips, take longer to grow and last longer when stored. Swedes are also sweeter than turnips.

Turnips will last for three to four months if stored in a cool, frost free place. To store swedes, twist off their leaves but leave the roots on, and place in a box of moist sand or vermiculite.

Sow turnips from early spring to late summer, about 2cm (¾in) deep in rows 30cm (12in) apart. Thin seedlings to 10cm (4in) apart. Swedes: Spring, about 2.5cm (1in) deep in rows 38cm (15in) distant. Thin seedlings to 22cm (9in) apart.

Turnip 'Snowball'

Swede 'Marian'

Turnip 'Purple Top Milan'

Root Vegetables

soil	Light/medium, manured for a previous crop. Turnips prefer soil to be slightly moist
site	Both swedes and turnips prefer an open but not exposed site
watering	Water enough to stop the soil from drying out. Too much watering boosts size but reduces flavour
feeding	Neither turnips nor swedes have any special feeding requirements
general care	Keep weeds down around the vegetables. Protect with fleece if flea beetle is a problem
pests and diseases	Flea beetles attack seedlings and both swedes and turnips are prone to violet root rot

Miniature Turnips

'Market Express': an attractive snowy white, cold tolerant variety. An early cropper. 'Tokyo Cross F1': a fast-growing, white variety with a fine flavour. 'Atlantic': a recent variety. It is purple topped and is disease resistant. It also has a long sowing and harvesting period.

	SPRING	SUMMER	AUTUMN	WINTER	
Turnip 'Purple Top Milan'	🌱🌱🌱	🌱🌱🌱🍃🍃	🍃🍃		Attractive white variety with purple tops. Early
Turnip 'Golden Ball'	🌱🌱🌱	🌱🌱🍃🍃	🍃🍃		Golden coloured skin and flesh. Outstanding flavour. Maincrop
Turnip 'Snowball'	🌱🌱🌱	🌱🌱🌱🌱	🌱🌱🌱		Fast growing, white skinned variety. Early
Swede 'Invitation'	🌱🌱🌱	🌱🌱 🍃	🍃🍃🍃		Very hardy variety with good disease resistance
Swede 'Marian'	🌱🌱🌱	🌱🌱🍃🍃	🍃🍃		High yielding, disease resistant variety with fantastic flavour
Swede 'Best of All'	🌱🌱🌱	🌱🌱		🍃🍃🍃🍃🍃	Mild flavoured, deep yellow flesh. Smooth texture

 planting   harvest

Potatoes

Solanum tuberosum

Potatoes originated in America, from where they have been introduced around the world since the sixteenth century. They are a mainstay of many people's diets, and probably more potatoes are eaten than any other vegetable. Books have been written solely about potatoes, a fact which indicates not only the huge interest in them, but that many people find the large number of varieties confusing.

Potato 'Santé'

Even if you are not especially interested in potatoes it is worth finding space for the earlies and salad potatoes which have such sensational flavour. There are also numerous rare and heritage varieties that are worth investigating.

Potatoes grow well in containers – there are even potato barrels, which open at the bottom, designed specifically for this purpose. These can be placed on a terrace or right outside the kitchen door for the ultimate convenience crop.

soil	Deeply dug, well manured and moisture retentive. High potash requirement; pH5–6
site	Potatoes do well in any open and frost free area in the garden
watering	Early potatoes should be watered in very dry periods. Do not water maincrops until tubers are marble sized
feeding	Maincrops will benefit from a supplement of bone meal or similar feed
general care	Earth up progressively to prevent light getting to tubers. Protect if frost threatens
pests and diseases	Potatoes are particularly prone to eelworm and blight but generally free from other pests and diseases

Potato 'Nadine'

They are able to grow in all soils, however they will do better on ground that is well manured and deeply dug. The type of soil will not only affect the size of the crop but also the taste of the potatoes; for example, if the soil is heavy or peaty, the potatoes may have a soapy flavour.

Every potato has its own characteristic which makes it suitable for one method of cooking but not another. There are varieties which roast well but turn into a mush when boiled, and others which make delicious mash but never become fluffy when baked.

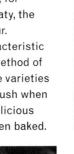

Potato 'Cara'

Root Vegetables

Potato 'Maxine'

Potatoes are purchased as seed potatoes, which are placed in trays in a frost free, light position and left to 'chit', or sprout – this generally takes about six weeks. They can be planted out once the sprouts are about 2cm (¾in) long.

Once the stems reach 20–23cm (8–9in) high the plants are ready to be earthed up. This is done to prevent any light getting to the tubers, which would then turn green and poisonous. Continue earthing up as they grow. An alternative is to use black polythene as a light excluder. This has the advantage of acting as a mulch, suppressing weeds and preventing water evaporation, however it will also attract slugs.

Plant out in early to mid-spring. Dig a trench 15cm (6in) deep and spread leaf mould along the bottom. Place the tubers

Potato Salad 'Nicola'

Potato Salad 'Pink Fir Apple'

25–30cm (10–12in) apart, leaving 45–52cm (18–21in) between rows. Allow slightly more space for second earlies and more again for maincrops.

Harvesting times vary, depending on the variety, from mid-summer (for first earlies), late summer (for second earlies) and early autumn (for maincrop).

		SPRING	SUMMER	AUTUMN	WINTER	
[FIRST EARLY]	Potato 'Pentland Javelin'	planting planting	harvest harvest harvest	harvest		Oval, smooth skinned variety. High yielding with excellent flavour
	Potato 'Rocket'	planting planting	harvest harvest harvest	harvest		Heavy cropper with fine texture and flavour. Very early
	Potato 'Maris Bard'	planting planting	harvest harvest harvest			Reliable, heavy cropper with pure white flesh
[SECOND EARLY]	Potato 'Charlotte'	planting planting	harvest harvest	harvest harvest		Fine flavoured, tender variety. Also excellent cold
	Potato 'Kestral'	planting planting	harvest harvest	harvest harvest		Traditional, white skinned type. Good for roasting and chips
[MAINCROP]	Potato 'Santé'	planting planting		harvest harvest harvest harvest harvest	harvest	Good in all soils, excellent disease resistance. Early maincrop
	Potato 'Maxine'	planting planting		harvest harvest harvest harvest harvest	harvest	Red skinned, white fleshed tubers. Good flavour. Early maincrop
	Potato 'Desiree'	planting planting		harvest harvest harvest harvest harvest	harvest	Very popular, high yielding, red potato. Compact and bushy
	Potato 'Nadine'	planting planting		harvest harvest harvest harvest harvest	harvest	Pale, cream-fleshed potato with firm, moist, waxy texture
	Potato 'Cara'	planting planting		harvest harvest harvest harvest harvest	harvest	Round, pink tinged skin and creamy flesh. Late maincrop
[SALAD]	Potato 'Pink Fir Apple'	planting planting		harvest harvest harvest harvest harvest	harvest	Old variety with fantastic flavour. Late maincrop
	Potato Salad 'Nicola'	planting planting		harvest harvest harvest harvest		Highly flavoured, waxy variety with smooth skin. Early maincrop
	Potato Salad 'Ratte'	planting planting		harvest harvest harvest harvest		Old French variety with lovely nutty flavour. Early maincrop

Celeriac

Apium graveolens var. *rapaceum*

With its swollen root-like stem and leaves resembling those of celery, celeriac looks like a strange hybrid. Unlike celery it is the root which is eaten. This has a lovely warm nutty flavour, with a hint of celery, and can be eaten cooked in soups and casseroles, puréed with potatoes, or raw, grated in salads.

When planting, be careful not to cover the young plant's crown in the ground. Instead, it should be level with the soil. Cut off any sideshoots in early autumn and lightly earth up to keep the bulbous stem white.

Sow indoors early to mid-spring at a temperature of 10–15°C (60–65°F). Prick out seedlings into 7cm (3in) pots and harden off before planting out in late spring. Space plants 30–38cm (12–15in) apart, allowing 40cm (16in) between rows. Harvest as required from late summer through to spring.

Celeriac

soil	Prefers a deeply dug, rich and moist soil. Ideal pH of between 6.5 and 7.5
site	Celeriac will thrive in an open position where there is plenty of sun
watering	In terms of watering requirements, as long as the soil is kept moist then celeriac will do fine
feeding	Add well rotted manure or compost to the ground in the winter before planting
general care	Mulch to preserve moisture. Protect with straw during winter and earth up late autumn. Remove side shoots
pests and diseases	Celeriac is prone to slugs and celery fly, but apart from that is fairly free from pests and diseases

	SPRING	SUMMER	AUTUMN	WINTER	
Celeriac 'Monarch'	sowing sowing planting		harvest harvest harvest harvest	harvest harvest harvest	Popular, high quality variety. Good disease resistance. Plant out late spring
Celeriac 'Alabaster'	sowing sowing planting		harvest harvest harvest harvest	harvest harvest harvest	Reliable variety with strong, upright foliage. Plant out late spring
Celeriac 'Prague Giant'	sowing sowing planting		harvest harvest harvest harvest	harvest harvest harvest	Smooth skinned and turnip shaped. Hardy. Plant out late spring

 planting harvest ▮ sowing

Kohl rabi

Brassica oleracea
Gongylodes
Group

Kohl rabi is an unusual looking vegetable which resembles a miniature flying saucer, bristling with antennae. It sits above the surface of the soil, and consists of a swollen stem with numerous narrow stems sprouting up out of it.

Kohl rabi leaves can be eaten, but it is the swollen base of the stems which it is mainly grown for. This should be harvested while still young and tender, and has a mild, distinctive flavour – resembling a mixture of cabbage and turnip – and a pleasant crunch to it. It is served raw in salads or coleslaw, or lightly cooked. Kohl rabi grows well out of season in a polytunnel or unheated greenhouse.

Sow from mid-spring to mid-summer in situ. Sow little and often, 1cm (½in) deep, in rows 30cm (12in) apart. Thin to 18cm (7in) apart. Harvest late spring to mid-autumn, when about the size of a tennis ball.

Kohl rabi is a peculiar looking vegetable

soil	Kohl rabi: light, fertile, sandy; pH5.5–7. Radish: light, sandy, rich, well drained; pH5.5–7
site	Kohl rabi: open site but sheltered from strong winds. Radish: open site
watering	Kohl rabi: water only in very dry periods. Radish: water well in dry weather
feeding	No special feeding requirements for either kohl rabi or radish
general care	As far as general care goes, keep weeds down as much as possible for both kohl rabi and radish
pests and diseases	Kohl rabi: prone to flea beetle, cabbage root flies and clubroot. Radish: prone to slugs and flea beetle

Radishes

Raphanus sativus

Radishes come in a wide range of shapes and sizes, from long, cylinder shaped ones to squat, globe shaped varieties.

They can be divided into two groups: summer and winter types. Summer types are very easy to grow and mature extremely fast. To ensure a constant supply, they should be sown in batches little and often. Winter radishes grow much larger and can be eaten raw or cooked – in stir fries, stews and soups.

Radishes have a peppery, spicy taste and are a good source of iron, calcium and Vitamin C.

For summer types, sow in succession from early spring to early autumn in situ; winter types from mid-summer. Sow in drills 1cm (½in) deep and 15cm (6in) apart. Winter radishes need 20cm (8in) space in all directions. Harvest in summer, three to six weeks after sowing; in winter, leave in ground and lift as required.

Radish 'French Breakfast 3'

	SPRING	SUMMER	AUTUMN	WINTER	
Kohl Rabi 'Kolibri'	planting	harvest harvest harvest	harvest		Fresh green leaves and dark purple skin. Very decorative and tasty
Kohl Rabi 'Green Vienna'	planting	harvest harvest harvest	harvest		Pale green with a delicious taste. Early
Radish 'Scarlet Globe'	planting	harvest harvest harvest harvest	harvest harvest		Popular, fast growing variety. Bright red skin
Radish 'French Breakfast 3'	planting	harvest harvest harvest harvest	harvest		Cylinder shaped, mild radish with white tips
Radish 'Mino Early'	harvest		planting harvest harvest harvest	harvest harvest harvest	Winter variety. Long, white radish. Delicious eaten hot or cold

planting   harvest

95

Beetroot

Beta vulgaris
subsp. *vulgaris*

Beetroot is often pickled, however it is delicious eaten fresh and hot. Some varieties, such as 'Golden', have edible leaves, which can be served raw in salads or steamed like spinach.

To stop the colour leaching away during the cooking process, just wash the beetroot – do not peel it.

Beetroot can be damaged by frost, so unless you live in a very mild area, do not leave it in the ground too long. Once lifted twist off the tops and store in polythene sacks or boxes of sand or soil. Kept like this it should last several months. Although it might be tempting, it is important not to wash beetroot before storing, and be careful not to cut or knock the roots or they will bleed.

Sow from early spring if the variety is resistant to bolting, otherwise the best

soil	Prefers well drained, fertile, light soil. Not recently manured. Ideal pH6.5–7.5
site	Although tolerant in most sites, beetroot prefers a sunny position
watering	Water only in very hot, dry periods to prevent the soil from drying out altogether
feeding	There are no specific feeding requirements for beetroot
general care	Hoe regularly to keep the weeds down and mulch to retain the moisture in the ground
pests and diseases	Beetroot is relatively free from most pests and diseases and so is very easy to grow

Beetroot 'Boltardy'

time is from mid-spring to mid-summer. Place the seed 2.5cm (1in) deep in rows 30cm (12in) apart. Thin the seedlings to about 15cm (6in) apart. Harvest the crop from around early summer up until late autumn.

	SPRING	SUMMER	AUTUMN	WINTER	
Beetroot 'Boltardy'	🌱🌱🌱	🌰🌰🌰 🍥🍥	🍥🍥		Fine flavoured, early variety which lives up to its name
Beetroot 'Forono'	🌱🌱🌱	🌰🌰🌰 🍥🍥	🍥🍥		Unusual long variety. Best eaten when young and tender
Beetroot 'Red Ace F1'	🌱🌱🌱	🌰🌰🌰 🍥🍥	🍥🍥🍥		Deep red flesh and fine flavour. Stands well
Beetroot 'Golden'	🌱🌱🌱	🌰🌰🌰 🍥🍥	🍥🍥		Unusual variety with yellow flesh and edible leaves. Tender and mild

Jerusalem artichokes

Helianthus tuberosus

A close relative of the sunflower, Jerusalem artichokes are hardy perennials which, if given free reign, could colonise large areas of the garden. However when growing them as crops it is better to replant every year.

One option, which is especially useful for small gardens, is to grow them in a large bin or tub. Filled with compost this will provide a big enough crop for most families.

Grown for their knobbly tubers which have a wonderful smokey flavour, they are delicious made into soups, baked, boiled with butter or a sauce, and roasted.

 planting   🌰 harvest

They will grow as tall as 3m (10ft) and as they are so fast growing are useful as windbreaks, although they may need support. If you do not want to use them as screens or windbreaks, cut back their stems by more than half their height near the end of the summer.

An excellent variety is 'Fuseau', which has longer, fatter tubers than other varieties. These are also smoother, which cuts down on waste when peeling.

Sow: late winter to early spring. Plant tubers whole or cut into pieces depending upon their size. Place in furrows about 15cm (6in) deep, about 25–30cm (10–12in) apart. If planting more than one row, leave a 90cm (36in) gap. Harvest from late autumn to late winter. Lift in the same way as potatoes.

Jerusalem artichoke 'Fuseau'

Salsify
Tragopogon porrifolius
&
Scorzonera
Scorzonera hispanica

Salsify, also known as the Oyster Plant or Vegetable Oyster, and scorzonera, have narrow, ribbon like foliage and long, skinny tap roots which have a delicate flavour and can be eaten steamed, boiled or fried.

Their flower buds are delicious fried in butter or added to an omelette and the young shoots and leaves of scorzonera can also be eaten.

The roots of salsify are white in colour and those of scorzonera black, although

soil	Jerusalem artichoke: prefers well dug, fertilized clay. Salsify/scorzonera: deep, light, rich
site	Jerusalem artichoke: unfussy. Salsify/scorzonera: open but not exposed site
watering	Jerusalem artichoke: water late summer if dry season. Salsify/scorzonera: none once established
feeding	Jerusalem artichoke: none. Salsify/scorzonera: do not freshly manure before sowing.
general care	Jerusalem artichoke: support if needed. Trim stems back in autumn. Salsify/scorzonera: hand weed
pests and diseases	Jerusalem artichoke: prone to slugs and sclerotina. Salsify/scorzonera: generally trouble-free

once peeled prior to cooking, the root of the latter is pure white.

Sow mid- to late spring in situ. Place two seeds 2.5cm (1in) deep and 20cm (8in) apart. Leave 30cm (12in) between rows. Thin to the strongest seedling of the two. Harvest in winter and fork up as required.

Scorzonera

Salsify

	SPRING		SUMMER	AUTUMN	WINTER				
Salsify 'Sandwich Island'	🌱	🌱			🌰	🌰	🌰	Hardy variety with excellent flavour and smooth texture
Salsify 'Giant'	🌱	🌱			🌰	🌰	🌰	Delicious, distinctive flavour. Reliable
Scorzonera 'Habil'	🌱	🌱			🌰	🌰	🌰	Undemanding, tasty variety
Scorzonera 'Russian Giant'	🌱	🌱			🌰	🌰	🌰	Tasty variety. Young leaves are delicious eaten raw

 planting   harvest

Fruit

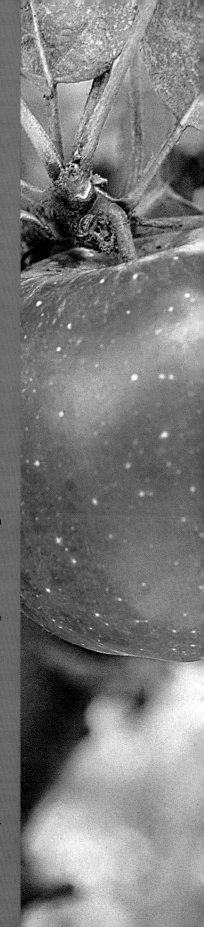

Tree Fruit

Fruit trees do not provide an instant crop. They are a long-term investment which will also enhance the beauty – and value – of your garden and property.

Planting a tree is an investment for the future. This one simple act shows a commitment to your garden and faith in what is to come. You will have to wait a few years for your first harvest, and many more years for the tree to mature fully and reach its ultimate size.

It is therefore all the more important to take your time when choosing which tree fruits to grow. Take into account all the factors, including space, position and the amount of time you can spend on care.

Space need not be the deciding factor when it comes to growing tree fruit. Some fruit trees, notably many varieties of apple and pear, will do very well in large containers, as long as they are fed and watered regularly. Just be sure to choose a dwarfing stock and prune to keep in check.

There are also family trees available, which have several varieties grafted on to one tree. These are an excellent idea for those with nothing more than a small courtyard. These family trees are available in apples, pears and plums, so that you could have a variety of fruit, both culinary and dessert, for picking from summer to the end of the year.

Apples

Malus sylvestris
var. *domestica*

Apples are hugely popular fruit, especially in those areas which have a cool, moist climate perfectly suited to growing them. They are easy to eat, requiring no preparation, and store well. They are also very easy to grow, being late to flower, and therefore safe from frost. There are numerous varieties to choose from, one to suit every taste from honey sweet to cleanly crisp and slightly sour.

The dwarfing rootstocks have become very popular in recent years, partly because amateur gardeners tend to have limited space and also because the trees fruit sooner and produce much heavier crops. The very dwarfing rootstocks produce trees which put all their effort into making fruit rather than wood. This means they are very productive and require very little pruning.

Being smaller, they also make pruning and picking easier.

Apples are available on five rootstocks, allowing the gardener a huge range of possibilities. The rootstock you choose will depend on what size of tree you want, as

Apple 'Cox's Orange Pippin'

soil	Apples will grow in most soils as long as they are well drained and manured
site	Sunny and sheltered sites are the best. Avoid planting in frost pockets
watering	Water the trees well at the early stages, then once established only during long, dry periods
feeding	Top dress with ammonium sulphate in spring if the trees need a boost
general care	Keep weeds down in a 1.2m (48in) circle around the tree. Mulch in spring. Support as necessary. Thin fruit
pests and diseases	Apple trees are particularly prone to canker, scab, powdery mildew, wasps and birds

Apple 'American Mother'

Apple 'Fiesta'

well as your soil type and how you plan to train the tree. For example, if you want to grow a semi-standard, however have very poor soil, then you can make up for this by choosing a slightly more vigorous rootstock than you would have done if you lived in an area with richer soil.

The rootstocks commonly available to amateur gardeners are 'M27', 'M9', 'M26', 'MM106' and 'MM111'. The most dwarfing rootstock, the 'M27', will reach only 1.5m (5ft) after ten years, given ideal growing conditions, while the most vigorous, the 'MM111', will reach 4m (12ft) without any difficulty. See page 23 for more on rootstocks.

Getting the pollination right is just as important as choosing the correct rootstock. To be certain of a large, tasty crop always grow more than one variety within the same flowering group, even if one of the varieties is self fertile. Flowering groups are simply lists of trees which blossom at the same time and so can pollinate each other. The flowering groups tend to

Apple 'Greensleeves'

overlap slightly, although to be totally safe, stay within the same group.

Choosing which trees will pollinate one another is complicated by the fact that some varieties are triploids, which means they have little pollen and will not pollinate other varieties. These triploids need two suitable varieties to cultivate them, rather than one. To be absolutely certain that you are choosing compatible varieties it is always best to check with the nursery or grower who is supplying the trees.

Apple 'Golden Delicious'

Apple 'Lord Lambourne'

Apple 'Bountiful'

It is generally better to buy bare-rooted trees to plant during their dormant period.

Many fruit trees are very fussy about which shape they are trained into, and will only fruit if trained a certain way. Apples, however, are very adaptable, and can easily be trained into numerous

Apple 'Golden Noble'

Apple 'Blenheim Orange'

shapes. You could choose a standard mophead, bush, cordon, fan, espalier or even a dwarf pyramid (see pages 36–8 for training instruction).

There are various tasks you can do which should be carried out regularly to keep the trees in top condition. Keep an area about 1.2m (48in) from the trunk weed free and mulch in late spring to preserve the soil's moisture.

It is also important to thin out the fruit, especially if you have a particularly heavy crop. This will protect branches from becoming overloaded but, more importantly, will improve the size and flavour of the crop. Wait until after the trees drop their infertile or deformed fruit in early summer, then go over the tree using sharp, clean secateurs to remove the excess fruit. It is worth repeating the operation in mid-summer. Aim for about a 10–15cm (4–6in) space between dessert – or eating – fruit, and 15–22cm (6–9in) between cooking varieties.

Apple 'Bramley's Seedling'

Precise pruning techniques will depend upon the shape you are training your tree into, although all trained trees should be pruned during the summer to keep their shape and get rid of excessive growth, as well as to encourage fruiting buds to develop.

Every winter you should cut out all dead and diseased wood, as well as removing overcrowded branches.

When pruning, remember that apple trees bear their blossom and fruit on shoots which are two years old or older.

Planting should be undertaken preferably in the autumn, but winter is also an acceptable time. Check with your supplier for planting distances as these vary according to a whole series of factors – from the rootstock, to the variety and how you plan to train it.

As for harvesting your apple crop, the time of year again varies according to variety. An easy way to test for ripeness is to hold the apple and give it a gentle twist. If it comes away easily from the shoot, then the apple is ripe. For more details on the harvest season for a selection of varieties, see the table below.

Apple 'Charles Ross'

Variety	SPRING	SUMMER	AUTUMN	WINTER	Notes
[EATING/DESSERT] Apple 'George Cave'		harvest	planting	planting	Early. Popular, red flushed dessert variety. Flowering group 3
Apple 'Charles Ross'		harvest	planting	planting	Early. Can also be used for cooking. Flowering group 3
Apple 'Greensleeves'			harvest/planting	planting	Early. Crisp, juicy dessert fruit. Reliable, heavy cropper. Flowering group 3
Apple 'Lord Lambourne'			harvest/planting	planting	Early. Lovely sweet dessert apple. Flowering group 2
Apple 'Egremont Russet'			planting/harvest	planting	Mid. Popular dessert apple with fantastic flavour. Good for containers
Apple 'Cox's Orange Pippin'			planting/harvest	planting	Mid. Excellent, juicy with plenty of aroma. Flowering group 3
Apple 'Fiesta'			planting/harvest	planting	Mid. Juicy, Cox-like variety. Flowering group 3
Apple 'American Mother'			planting/harvest	planting	Mid. Easy to grow dessert apple. Longer, thinner looking apple
Apple 'Golden Delicious'			planting/harvest	planting	Late. One of the most popular shop-bought varieties. Flowering group 4
Apple 'Laxton's Superb'			planting/harvest	planting	Late. Sweet and juicy dessert variety which keeps well. Flowering group 4
Apple 'Jonagold'			planting/harvest	planting	Late. Vigorous dessert apple. Triploid. Flowering group 4
Apple 'Cox's Orange Pippin'			planting/harvest	planting	Late. Crisp, greeny brown dessert variety. Keeps well. Flowering group 3
[COOKING] Apple 'George Neal'			planting/harvest	planting	Early. Cooking apple with excellent flavour. Flowering group 2
Apple 'Golden Noble'			planting/harvest	planting	Early. Excellent flavour, breaks down in cooking. Reliable. Flowering group 4
Apple 'Lord Suffield'			planting/harvest	planting	Early. Reliable cooking apple. Flowering group 1
Apple 'Blenheim Orange'			planting/harvest	planting	Mid. Excellent cooking apple. Keeps well. Vigorous grower, self sterile
Apple 'Cox's Pomona'			planting/harvest	planting	Mid. Reliable cooker. Quite vigorous. Flowering group 4
Apple 'Norfolk Beauty'			planting/harvest	planting	Mid. Reliable culinary variety with lovely flavour. Flowering group 2
Apple 'Bramley's Seedling'			planting/harvest	planting	Late. Possibly the best cooking apple. Quite vigorous. Triploid
Apple 'Bountiful'			planting/harvest	planting	Late. New culinary variety. Good disease resistance. Flowering group 3
Apple 'Newton's Wonder'			planting/harvest	planting	Late. Vigorous culinary variety. Keeps very well. Flowering group 5

 planting   harvest

Pears

Pyrus communis var. *sativa*

The pear tree is a native of the Mediterranean, which gives an indication of its growing requirements. Put bluntly, unless they have warmth, sunshine plus shelter from strong winds and frost, pear trees will not bear fruit.

One way of helping the pear to mature and fruit, which works well in cooler regions, is to grow it against a sunny wall, where it can enjoy the warmth radiated by the brick or stone. The best form for growing in this way is the espalier (see page 38).

There are some self fertile pears, however to be sure of a good crop it is important to have another pear from the same group nearby – in others words, one which flowers at the same time.

Pears are sometimes divided into three pollination groups, however some growers divide them into four groups to be more precise. The flowering season will overlap slightly, so trees from adjoining groups may be able to pollinate each other. Bear in mind that some pears are self sterile and others are triploid, so they are not suitable as pollinators, while others will not pollinate trees within their own group. It is always best to seek advice from the nursery or garden centre when you buy your trees.

Pear 'Beaurré Hardy'

Pears are generally grown on quince rootstock to prevent them growing too large and to make them fruit early. The rootstock which produces the smallest tree after ten

soil	Will grow in most soils, but performs rather badly on chalk
site	Warm, sheltered and sunny is the preferred location for these trees
watering	Water well at the early stages of development, then during hot dry periods once established
feeding	Soil should be well manured before planting. Ensure there is adequate nitrogen
general care	Remove all weeds and grass in a wide circle around the tree and provide a good mulch in spring
pests and diseases	These particular trees are especially prone to aphids, wasps, rabbits, birds and scab

Pear 'Conference'

years – 3m (10ft) maximum – is 'Quince C', while trees grown on a 'Quince A' rootstock will reach 4m (13ft) in the same time. Fully mature trees grown on quince rootstock may reach at least 6m (20ft), while if they were grown on pear rootstock they could easily make double the height.

The rootstock you choose will depend upon the form in which you intend to train your pear. Pears can be grown as standards, bushes, pyramids, stepovers, cordons or espaliers (see pages 36–8 for instructions on training).

If you are going for the more restricted forms, such as pyramids, stepovers, cordons and espaliers, then you need

Pear 'Joséphine de Malines'

'Quince C' as it is quite dwarfing, however a standard would need the more vigorous 'Quince A'.

Pears have few pruning requirements while very young – as far as standards are concerned, all that is necessary is the removal of any dead or diseased wood. Prune the more restricted forms in summer.

Mid-summer is also the time to thin the fruit. Aim for one or two fruit per cluster, depending on the overall size of the crop.

When harvesting it is important to note that the fruit ripen in stages and, if left, quickly deteriorate. To avoid this, pick over the tree several times, being careful not to bruise the delicate fruit. Best planting time is in the autumn, with a harvest from mid-summer to mid-spring.

Pear 'Packham's Triumph'

	SPRING	SUMMER	AUTUMN	WINTER	
Pear 'Early Jargonelle'					Early. Hardy variety bearing tender dessert fruit. Flowering group 3
Pear 'Williams' Bon Chrétien'					Early. Medium to large, sweet dessert pear. Flowering group 3
Pear 'Beth'					Early. Prolific sweet and juicy dessert pear. Flowering group 4
Pear 'Beurré Hardy'					Mid. Vigorous, hardy dessert variety. Flowering group 3
Pear 'Conference'					Mid. Delicious dessert fruit, good for containers. Regular cropper
Pear 'Joséphine de Malines'					Mid. Small fruits but with a great flavour
Pear 'Packham's Triumph'					Mid. Juicy and sweet dessert fruit. Flowering group 1
Pear 'Winter Nelis'					Late. Excellent culinary variety with good frost resistance
Pear 'Easter Beurré'					Late. Reliable cooking pear with rich flavour. Will keep until mid-spring
Pear 'Black Worcester'					Late. Cooking pear with lovely flavour. Flowering group 3
Pear 'Catillac'					Late. Cooking variety to be picked late autumn, but will keep until late spring

🌱 planting   🥭 harvest

Plums, Gages & Damsons

Prunus domestica

The plum family is extremely extensive, with numerous rarely seen relatives – bullaces, cherry plums, Saline or Japanese plums – lurking neglected in the shadows, along with the more widely seen gages and damsons.

The most well known group within this family, the *Prunus domestica*, include the common plums, gages and damsons, which are all excellent fruit trees for the amateur gardener to grow. Most of these are self fertile. However, if there is another variety in the same pollination group nearby, then you are more likely to get a bumper crop.

The key to a successful crop is frost. Plums flower very early, often by mid-spring, which means they are prone to frost damage. So if your garden is subject to frost attack, then either choose a late flowering variety or a damson, which is more hardy.

There are four rootstocks used for plums, gages and damsons. These are, in order of size: 'Pixy', 'St Julian A', 'Brompton' and, less commonly, 'Myrobalan B'. The smallest, 'Pixy', is a dwarfing rootstock which may reach about 2m (7ft). 'St Julian' is moderately vigorous and can reach 3m (10ft), while the two others can grow as tall as 4.5m (15ft), so are only suitable for large gardens.

Some rootstocks are more suited to particular methods of training than others. If you are aiming for a bush or fan shape then choose 'St Julian A'; if you want a pyramid, choose 'St Julian A' or 'Pixy'; however, 'Brompton' and 'Myrobalan B' are the rootstocks to pick if you want to grow a half standard tree.

soil	Well drained but moisture-retentive soil is best. Likes high nitrogen levels
site	Position in a warm, sunny and sheltered site. Important that it is frost free
watering	Water regularly at the early stages of development, then as required, especially during dry spells
feeding	Well manured soil before planting. Top dress in spring with nitrogen rich fertilizer
general care	Keep weeds down and mulch in spring with well rotted manure or compost. Protect from frost; net to deter birds
pests and diseases	These trees are particularly prone to silver leaf, bacterial canker, aphids, wasps, rabbits and birds

Plum 'Victoria'

Plum 'Marjorie's Seedling'

You are more likely to get early crops if you leave your trees unpruned until after they have fruited for several years. This allows them to get into the habit of fruiting. If you are training them into a shape then you will have to prune before then, but keep it to a minimum.

Unusually among fruit trees, early autumn pruning is not a good idea for *Prunus domestica* as it leaves the trees vulnerable to silver leaf disease. Instead, prune between late spring and late summer, removing all diseased or damaged wood and thinning as necessary. Remember that the fruit is borne on two-year-old wood and the base of one-year-old shoots.

If you want abundant crops, then the fan is by far the best shape for plums, gages and damsons (see page 37 for details).

Pyramids are formed by cutting back the leader to about 1.5m (5ft) from the ground above a healthy bud. You need about five laterals, evenly spaced on either side of the leader. Remove all others and then trim the remaining laterals so that they form the basic pyramid shape.

Damsons are a less commonly grown form of plum

It is vital to thin the fruit if you want to ensure the remainder grows as large as possible. The smaller varieties should be thinned to about 5–8cm (2–3in) apart, while larger fruit need a fraction more space. Plant in late autumn or early winter.

Variety	Season	Description
Plum 'Laxton'	harvest summer; plant autumn–winter	Early. Tasty dessert variety only suitable for frost free areas. Partly self fertile
Plum 'Opal'	harvest summer; plant autumn–winter	Early. Red-purple dessert fruit with superb flavour. Self fertile
Plum 'Stint'	harvest summer; plant autumn–winter	Early. Reliable dessert fruit. Partly self fertile, flowering group 4
Plum 'Czar'	harvest summer; plant autumn–winter	Early. Reliable dessert/culinary plum. Self fertile, flowering group 3
Plum 'Pershore'	harvest summer; plant autumn–winter	Early. Large yellow culinary fruit. Self fertile, flowering group 3
Plum 'Rivers'	harvest summer; plant autumn–winter	Early. Prolific, juicy fruit for cooking. Self fertile, flowering group 3
Plum 'Victoria'	harvest summer; plant autumn–winter	Mid. A favourite dessert/cooking plum. Self fertile, flowering group 3
Plum 'Purple Pershore'	harvest summer; plant autumn–winter	Mid. Cooking variety. Good and reliable
Plum 'Cox's Emperor'	harvest summer; plant autumn–winter	Mid. Popular culinary plum with good flavour
Plum 'Marjorie's Seedling'	harvest autumn; plant autumn–winter	Late. Vigorous variety, bearing large fruit for cooking. Self fertile
Plum 'Warwickshire Drooper'	harvest autumn; plant autumn–winter	Late. Fine flavoured culinary variety. Self fertile, flowering group 2
Gage 'Denniston's Superb'	harvest summer; plant autumn–winter	Extremely reliable dessert gage. Self fertile. Also known as 'Imperial Gage'
Gage 'Oullins Golden Gage'	harvest summer; plant autumn–winter	Delicious dessert gage. Pick early to cook. Self fertile, flowering group 2
Gage 'Laxton's Gage'	harvest summer; plant autumn–winter	Dessert gage with lovely flavour. Self fertile, flowering group 3
Gage 'Cambridge Gage'	harvest summer; plant autumn–winter	Small juicy dessert gage. Self fertile, flowering group 2
Gage 'Transparent'	harvest summer; plant autumn–winter	Small, sweet and golden dessert fruit. Self fertile, flowering group 2
Damson 'Merryweather'	harvest autumn; plant autumn–winter	Reliable, large fruit for cooking. Self fertile, flowering group 3
Damson 'Shropshire Damson'	harvest autumn; plant autumn–winter	Culinary fruit with excellent flavour. Self fertile, flowering group 5
Damson 'Farleigh Prolific'	harvest autumn; plant autumn–winter	Reliable culinary damson. Partly self fertile, flowering group 4
Damson 'Bradley's King'	harvest autumn; plant autumn–winter	Cooking fruit. Self fertile, flowering group 4
Damson 'Frogmore Damson'	harvest autumn; plant autumn–winter	Cooking fruit, with good texture and flavour. Partly self fertile

 planting   harvest

Sweet/ dessert cherries

Prunus avium

&

Acid/ cooking cherries

Prunus cerasus

Cherries, with their deep red-black, glossy, silky smooth skins, are inspirational fruits, and well worth growing as they are so expensive and generally such poor quality in many supermarkets.

There are two types of cherry – sweet/dessert (*Prunus avium*) and acid/cooking (*Prunus cerasus*). They have the same requirements as far as cultivation is concerned. The main differences between the two groups, apart from flavour, are that acid cherry trees tend to be slightly smaller than their sweet counterparts; most acid varieties are self fertile; they are more hardy, so can be grown against a wall that does not get quite as much sun; and instead of cropping on two-year-old or older wood, acid cherries fruit on one-year-old shoots.

The first things to consider when choosing varieties are pollination groups and rootstocks. Most acid cherries are self

soil	Prefers dry, well drained soil that is rich in potash and lime
site	Warm, dry, sunny and sheltered. *Prunus cerasus* can cope with milder sites
watering	Water well at the early stages of development and during summer, especially very hot and dry ones
feeding	Top dress the soil with sulphate of potash during mid-spring
general care	Keep weeds down as much as possible and mulch in spring. Tie in as necessary and net to protect from birds
pests and diseases	This group is particularly prone to bacterial canker, silver leaf disease, aphids and birds

fertile which simplifies matters, however there are fewer self fertile sweet cherry varieties.

It is worth seeking these self fertile sweet varieties out as it can be very complicated choosing the correct trees to pollinate one another. Besides needing to ensure that flowering times coincide, there is the added complication that certain cultivars are self sterile, so will not pollinate themselves. Also, some varieties will not pollinate other varieties within their own group. However, on the plus side, there are some varieties which are universal pollinators – in other words they will pollinate any variety that flowers simultaneously. One final point on pollination – bear in mind that sweet cherries will not pollinate the acid varieties.

The two most common rootstocks are 'Colt' and the snappily named 'Malling F12/1'. This is extremely vigorous, so needs plenty of space. 'Colt' is semi dwarfing and so is ideal for the average sized garden.

There are also some dwarfing rootstocks which have recently become available, notably 'Tabel', which are excellent for containers or where space is very restricted.

Pruning and training cherry trees is a time consuming task as they are constantly trying to outgrow their boundaries. A fully grown sweet cherry can reach 7.5m (25ft) tall, and spread by as much. Expect a fan-trained tree to grow to about 2.5m (8ft) high and spread to double that measure.

Fan-trained trees must be securely fixed to strong horizontal wires held away from the wall by vine eyes. Allow the main stem to reach about 38cm (15in) from the ground, then find the two strongest laterals just below this point (one on either side of the stem) and cut the main stem back to just above them. As these laterals grow, tie them on to canes attached to the support wires at an angle of about 45°. Remove all other laterals. As the laterals grow they will produce sideshoots; tie the strongest six (three per lateral) of these on to the support wires to form the fan shape. Remove all other sideshoots.

Cherry 'Nabella'

Cherry 'Morello'

Remember that sweet cherries crop on two- or three-year-old wood, while acid cherries fruit on one-year-old shoots.

If your tree is putting on excess growth then root prune it. This involves digging a trench around the tree, about 1m (3ft) from the main stem, and cutting through the biggest roots.

The best time to plant is in late autumn. Harvesting is generally from early summer to early autumn, depending upon variety. Check the variety table below for more precise times of the year.

		SPRING	SUMMER	AUTUMN	WINTER	
[SWEET]	Cherry 'Early Rivers'		harvest		planting	Early. Juicy and sweet, black fruit. Incompatible within own group
	Cherry 'Waterloo'		harvest		planting	Mid. Flowering group 2. Incompatible within own group
	Cherry 'Merton Bigarreau'		harvest		planting	Mid. Very fast growing. Lovely large, black fruit. Flowering group 3
	Cherry 'Merton Glory'		harvest		planting	Mid. Self sterile and flowering group 2. Universal pollinator
	Cherry 'Stella'		harvest		planting	Late. Shiny deep red fruit. Self fertile and flowering group 4
	Cherry 'Lapins'		harvest		planting	Late. Very popular variety. Self fertile and flowering group 4
	Cherry 'Noir de Guben'		harvest		planting	Late. Self sterile and flowering group 1. Universal pollinator
[ACID/COOKING]	Cherry 'Kentish Red'	harvest			planting	Early. Hardy with excellent fruit. Self fertile
	Cherry 'Morello'		harvest		planting	Excellent against a cooler wall. Self fertile
	Cherry 'Nabella'		harvest		planting	Excellent for cooler walls. Self fertile and flowering group 4

planting   harvest

Peaches
Prunus persica
&
Nectarines
Prunus persica
var. nectarina

Unlike many tree fruits, you will not have to wait years for your peach or nectarine tree to produce their first golden offerings. As little as three years after planting, you could be picking your first fruit.

Peaches and their smooth skinned cousins – nectarines – originate from China, and need a great deal of sunshine, warmth and shelter to bear fruit. They also need to be protected from frost and do not like very wet winters, although they can cope with the cold for short periods. These requirements mean that in cooler, more temperate climates, peaches and nectarines will be more likely to bear fruit if grown under glass.

Nectarines are especially demanding when it comes to temperature. They require slightly more warmth, so are unlikely to bear fruit if they are grown out of doors in temperate areas.

Traditionally, peaches and nectarines are trained in a fan shape against a sunny, sheltered wall. Out of doors this would have to be on the wall or side of the house which gets the most sun during the day. They can also be grown as bushes and free standing trees in containers – for which the dwarf varieties are most suited. However, the fan method is the most reliable as it allows the maximum amount of sunlight and heat to get to every part of the tree. You should allow a good amount of space, as they can spread to as much as 4.5m (15ft).

As well as choosing a variety you must also consider which rootstock to use.

Peach 'Peregrine'

Occasionally, peach rootstocks are used. However, the most common rootstocks are the plum rootstocks – 'St Julian A' and 'Brompton'. Of the two the most vigorous is 'Brompton'.

When deciding upon a rootstock take into account the growing conditions. For

Peach 'Autumn Rose'

soil	Peaches and nectarines like deep, fertile, moisture-retentive soil – ideally pH 6.5–7
site	A sun-drenched, sheltered, warm and frost-free position is best, or grown indoors
watering	Water well at the early stages, then during dry spells. Extra water is required if the soil is sandy
feeding	Add bone meal, or a similar slow release, nitrogen-rich manure
general care	Spray and damp down trees grown under cover (although not during flowering period)
pests and diseases	Prone to die back, bacterial canker, peach leaf curl, red spider mite, aphids, earwigs and birds

Peaches prefer a sun-drenched position in the garden

Peach 'Autumn Rose'

example, if your soil is not absolutely ideal for growing peaches or nectarines, then it may be worth choosing the more vigorous 'Brompton' rootstock to make up for this.

Peaches are self fertile, so you do not need to grow more than one tree. However, it is sensible to give pollination more of a chance of success by hand pollinating. This is especially advisable in colder, more temperate climates and when you are growing under cover.

Growing under cover is the surest way of guaranteeing a crop in the cooler regions, yet it is not a task to be undertaken lightly.

Firstly you need the space – an above average-sized greenhouse is vital as the tree may spread up to 3m (10ft) wide – plus you must have the time to lavish care on it. In addition to needing good fertile soil, it will require constant watering, feeding and damping down, as well as careful hand pollination.

Also be prepared to keep an eye on the ventilation of the greenhouse – vital for health and development – and on top of all these tasks you must ensure there are adequate supports for training the tree (see page 112 for method).

As with all greenhouse-grown plants and trees, temperature is the key to a successful crop. Start off with a steady spring-time temperature of 8–10°C (40–50°F) for about fourteen days, then double it to 20°C (68°).

If the conditions are right the tree will put on growth very rapidly. This is extremely satisfying, although it does mean that you will need to work hard making sure that its requirements for food and water are completely satisfied.

Peaches and nectarines are prone to a few problems, the main one being leaf curl, which is particularly likely to occur in wet areas. This can be avoided by spreading polythene over wall trained trees as soon as the buds burst through in late spring. Make sure you leave gaps for ventilation and pollination.

Correct pruning is especially important. Bush trained trees need to be cut back heavily in late spring, after which time any excess growth can be curbed by cutting back the roots (also known as root pruning); over-vigorous trees should also be root pruned.

To root prune a tree, wait until about five years after planting then dig a ditch in a circle around the tree, about 1m (3ft)

from the main stem, cut through the longer roots, then replace the soil, firm in and water well.

To train a fan shaped tree, wait until two strong laterals have developed on either side of the leader about 30cm (12in) above the ground, then cut the leader off just above the laterals. The next step is to tie these laterals on to canes, themselves tied on to supporting horizontal wires at an angle of about 45°, and trim off all other laterals. Allow a couple of sideshoots to grow up and one to grow from underneath each lateral and trim off all the others. Tie in these sideshoots as they develop to create the fan shape.

Once the shape is established, prune in spring to encourage new growth. Also prune after fruiting to remove fruited wood, old dead wood and to maintain the fan shape. Always remember that peaches and nectarines fruit on the previous season's shoots.

Nectarine 'Alba Red'

Nectarine 'Pacer'

Nectarine 'Lord Napier'

Like other tree fruit you will get a better crop if you thin the fruit. Initially thin to one fruit a cluster, then once they have grown larger, reduce so that there is a minimum of 15cm (6in) between fruit.

The best time for planting is in the late autumn to mid-winter, allowing for a space of about 5.5m (18ft) between trees.

The fruit is generally harvested from mid- to late summer into the early autumn, depending upon the variety. Check the table below for the different times of each variety.

	SPRING	SUMMER	AUTUMN	WINTER	
Peach 'Amsden June'		🥚🥚		🛠 🛠 🛠	Early. White fleshed, sweet and juicy. Heavy cropper
Peach 'Early Alexander'		🥚		🛠 🛠 🛠	Early. White fleshed, medium sized fruit
Peach 'Duke of York'		🥚		🛠 🛠 🛠	Early. Large, white fleshed fruit with excellent flavour
Peach 'Waterloo'		🥚🥚		🛠 🛠 🛠	Early. Delicious, tender white flesh
Peach 'Bonanza'		🥚		🛠 🛠 🛠	Mid. Dwarf variety, therefore good for containers. Yellow flesh
Peach 'Crimson Galande'		🥚		🛠 🛠 🛠	Mid. White fleshed, sweet and juicy fruit
Peach 'Peregrine'		🥚		🛠 🛠 🛠	Mid. White fleshed, fine flavoured fruit. Reliable
Peach 'Royal George'		🥚		🛠 🛠 🛠	Mid. Large, yellow fleshed fruit
Peach 'Autumn Rose'			🥚 🛠	🛠 🛠	Late. Fine flavoured, yellow fleshed variety
Peach 'Bellegarde'			🥚 🛠	🛠 🛠	Late. Yellow fleshed, delicious fruit
Peach 'Dymond'			🥚 🛠	🛠 🛠	Late. Juicy, yellow flesh
Nectarine 'Early Rivers'		🥚		🛠 🛠 🛠	Early. Fantastic flavour. Reliable outdoors
Nectarine 'John Rivers'		🥚		🛠 🛠 🛠	Early variety bearing heavy crops. Excellent flavour
Nectarine 'Lord Napier'		🥚🥚		🛠 🛠 🛠	Mid. Delicious, white fleshed fruit. Good for out doors
Nectarine 'Alba Red'		🥚		🛠 🛠 🛠	Mid. Juicy, fine flavoured, deep orange/red tinged fruit
Nectarine 'Pacer'			🥚🥚 🛠	🛠 🛠	Late. Distinctively flavoured, succulent fruit

🛠 planting 🥚 harvest

Apricots

Prunus armeniaca

Apricots can be tricky to grow in more temperate climates. They suffer from various problems, firstly they are very susceptible to frost damage, due to the fact that they flower so early, but the main problem is die back, which strikes quite unexpectedly, often affecting the healthiest, most vigorous limbs first.

By far the best position for *Prunus armeniaca* is trained against a sun-drenched wall in a fan shape, or indoors.

Apricots are self fertile, so you only need one variety, but you stand a better chance of pollination if you have two or three and you help the process along by hand pollinating with a soft camel hairbrush.

Correct pruning and training are essential to the health and size of crop the tree will produce. Apricots fruit on the previous season's stems, so you must try to encourage new growth by cutting back old wood in early spring, as well as taking out any dead or diseased branches. Concentrate on pinching back side shoots during the early summer to about 5cm (2in), and then pinch back the shoots which spring from these side shoots to one leaf. The key to training is constantly tying in all new growth to maintain the shape.

soil	Prefers well drained loam with high lime levels. Not too rich, however
site	A sun-drenched, sheltered, warm and frost-free position is best or grown indoors
watering	Water well at the early stages of development, and then once established only during dry spells
feeding	Do not overfeed, as a soil too rich in nutrients may be one cause of die back
general care	Keep weed free. Protect against frost (with horticultural fleece) and birds (with netting)
pests and diseases	Apricots are only vulnerable to a few pests and diseases, such as die back, rust, earwigs and birds

Apricots are ideal for growing indoors

Thin fruit in mid- to late spring to ensure the rest have the opportunity to grow to their full size. Aim for three fruit to a cluster, then thin again when the fruit starts to mature, leaving a gap of 10cm (4in) between each one.

The fruit is susceptible to bruising, so be gentle when picking them. Wait until they are fully ripe, then lie them on a bed of cotton wool. Use immediately or freeze.

Plant in the late autumn or early winter. If growing more than one, space 5.5m (18ft) apart; if training against a wall, plant about 30cm (12in) away and angle the stem back.

	SPRING	SUMMER	AUTUMN	WINTER	
Apricot 'Hemskerk'		harvest harvest	planting planting		Early variety with excellent flavour
Apricot 'New Large Early'		harvest harvest	planting planting		Early. Good disease resistance
Apricot 'Alfred'		harvest harvest	planting planting		Mid. Heavy cropping Canadian variety. Large fruit
Apricot 'Breda'		harvest harvest	planting planting		Reliable, mid-season fruiter
Apricot 'Farmingdale'		harvest harvest	planting planting		Mid. Juicy with good flavour
Apricot 'Shipley's/Blenheim'		harvest	planting planting		Mid to late season. Very hardy, heavy cropper. Small fruit
Apricot 'Moorpark'		harvest	planting planting		Late, old variety. Top class fruit. Also has early type

planting   harvest

Figs
Ficus carica

These long lasting, architectural trees are so handsome with such striking, large leaves that they would be worth growing for their appearance alone, even if they did not bear such sweet, juicy fruit.

Figs – in brown and green varieties – prefer a long, hot season to grow and ripen. However, if people living in cooler areas choose their site and variety well, there is no reason why they should not enjoy a late harvest.

They are relatively hardy and can cope with quite adverse conditions. Figs can be trained into a bush shape, but thrive grown against a sunny, sheltered wall. They respond especially well to being trained into a fan shape, which allows every part of the plant maximum exposure to light and heat.

Figs also do well in containers, which are the best option for really cool areas as they can be kept in a conservatory or greenhouse during cold periods, then taken outside as soon as the weather warms up. The containers need to be about 38cm (15in) across to allow the tree to grow large enough to produce fruit.

Figs planted in the ground can grow quite large and produce masses of foliage at the expense of the fruit. You can prevent this from happening by restricting the fig's roots. Dig a hole about 1m (3ft) wide and deep, then line the bottom with a 25cm (10in) layer of broken bricks or stone. Next place paving slabs against the sides of the hole and fill with earth, adding lime if necessary.

As fruit grows on the previous season's wood, prune with care, aiming to remove excessive growth and damaged branches rather than all the old wood. This is best done in spring, although you can cut off more growth in the summer if necessary.

Plant in the spring in cool areas and late autumn elsewhere. Harvest just as the fruit begin to split.

Figs are tasty fruits and can be eaten hot or cold

soil	Figs prefer well drained but moisture-retentive soil and preferably alkaline
site	A sun-drenched, sheltered and warm position is the best site for this tree
watering	Water well in the early stages, then during hot, dry spells, paying attention to pot grown plants
feeding	Give the tree occasional liquid feeds throughout the summer
general care	Keep the weeds down. Mulch in spring with decayed compost or well rotted manure
pests and diseases	Figs are only vulnerable to a few pests and diseases, such as grey mould/botrytis, wasps and birds

	SPRING	SUMMER	AUTUMN	WINTER	
Fig 'Black Ischia'		harvest	planting		Early. Hardy variety, excellent for cooler areas
Fig 'St John's'		harvest	planting		Early. Deliciously sweet and juicy white flesh
Fig 'White Marseilles'		harvest	planting		Early. Crops especially well under glass
Fig 'Brown Turkey'		harvest harvest	planting		Mid. Best all round variety. Hardy
Fig 'Brunswick'		harvest harvest	planting		Mid. Large pale green fruits with succulent white flesh
Fig 'Negro Largo'		harvest harvest	planting		Mid. Dark fruit with excellent flavour

🖊 planting   🌰 harvest

Olives

Olea europaea

It is amazing how important a place such a small, not particularly prepossessing, fruit can have. Olive trees have been cultivated for centuries, with their fruit and wood being vital to the survival of whole communities – and the shade they provide being no less important.

Olives and their oil have enormous health-giving properties, and their flavour adds so much to cooking that it is hard to imagine a world without this wonderful fruit.

Evergreen, with beautiful tiny leaves that seem to sparkle in the sunlight, olive trees can live for hundreds of years, remaining productive for virtually all that time. Old trees develop a venerable, gnarled appearance.

Olives will not flower or fruit for at least three years and crops may be light for the first 15 years. They are self fertile, however it is advisable to grow more than one in cooler areas to be certain of pollination.

In cooler areas, olive trees may not produce flowers or fruit unless grown under cover. As the trees can reach 12m (40ft) high and 9m (28ft) wide, this is rarely practical in anything less than a stately home-sized greenhouse. They can, however, be grown in 35cm (14in) wide containers which can be moved outside once the weather becomes warm and sunny. Obviously the size of container will restrict the tree's growth, and the size of the crop.

Olives can either be harvested when green but ripe for fermenting or left on the tree to turn black if they are intended for eating. Olives to be pressed for oil should be harvested last of all, when they are completely ripe. Do not pick these, instead follow the traditional method

Green olives can be harvested for oil

and place fine netting beneath the tree, then shake it so that the fruit fall into the netting.

Cut back the leading shoot once the tree reaches 1.5m (5ft) and later cut away old wood to encourage fresh growth. Remember the fruit is borne on one-year-old wood.

soil	Olives prefer a well drained, with low to medium fertile soil, preferably alkaline
site	Thrives in a sun-drenched site sheltered from strong winds
watering	Water well for the first few years of growth, then regularly during dry periods once established
feeding	Top dress during the growing period with moderate to high nitrogen fertilizer
general care	Keep the tree as weed free as possible and give a good mulching. May need to thin fruit
pests and diseases	Particularly prone to scale insects, verticillium wilt, red spider mites, thrips and whiteflies

Black olives have simply been left on the tree longer

	SPRING	SUMMER	AUTUMN	WINTER	
Olive 'El Greco'					Popular, reliable variety. Wonderful flavour
Olive 'Sevillano'					Superb flavour and rich in oil
Olive 'Manzanillo'					Consistently delicious

planting   harvest

Mulberries

Morus nigra

Planting a mulberry tree demonstrates a faith in the future, for it is your children's children who will enjoy it in its full glory. You also need a good sized garden even to contemplate growing a mulberry.

Mulberries are large trees – black mulberries can reach 10m (30ft) high – with an extremely spreading habit. There are actually two types of mulberry, the black mulberry (*Morus nigra*) and the white mulberry (*Morus alba*). The white mulberry is smaller and generally grown as a specimen tree. It is the black mulberry which provides the raspberry-like fruit and is so handsome that it deserves to stand alone in a prominent position where it can be admired all year round.

Unusually for a tree, the mulberry will do better in cold areas if it is planted during the spring; everywhere else, late autumn to winter is the best time to plant. As the mulberry is self fertile there is no need to plant more then one.

Mulberries do not need to be pruned regularly. In fact, they bleed heavily when cut, so pruning should be confined to the removal of dead or diseased wood and overlapping branches during the winter. Any bleeding limbs should be cauterized with a hot poker.

The fruit of the mulberry ripens at different times during late summer so it is

soil	Thrives in well drained but moist soil as long as it is deep, rich and slightly acid
site	Prefers an open and sunny position with plenty of space around it
watering	Water well at the early stages of development, then once established, only water during dry spells
feeding	The ground should be well dug and manured before planting
general care	Try to keep the area around the tree weed free. Provide a mulch to retain moisture in the spring
pests and diseases	Apart from mulberry canker, this tree is relatively free from most pests and diseases

more a case of picking over the tree regularly rather than having one long harvesting session. Another method is to spread a sheet of polythene under the tree to catch the fruit as it falls.

Once harvested the fruit is delicious eaten raw and also freezes extremely well, using the tray freezing method (see pages 39–40).

Young mulberry trees are not widely available, and should be bought from specialist nurseries. There are not many varieties on the market, but one to look out for is 'Wellington', an extremely reliable cropper, which produces a mass of delicious fruit.

The best time to plant mulberries is in the late autumn to the beginning of winter. In more temperate climates, however, it is best to wait until spring. Remembering that mulberry fruit can ripen at different times during the summer, a general rule for harvesting times is mid- to late summer.

Morus nigra

Soft Fruit

**What soft fruit loses in shortness of season, it more
than makes up for in richness of taste. This group
includes some of the most popular fruits of all,
including that star whose arrival signals summer
has really arrived, the strawberry.**

Lacking the high glamour of the strawberry, but just
as delicious, raspberries, blackberries and their
offspring the hybrid berries, are bursting with flavour,
and can be frozen to bring a taste of sunshine to the
depths of winter.

Gooseberries and the currants – red, white and black
– are rarely available fresh in supermarkets, so most
people associate them, in the case of gooseberries, with
the tart canned version or, in the case of the currants,
with soft drinks. This is a pity as it means that few
people nowadays have the chance to enjoy the fine
flavour of the fresh fruit.

As if the taste of soft fruit were not enough, most
are also very decorative and can be trained to grow
against walls and fences or left, like the blueberry, to
provide a blaze of colour in the autumn. The low-growing
strawberries are an obvious exception to this, yet
they look extremely pretty edging paths – especially
the alpine varieties, which somehow escape the
attention of birds.

Strawberries

Fragaria x ananassa
&

Alpine Strawberries

Fragaria vesca

Forget supermarket strawberries – those disturbingly large, crisp, artificially red and completely tasteless offerings available all year round. 'Real' strawberries are generally only available during the summer, do not look as though they have come off a production line and have an unequalled taste.

Strawberries need not be a troublesome crop; a lot of varieties have had disease resistance bred into them and are tolerant of many different soil types, although they thrive best in a light, humus-rich loam.

The important thing to remember when establishing a crop, is to make sure the ground is completely free from perennial weeds and then to work in as much well rotted manure as you can manage. Anything from farmyard manure to compost or seaweed would be ideal.

A good feed of fish meal is excellent for its nitrogen, potash and phosphorus content. Avoid chemical manures; they will do nothing to improve flavour and will actually cause yields to drop.

Besides feeding the soil, digging in large amounts of manure and humus-creating materials will ensure that light soils are more able to retain moisture, while heavy ones become more open. Strawberries need to absorb a great deal of moisture, particularly

soil	They prefer a well manured, humus-rich, light loam. Ideal pH between 6 and 6.5
site	Warm with full sun, some shade for summer fruiting. Shelter from strong winds
watering	Plants need plenty of moisture during spring and summer while the fruit are growing
feeding	Apply a top dressing of potash before planting, especially if the soil is light
general care	Keep weed free. Spread thick layers of newspaper or straw under plants to keep fruit clean
pests and diseases	Prone to red core root rot, botrytis (grey mould), wireworm, strawberry beetle, slugs and birds

Strawberry 'El Santa'

as the fruit is forming, in order to help them swell. However, they do not like the ground to be waterlogged during the winter, so a free draining yet moisture-retentive soil is ideal. Again, digging in plenty of organic material will help ensure this.

There are three types of strawberries: those which fruit in the summer (either early or late), those which fruit in late summer and autumn – known as perpetuals or ever-bearing strawberries – and alpines.

Alpine strawberries are ideal for amateurs as they need little or no care and will happily occupy shady spots that are unsuitable for ordinary strawberries. Those with runners spread themselves freely, others are easily divided and all are simple to raise from seed. They look pretty edging a border or path, or growing from cracks between paving stones in the terrace. The fruit is smaller than ordinary strawberries, but has a lovely flavour.

All types of strawberries are excellent candidates for growing in pots. There are attractive terracotta planters specifically designed for them, which look wonderful on a terrace – very convenient for a pick your own pudding.

Strawberry plants tend to crop well for about three years, after which they lose much of their vigour and are best dug up and replaced with new plants – although alpines will last longer. It is also advisable to plant your new stock in a different area, leaving the previous site until you next renew your plants.

While strawberries can be raised from seed, it is easier to buy in your initial stock – check that the plants are certified virus free – and then propagate by rooting runners or, in the case of certain alpines, dividing the plants.

Strawberries can be grown under cover, which allows you to raise a much earlier crop – possibly up to four weeks earlier. There are disadvantages, however, as the resulting fruit will not have the rich, mouthwatering flavour so attractive in later crops.

Such a crop can only be achieved with the help of a heated greenhouse. It is important to get the temperature right. It should be at least 10°C (50°F) during the day, although during the night it need only be 7°C (45°F).

Strawberry 'Cambridge Favourite'

Keep an eye on the humidity, damping down the greenhouse if it seems too dry. Airflow is also important to the health of the plants.

Once the flowers start to develop the temperature can be dropped by a few degrees, although it should be raised to its original level once flowering proper begins.

Cloches will also speed up ripening, and have the advantage of protecting the crop from birds. Do not cover the plants too early, however, or they may develop mildew or botrytis. Late winter is ideal.

For sowing purposes, plant summer fruiters in late summer or early autumn, perpetuals in autumn or spring and alpines in spring or summer. Allow 45–60cm (18–24in) space between plants, 30cm (12in) for alpines. Summer fruiters are ready the summer after planting; perpetuals the following late summer and autumn; and alpines are ready to harvest within a few weeks of planting.

Another way to propagate strawberries is from 'runners' sent out by an established

Strawberry 'Honeoye'

plant. The plant should be strong growing, free from pests and diseases (as far as possible), and a good cropper. The 'runners' grow from the main plant during summer and produce small plantlets at the end. Sometimes, several plantlets can be found on one runner, but it is best to use the strongest one.

Strawberry 'Claire-Maree'

Strawberries have a distinctive 'summer' taste

Peg down the plantlet with looped wire – leaving it attached to the parent – either straight into the ground or sink a pot with potting compost in the ground and peg the plantlet into the potting mixture. Water the plantlet once it is settled in its new home, but after that watering should not be necessary.

After about a month, the plantlet should have developed a good root system and will be ready to be separated from the parent's runner. Simply cut off the remains of the runner and remove any dead leaves and stalks. Dig a hole deep enough to accommodate the rootball and transplant your new strawberry plant into its position. Water in and the following summer, expect a good crop of fruit from your new plant.

	SPRING	SUMMER	AUTUMN	WINTER	
Strawberry 'Honeoye'		harvest / planting	planting		Early. Heavy cropper, good disease resistance. Delicious red-orange fruit
Strawberry 'Claire-Maree'	harvest	harvest	planting	planting	High-yielding, early fruiter. Delicious large, sweet rich flavour
Strawberry 'Cambridge Favourite'		harvest / harvest	planting	planting	Mid. Provides the heaviest yields. Good under glass. Very reliable
Strawberry 'El Santa'		harvest / harvest	planting	planting	Mid. Good grower with large, succulent berries. Good disease resistance
Strawberry 'Everest'		harvest / planting	planting		Late. Hardy, heavy cropper. Top quality, delicious berries.
Strawberry 'Cambridge Late Pine'		harvest / planting	planting		Very sweet, deep crimson berries. Very late fruiting.
Strawberry 'Aromel'	planting planting planting	harvest harvest harvest	planting planting planting	Perpetual variety. Excellent for containers. Sweet and juicy berries
Strawberry 'Calypso'	planting planting planting	harvest harvest harvest	planting planting planting planting	Perpetual variety. Shiny red berries. Crops under cloches to late autumn
Alpine Strawberry 'Baron Solemacher'	planting planting	planting planting planting	harvest	Popular tall variety. Long, rich flavoured fruit
Alpine Strawberry 'Alpine Yellow'	planting	planting planting planting	harvest	Decorative variety with sweet berries
Alpine Strawberry 'Belle de Meaux'	planting	planting planting planting	harvest	French variety with small, sweet crimson fruit. Forms runners

 planting   harvest

Raspberries

Rubus idaeus

Raspberries are extremely delicate looking with a melt-in-the-mouth flavour that implies they are a high summer fruit. In fact, they are a cool season crop which will carry on yielding fruit into winter.

There are two types of raspberry: those which fruit in the summer and those which are ready in the autumn through to early winter. The summer fruiting varieties have quite a short season, however they do produce high yields, while the autumn fruiters will bear berries from the end of summer through to the first frosts.

Raspberries will not thrive on light, dry soil. Instead, for best results, they need a really moisture-retentive soil packed full of manure, whether it be poultry, farmyard or garden compost. Once planted, the canes will also appreciate a light top dressing of sulphate of potash. Wood ash is an excellent source of this.

The canes require support once they reach about 45cm (18in) high. The best method of supporting new growth is to tie it to a series of horizontal, parallel wires strung between stakes. Choose 1.8m (6ft) high stakes and set them about 3m (10ft) apart, then attach three runs of wire to the

Raspberry 'Glen Moy'

stakes at about 75cm (30in), 1.1m (3½ft) and 1.5m (5ft) off the ground.

You can tie in the canes in many different ways. The most important thing to remember is that you must ensure the canes are securely tied so that they are safe from damage in windy weather and that they are arranged in a way that makes picking easy.

Summer fruiting raspberries will need to be netted, otherwise the birds will have a field day stripping the plants of fruit in minutes. Autumn fruiting varieties seem to escape the attention of birds, and also grow in fairly tight clumps, making them useful as screens.

soil	Prefers heavy loam, moisture-retentive but not waterlogged soil
site	A sunny, sheltered frost-free site, although can cope with some shade
watering	Make sure you water well during the summer when the canes are flowering and fruiting
feeding	The ground should be well manured before planting the canes
general care	Keep weed free. Net to protect summer fruiters from birds. Mulch monthly during the summer
pests and diseases	Raspberries are particularly prone to mosaic virus, botrytis, raspberry beetle and birds

Raspberry 'Driscolls'

Pruning is equally as important as training. This is carried out in two periods – mid-summer and after the last fruit has been picked. In mid-summer, the canes that were cut back after planting should be removed altogether. After cropping, summer fruiting varieties should have all fruiting canes removed, while autumn fruiting types should have every cane cut back to about 15cm (6in) from the ground in late winter or early spring. Also remove any weak growth.

Raspberries are bought as canes, rather than seeds. Check that these have a certificate stating that they are virus free. They are propagated by removing suckers which are growing away from the parent plant.

Raspberry 'Autumn Bliss'

Raspberry 'Glen Magna'

A bit of patience is needed when growing raspberries. Do not expect your canes to provide a crop the first year – raspberries need time to establish themselves.

For sowing purposes, plant your canes between late autumn and early winter, around 38–60cm (15–24in) apart, with the roots about 5cm (2in) below the soil surface. Cut the canes down to 30cm (12in) from the ground after planting.

The time to harvest fruit depends on the different varieties. Early summer fruiting varieties are normally ready from early to mid-summer. Mid-season summer fruiters can be harvested in mid-summer. Late summer fruiters are ready from mid-summer up to the beginning of early autumn. Finally, autumn fruiting varieties can be picked from late summer up until the first frosts.

	SPRING	SUMMER	AUTUMN	WINTER	
Raspberry 'Glen Moy'		🍓🍓		🌱🌱	Early. Richly flavoured, large berries. No spines
Raspberry 'Malling Jewel'		🍓🍓		🌱🌱	Early. Among the best earlies. Luscious and sweet berries. Very abundant
Raspberry 'Glen Prosen'		🍓		🌱🌱	Mid. Fantastic flavour, juicy and sweet
Raspberry 'Malling Orion'		🍓		🌱🌱	Mid. Vigorous and heavy cropper. Freezes well
Raspberry 'Glen Magna'		🍓🍓		🌱🌱	Late. Huge, crimson fruit. Fantastic flavour. Freezes well
Raspberry 'Malling Joy'		🍓🍓		🌱🌱	Late. Juicy, richly coloured fruit with wonderful taste
Raspberry 'Autumn Bliss'		🍓🍓🍓		🌱🌱	Autumn. Popular variety with large, delicious berries
Raspberry 'All Gold'		🍓🍓🍓		🌱🌱	Autumn. Yellow variety. Hardy with luscious fruit

🌱 planting   🍓 harvest

Blackberries
Rubus fruticosus

Blackberries are generally dismissed as, at worst, a nuisance to be eliminated, and at best as wild berries – fun to pick from hedgerows, yet not worth growing. However, if you cultivate blackberries you will harvest a more bountiful crop than wild berries ever produce and, because you can control the amount of humus and nitrogen they receive, you can ensure the berries are large and juicy.

Blackberries are extremely hardy, and are untroubled by spring frosts and all but the very driest soil. They do, however, spread and so need a great deal of space. This requirement makes them extremely suitable for those with large gardens, where their rampant habits would not be so disastrous.

Blackberries are generally sold as one-year-old canes. It is very important to only choose stock which has a certificate to guarantee it is virus free. Choose thornless varieties if possible – these are slightly less vigorous and immeasurably easier to handle and harvest.

Dig plenty of well rotted manure or compost into the ground before planting and treat the young canes with care. This is because although the blackberry is very hardy, the young canes are quite brittle

Blackberry 'Black Bute'

and once damaged take a whole season to recover. Blackberries tolerate partial shade, particularly in very hot summers, and appreciate some protection from strong winds.

There are many ways of training blackberries, and many involve tying the canes to horizontal wires so that they can be easily picked and tended. As the blackberry grows, train the canes up supports and parallel wires, similar to those used for raspberries (see pages 122–3). Blackberries will also grow extremely well set against walls and fences. The canes become extremely heavy as they get larger and start to produce fruits, so make sure that the wires are thick enough and tightly strung to avoid sagging.

Once the berries have been harvested

Blackberry 'Loch Ness'

they need to be pruned. Again, the method is very similar to that used for raspberries. Cut down to ground level all canes that have fruited and then tie in the new canes. As blackberries fruit on one-year-old canes, be careful not to remove canes until after they have borne berries.

Controlling the number of new canes in the growing season is beneficial not only for keeping the plant within your required bounds in the garden, but also for producing better quality canes for the following year, thereby improving the size and taste of the fruit produced.

Watering when the fruit starts to change colour will improve the size and weight of the fruit. Water the soil to avoid wetting the canes and fruit, which could lead to disease.

Blackberries are extremely easy to propagate, as anyone who has ever battled with brambles will know. Simply place the tip of a shoot in a hole about 10cm (4in)

soil	Blackberries prefer well manured and moisture-retentive soil
site	A sunny or partially-shaded site, sheltered from strong winds, is best
watering	Once blackberries are established, keep well watered during dry spells in the summer
feeding	The ground should be well manured before planting the canes
general care	Try to keep the area around the canes weed free and mulch in spring. Provide as much support as possible
pests and diseases	Apart from botrytis, raspberry beetles and birds, blackberries are generally trouble-free

deep and cover with soil. This tip will then form roots and, when it is established, can be separated from the parent plant and be replanted.

The best time of year to plant blackberries is in the late autumn or winter. Plant to quite a shallow depth, then immediately cut the canes back to 23cm (9in) above the ground. Allow about 4m (12ft) between canes. The best time of year for harvesting is between late summer and early autumn. Pick the fruit, when ripe, every two to three days to avoid any over-ripe fruit rotting and picking up any diseases. When picking, try to get the fruit with the core, or plug, still complete as this will help the fruit retain its shape.

Blackberries, as well as being superb in cooking, make wonderful jam and are excellent to keep in the freezer or stored in a bag in the fridge for a few days.

By controlling humus and nitrogen levels, you can guarantee large, juicy fruit

	SPRING	SUMMER	AUTUMN	WINTER	
Blackberry 'Loch Ness'		harvest harvest	planting planting	planting planting	Not so rampant. Neat and upright. Thornless and bountiful
Blackberry 'Black Bute'		harvest harvest	planting planting	planting planting	Probably the largest blackberry – fruits 5cm (2in) long by 2.5cm (1in) wide
Blackberry 'Merton Thornless'		harvest harvest	planting planting	planting planting	The most manageable variety, not too vigorous

 planting   harvest

Blueberries

Vaccinium corymbosum spp.

Cultivated blueberries, otherwise known as highbush blueberries, are descended from the North American wild blueberry. They are attractive berries, often so dark as to look almost purple-black, with a delicate, dusty bloom. Their flavour verges on the bitter and so they are generally cooked rather than eaten raw.

Blueberries are worth growing for their pretty flowers, which resemble the flowers of heather, and for the fantastic display of colour produced by the foliage in the autumn. The leaves turn every hue from a deep, rich bronze, through vivid crimson to a fiery gold.

Blueberries do not need another variety to fertilize them, but your yield will be heavier if you plant more than one cultivar. You will also find that the yield increases after a couple of seasons, and that mature bushes produce by far the heavier crop. Bushes may continue to bear fruit for as long as 30 years.

As blueberries grow so well in containers, they are an excellent choice for a small garden. This is also a way of cultivating them in an area with very alkaline soil. The containers need to be at least 38cm (15in) wide and filled with ericaeous compost.

soil	Weed free, moist but well drained and acidic – prefers a pH of about 4.5
site	Sunny or partially shaded, open but sheltered from strong winds
watering	Once blueberries are established, keep them watered with rainwater during dry spells
feeding	Unless acid, the ground should be treated with acidic compost before planting
general care	Keep weed free, mulch with acid compost or leaf mould in early summer. Net to protect against birds
pests and diseases	Apart from chlorosis and birds, this plant is fairly trouble-free from pests and diseases

Do not prune for about three years, apart from removing any diseased or weak shoots. After that time cut out old wood, bearing in mind that the fruit are borne on two- or three-year-old wood.

Blueberries are easily propagated through layering shoots in the autumn or by taking softwood cuttings in late summer. These should be taken just above a leaf joint and need to be about 10cm (4in) long.

Plant in late autumn to late winter about 5cm (2in) deep, and allow about 1.5m (5ft) between plants. The best time to harvest is over a few weeks in mid- to late summer.

Blueberry 'Darrow'

	SPRING	SUMMER	AUTUMN	WINTER	
Blueberry 'Bluecrop'		🌱🌱		🌿🌿🌿🌿	Early. Foliage turns fantastic colours in the autumn
Blueberry 'Earliblue'		🌱🌱		🌿🌿🌿🌿	Early. Copes well with cold. Produces high yields of sweet, juicy berries
Blueberry 'Berkley'		🌱🌱		🌿🌿🌿🌿	Mid. Popular variety. Vigorous and prolific
Blueberry 'Herbert'		🌱🌱		🌿🌿🌿🌿	Mid. Reliable, with high quality fruit
Blueberry 'Darrow'		🌱🌱		🌿🌿🌿🌿	Late. Excellent choice for late harvest. Freezes well
Blueberry 'Jersey'		🌱🌱		🌿🌿🌿🌿	Late. One of the most vigorous varieties. Heavy crops of large berries

🌿 planting   🌱 harvest

Loganberries & Tayberries

Rubus hybrids

The hybrid berries, loganberries and tayberries, are the result of a cross between a raspberry and blackberry. The first cross produced the loganberry, and took place in California in the late 18th century; the tayberry followed shortly afterwards.

Loganberries and tayberries combine the size and juiciness of blackberries with the sweetness of raspberries – tayberries being the slightly sweeter of the two. They freeze especially well, losing none of their flavour and staying firm.

Like all canes they are susceptible to virus, so it is vital to buy only stock certified disease free.

The hybrid berries are very accommodating, enjoying most soils and being hardy enough not to be troubled by frosts. The main way they differ from blackberries is that the canes are less supple and whippy, so must be treated with care, rather like raspberry canes. Support and tie in following the same techniques used for blackberries, although aim for a fan

Loganberry 'LY654'

The hybrid tayberry fruit is elongated

shape rather than tying the canes along wires. Allow at least one season before expecting a crop; this delay is more than made up for by the fact that the canes will carry on being productive for many years.

As far as pruning is concerned, follow the method used for raspberries, cutting back canes which have fruited to within 7.5cm (3in) of the ground and tying in the new growth ready for the next season.

Propagate the hybrid berries by tip layering. This could not be easier: simply bury the tip of a healthy, vigorous shoot and once it has rooted detach it from the parent plant and move it to its permanent position.

Ideally, plant during late autumn. However, any time from late autumn to early spring is acceptable. Leave spaces of 3m (10ft) between each cane. The best time for harvesting is mid- to late summer.

soil	Avoid waterlogged soil, otherwise no special requirements
site	A sunny or partly shaded spot, sheltered from cold winds is preferable
watering	Generally unfussy. Apart from watering during dry spells, you do not need to spend time watering
feeding	Treat the soil with any manure that is rich in nitrogen
general care	Keep the area weed free and provide a good mulch in spring. Net to protect against birds
pests and diseases	Apart from raspberry beetle, both of these are relatively free from pests and diseases

	SPRING		SUMMER		AUTUMN		WINTER			
Loganberry 'LY654'	🌱		🍃 🍃				🌱	🌱	🌱 🌱	Reliable with good disease resistance
Loganberry 'LY59'	🌱		🍃 🍃				🌱	🌱	🌱 🌱	Heavy cropper, extremely vigorous – grows to 2.4m (8ft). Virus-free strain
Tayberry 'Medana'	🌱		🍃 🍃				🌱	🌱	🌱 🌱	Good disease resistance. Excellent flavour

 planting   harvest

Gooseberries

Ribes uva-crispa

The gooseberry is the ideal fruit for the amateur soft-fruit gardener to start growing, as it is so hardy and wonderfully able to thrive in conditions that other soft fruit would find quite intolerable.

Partial shade, wind, high ground and heavier soils – all these things the gooseberry will shrug off. In fact, the fruit can even be left on the bushes without going bad far longer than any other soft fruit. As an extra bonus gooseberries do not require regular pruning. Simply remove any dead or diseased wood, and thin out if necessary to make picking easier and to allow air to circulate.

Gooseberries have fallen slightly out of favour as many people associate them purely with the unripe, slightly sour, green fruit, picked early for cooking and available in cans at the supermarket. These bitter fruit do nothing for the reputation of gooseberries, which come in many varieties and colours – white, yellow and red – and which can be deliciously sweet and soft.

The trick is to leave the fruit intended to be eaten raw – the dessert fruit – on the bush longer. In fact, they should not be picked until they have had the chance to

Gooseberry 'Invicta'

ripen fully. You will know when they have reached this point as their colour will have developed and deepened to its maximum.

Such ripe gooseberries are seldom seen in supermarkets, possibly due to the difficulties and costs of getting them packed and transported undamaged to their destination within such a tight time frame. So it is definitely worth finding a corner for them in your garden.

There are various different ways of training gooseberries and they are amenable to most forms. They can be left as bushes, tied to wires strung between stakes or trained into smart standards.

The best method for smaller gardens is the cordon – either double or single. Cordon-trained gooseberries can be

soil 	Avoid waterlogged or very dry soil. Light, well drained, cool and humus rich is ideal
site	Gooseberries thrive in positions that are sunny or partly shaded
watering	These are fairly unfussy plants, although they do require watering during dry spells
feeding	Top dress the plants with sulphate of potash in the spring
general care	Keep the area free of weeds and mulch in spring. Put nets over to protect against birds
pests and diseases	Apart from American gooseberry mildew and birds, these are fairly trouble-free

Gooseberry 'Leveller'

Gooseberry 'Whinham's Industry'

grown against a wall or fence, taking up very little room – the perfect solution if space is tight. (For more details of the various shapes of training, see pages 36–8.)

Propagate gooseberries by means of 30cm (12in) softwood cuttings, taken in early autumn.

Choose the newest wood available – it will be lighter in colour – and remove all buds bar the top four. The next step is to dip the end of the cutting in hormone rooting powder and place it in moist, sandy soil, about 10cm (4in) deep. After a while the buds will start to develop into branches.

It is vital to plant the cutting as soon as possible after taking it. If there is any delay and it starts to dry out, it is likely they will not take root.

Late autumn is the best time for planting, however they can be planted any time during the winter – unless your soil is especially heavy or badly drained, in which case wait until early spring. Place the

bushes 1.5m (5ft) apart or if you are growing cordons, make sure they are 30cm (12in) apart.

Water gooseberries during dry periods and especially once the fruits start to swell, as this will improve their size and weight. Mulch to keep in moisture and protect from weeds in early to mid-spring using well-rotted manure or compost.

Suckers – ground-level shoots – may sprout from bushes that are stressed and unhealthy. Rather than cutting them back with secateurs, pull them off at source as this will discourage others forming the following year.

The best time to harvest crops is early to mid-summer. Pick fruit with a short stalk still left on it or you could tear the skin trying to prise it off its stalk.

	SPRING	SUMMER	AUTUMN	WINTER	
Gooseberry 'Broom Girl'	planting	harvest harvest		planting planting planting planting	Early, cooking/dessert. Outstanding flavour and attractive looking
Gooseberry 'May Duke'	planting	harvest harvest		planting planting planting planting	Early. Pick late spring for cooking and early summer for dessert
Gooseberry 'Invicta'	planting	harvest harvest		planting planting planting planting	Mid. Cooking variety. Extremely disease resistant. Fast growing, spreading
Gooseberry 'Leveller'	planting	harvest harvest		planting planting planting planting	Mid. Very popular dessert variety with marvellous taste
Gooseberry 'Careless'	planting	harvest harvest		planting planting planting planting	Mid. Well known, white spreading variety, providing bumper crops
Gooseberry 'Whinham's Industry'	planting	harvest harvest		planting planting planting planting	Mid. Lovely dark fruit with fine flavour. Reliable cooking/dessert variety
Gooseberry 'Warrington'	planting	harvest		planting planting planting planting	Late. Dark crimson fruit makes fantastic jam
Gooseberry 'White Lion'	planting	harvest		planting planting planting planting	Late, heavy cropper, vigorous with superb flavour for cooking/dessert

planting   harvest

Blackcurrants
Ribes nigrum

Red & Whitecurrants
Ribes rubrum

If you think that currants are so fiddly to prepare that they are not worth growing, think again. These tiny fruits are bursting with Vitamin C and have such a rich flavour that a few will go a long way. They are unbeatable made into jams, preserves and soft drinks, and yet are rarely seen on supermarket shelves.

The currants are quite undemanding plants, and with their glossy berries, they are decorative enough to enhance any garden.

Buy as one- or two-year-old certified plants and either leave them to grow in their

natural state as bushes – they may reach about 1.5m (5ft) – or tie them on to wires against a wall or fence. Red and whitecurrants tend to have a more upright habit than blackcurrants, which are more spreading. Red and whitecurrants also respond well to being trained as cordons, either single or double. These can be used to great effect to separate areas of the garden and are very space saving.

Currants like ground which has been well dug and manured; blackcurrants are especially greedy, requiring extra manure. They are also more tender than the red and whitecurrant varieties, needing a warm site, sheltered from any cold winds and late frosts.

soil	Well dug and manured (if growing blackcurrants, dig in extra manure)
site	Open but sheltered. Blackcurrants need more warmth and protection
watering	Make sure currants are watered during dry spells, although not when the fruit are ripening
feeding	Top dress with manure and sulphate of ammonia in the spring
general care	Hand weed around bushes to keep weed free and mulch in spring. Net to protect against birds
pests and diseases	All currants can be particularly prone to botrytis, reversion disease, aphids and birds

Blackcurrant 'Ben Connan'

Whitecurrant 'Blanka'

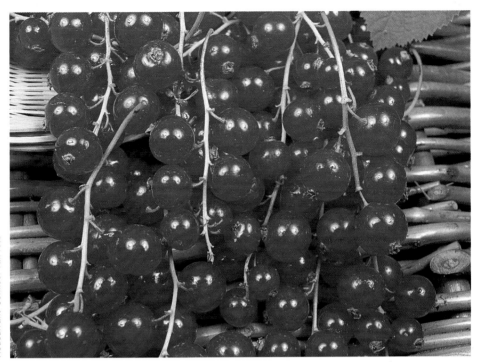

Redcurrant 'Jonkeer van Tets'

Again, blackcurrants need a slightly different treatment from red and whitecurrants when it comes to pruning. This is because blackcurrants fruit on one-year-old wood, unlike their cousins which fruit on old wood. After, harvesting prune out all the blackcurrant's old wood to encourage fresh new growth. However, with red and whitecurrants you only need to remove any dead or damaged wood, and cut back to open up the plant and shape. Cordons need more work, as the laterals should be cut back to about 3cm (1⅛in) of the main stem.

Reversion virus can be devastating, progressively reducing yields, so it is advisable to replace the plants every ten years as a precaution. If you see any signs of the disease, then dig up and burn affected plants.

Only start to pick fruit when whole bunches have formed, and remove the berries by combing them off the bunch with a fork. They freeze extremely well, retaining their flavour and staying firm.

To propagate currants take cuttings in the autumn of young, healthy wood. The cuttings should be about 20cm (8in) long and you should leave all the buds on. Dip the cut end in hormone rooting powder and plant immediately in damp, sandy soil.

The best time to plant is in the late autumn. Place about 1.2m (4ft) apart, immediately cutting back to 5cm (2in) above the ground. Harvest the crop from mid- to late summer.

	SPRING	SUMMER	AUTUMN	WINTER	
Blackcurrant 'Ben Connan'		harvest	planting		Top performer with juicy, flavourful berries. Good disease resistance
Blackcurrant 'Ben Sarek'		harvest harvest	planting		Very compact, excellent for small gardens. Late
Whitecurrant 'Blanka'		harvest harvest	planting		Heavy cropping variety. Berries are bursting with flavour
Whitecurrant 'White Grape'		harvest harvest	planting		Large, tasty berries. Lovely flavour. Very reliable
Redcurrant 'Jonkeer van Tets'		harvest	planting planting		Good sized, juicy berries, full of flavour. Early
Redcurrant 'Red Lake'		harvest harvest	planting		Well known variety bearing large, tasty fruit. Upright habit

 planting   harvest

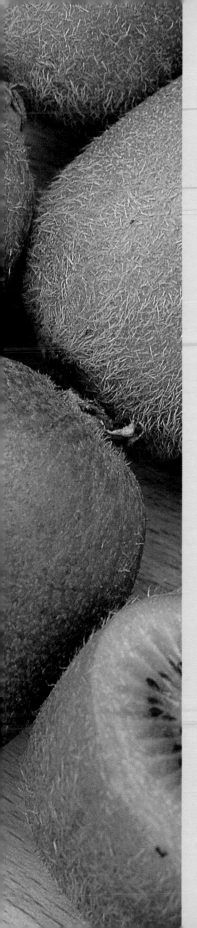
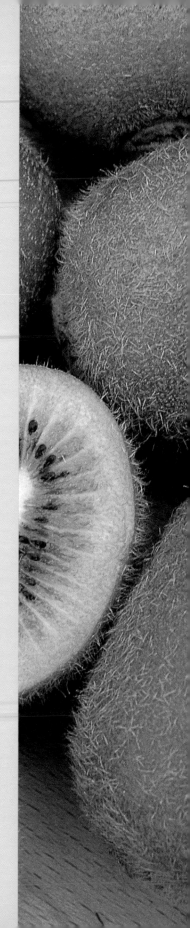

Vine Fruit

The vine fruit scramble, tumble and twine, brightening up the garden with their attractive foliage and the kitchen with their delicious fruits.

This group includes the world's most widely grown and popular fruit – grapes. For many centuries these have been cultivated and cosseted by growers appreciative of their many star qualities. Whether grown as a dessert fruit, for wine making or even to create a decorative, shady bower, grapes are unbeatable.

Melons, sometimes classified as vegetables rather than fruit, have a great deal in common with squash – including their lovely large leaves. Both the sweet varieties and watermelons are so refreshing and delicious that it takes a strong will to eat only one slice. Like the kiwi and passion fruit, melons need a great deal of warmth and sunshine, however it is amazing what can be achieved with a greenhouse or even a cold frame.

Kiwi and passion fruit are also extremely attractive plants that are worth growing purely for their handsome foliage and wonderfully vigorous habit. The fruit are a fantastic bonus, but one which cannot be relied upon if the plants are grown outside in cooler areas. However, these plants will add such a spectacular extra dimension to any garden that they fully deserve their place.

Grapes

Vitis labrusca and
Vitis vinifera

The world would be a considerably less enjoyable place without grapes and their life enhancing potion – wine. Both the European grape (*Vitis vinifera*) and its American cousin (*Vitis labrusca*) are truly magical fruit. The European grape varieties are of an unrivalled quality, yet do not have the tolerance of the American cultivars, which are by far more suitable for a cool climate.

Apart from the obvious distinction of whether they are white or black, grape varieties can be divided into groups of dessert (sweet) grapes, wine grapes and dual purpose grapes; then within these categories they can be broken down into early, mid- or late season.

The dessert grapes are divided into three further groups – sweetwater, the earliest and sweetest; muscat, next to mature with an unparalleled flavour; and vinous, last to mature with less flavour but plenty of vigour.

Vines are a mass of contradictions. They are hardy – many can cope quite easily with severe frosts – however, they do need long, sunny, dry summers to ripen, which is why they are not commonly grown in kitchen gardens in more temperate, cooler climes.

Different types are suitable for different areas and weather conditions, and it is possible to make up for less than ideal

soil	Well drained, deep, fertile and loamy. Vines love a limestone subsoil
site	A warm, sheltered and sunny position or otherwise grow indoors
watering	Water throughout the growing season, especially if hot and dry, until fruits begin to ripen
feeding	Liquid feed every 10–12 days as grapes are developing; stop once fruits begin to ripen
general care	Spray with water when buds break out, but stop once fruit start to ripen. Mulch outdoor grown vines in early spring
pests and diseases	Grape vines are particularly prone to powdery mildew (grey mould) and red spider mite

Grape 'Thompson White'

weather through clever choice of variety and site. For example, if you live in an area with shorter or colder summers, it makes sense to choose an early variety, which does not need so long to ripen. Plant it against a sun-drenched, sheltered wall, or in a greenhouse or polytunnel where the fruit can get maximum heat and protection. Some fruit even improve after being exposed to frost, although it is vital that the young growth in spring does not get frost bitten or it will shrivel.

Grapes grown indoors like their roots to be cool, hence the tradition of planting vines with their roots outside the greenhouse or conservatory and their top growth taken through a hole or window and trained up inside.

Correct pruning is vital to the health and vigour of your vine and will determine the size of the crop. There are various different ways of pruning, and which method you choose will depend on whether you are growing wine or dessert grapes. The aim when growing wine grapes is to produce the heaviest crop possible, while dessert grape growers are aiming for a lighter crop, yet of the very highest quality.

Pruning takes place in the summer and winter months. Winter pruning, when the plant is dormant, is more radical and aims

Black grape 'Napoleon'

to remove dead and old wood and to encourage the plant to produce masses of new shoots. These shoots are then summer pruned and the tips are pinched out to prevent overcrowding and encourage the vine to grow in a shape suitable for the training method you have chosen, as well as ensuring there is only one bunch of grapes per spur.

Training goes hand in hand with pruning. Dessert grapes are often grown as single, double or multiple cordons, while wine grapes are very successful trained in the Guyot system. This intensive method ensures maximum crops in a minimum space, and involves training a selection of parallel fruiting shoots vertically and securing them on to horizontal wires.

Indoor vines can be trained up wires strung between upright posts high up near the roof to ensure they receive as much air and sunshine possible.

Vines can be grown as vertical cordons with slightly longer laterals than other fruit. To ensure a good number of laterals, cut the leader back by about a third and the laterals to two buds in the first autumn. These two buds will develop into spurs, which you can then thin the following spring down to two laterals. In the next summer

White grape 'Festival'

Black grape 'Crimson'

prune these back to just beyond the final cluster of grapes.

Grape vines are generally self fertile and can be wind pollinated. However, it is a good idea to help the pollination process along by hand pollinating. This is especially important for crops grown under cover and is easily done with a soft paintbrush, which is used to transfer pollen from one flower to another.

Once buds begin to develop, indoor crops must be kept moist. Spraying the floor of the greenhouse is extremely useful – when the water evaporates it creates a moist atmosphere.

As fruit develops it is necessary to thin bunches to one per stem to allow the fruit to reach their maximum size and to aid air circulation.

Propagate grapes through hardwood cuttings taken from one-year-old shoots in the winter and potted on the next summer. Harden off before planting out.

The best time of year to plant is mid-autumn to late winter, about 1.5m (5ft) apart. Cut the stems of wine grapes back to a bud about 15cm (6in) from the ground, while dessert grape vines should be cut back by about two thirds, also to a strong bud. Harvest the crop according to variety.

	SPRING	SUMMER	AUTUMN	WINTER	
[WHITE] Grape 'Siegerrebe'					Outdoor, dessert and wine. Sweet, perfumed flavour. Early variety
Grape 'Foster's Seedling'					Indoor, dessert. Early variety bearing heavy crops
Grape 'Muscat of Alexandria'					Most delicious dessert variety. Late and needs heat, so grow under cover
Grape 'Madeleine Sylvaner'					Outdoor, wine. Early variety, so good for cooler areas
Grape 'Muller Thurgau'					Outdoor, wine. Mid-season grape, best grown in warmer areas
[BLACK] Grape 'Mrs Prince's Black Muscat'					Outdoor, dessert. Late with fantastic taste
Grape 'Napoleon'					Indoor, dessert and wine. Possible to grow outdoors in very warm areas
Grape 'Brant'					Outdoor, wine. Very vigorous, bearing heavy crops
Grape 'Concord'					Outdoor, wine. American grape. Best choice for cooler climates

planting   harvest

Melon
Cucumis melo

Watermelon
Citrullus lanatus

Both sweet melons and watermelons are tropical fruit, which need high temperatures and plenty of sunshine to stand any chance of germinating and fruiting. This means that in more temperate climates, most varieties need to be grown under cover in order to ripen, unless it is an especially warm summer.

Cold frames, greenhouses or polytunnels are ideal for growing sweet melons, however as watermelons grow so large – their stems can spread to as much as 4m (12ft), and their fruits can grow to 60cm (24in) long – a polytunnel is more suitable than a greenhouse. This should be opened occasionally to prevent the build up of humidity, which in turn could encourage viruses to develop.

Melons are greedy feeders, so the soil must be incredibly rich in nutrients – masses of well rotted manure is required. Another option would be to grow the plants in grow bags. The downside with these is that they are quite shallow, so it would be advisable to put one grow bag on top of another and cut through the base of the top bag to give the melon's roots plenty of room.

Melons are annuals and the sweet melons are divided into three groups – cantaloupe, casaba/winter and musk.

Melon 'Honeydew'

The melons in these groups look quite different. The musk melons are the smallest, with the cantaloupes being next up in size with thick, rough skin, and the casabas – or winter melons – being the largest, with smooth skins.

All melons need to be pollinated to produce fruit. Insect pollination is possible, although to be absolutely certain of a crop it is worth hand pollinating. This is not difficult, as the female flowers are easy to identify by the swelling they have behind the bloom. Simply dab a little pollen from a male flower on to the female.

As the plants begin developing, they require proper support. Small nets strung to the frame of the greenhouse or polytunnel are ideal for this. Also place plastic underneath the plant to protect developing fruit.

It is important to control growth to ensure the plant's efforts go into producing fruit rather than foliage. This is done by pinching off the tips of side stems once they have reached about five leaves, then doing the same with the stems that grow from these side stems once they reach about three leaves.

soil	Well manured, well drained and fertile. Sweet melons: pH 6.5–7; watermelons: pH 5.5–7
site	A very sunny, warm and sheltered site needed, otherwise under cover
watering	Both sweet melons and watermelons require regular watering to produce juicy fruit
feeding	Supplement with a liquid feed every couple of weeks until the fruits develop
general care	Keep weed free. Mulch to retain moisture and provide support. Pinch out growing tips and thin fruit
pests and diseases	Both sweet and watermelons are prone to aphids, powdery mildew and mosaic virus

As the fruit start to develop they should be thinned to one fruit per shoot, then all growth two or three leaves beyond this fruit should be removed. Thinning in this way allows the remaining fruit to reach their full potential.

Watering, especially during the flowering period, is necessary to produce the best crop. The soil should be kept nutrient rich by adding plenty of organic material.

For growing indoors, the best time to sow seed is from late winter to late spring. The seeds need a steady temperature of about 18–20°C (65–68°F) to germinate.

Sweet melon 'Sweetheart F1'

Place seeds on their side in individual pots of compost roughly 1cm (⅓in) deep. Keep them moist and cover with plastic until they germinate. Harden off and transplant them out once all risk of frost has passed and the seedlings have grown about four leaves. Place them in the ground but on a slight mound about 1m (3ft) apart. (For more details on this, see pages 20–1.)

The time to harvest melons is from mid-summer onwards. Wait until the fruit are fully ripe before harvesting, though. Sweet melons start to smell sweet when they are ripe, and the stalk begins to crack; with watermelons, they are close to ripening when the stem dries and the fruit changes colour. They should also sound hollow when tapped.

Watermelons need a large, very warm area to fully mature

	SPRING	SUMMER	AUTUMN	WINTER	
Sweet melon 'Sweetheart F1'	sow sow sow	transplant harvest harvest harvest	harvest	sow	Prizewinning cantaloupe variety with tasty orange flesh. Early to mature
Sweet melon 'Ogen'	sow sow sow	transplant harvest harvest harvest	harvest	sow	Small, sweet cantaloupe. Needs to be grown indoors in cooler climates
Sweet melon 'Minnesota Midget'	sow sow sow	transplant harvest harvest harvest	harvest	sow	Very small, but very sweet cantaloupe. Fast growing
Sweet melon 'Blenheim Orange'	sow sow sow	transplant harvest harvest harvest	harvest	sow	Attractive musk melon with wonderful taste
Sweet melon 'Tiger'	sow sow sow	transplant harvest harvest harvest	harvest	sow	Very striking musk fruits. Bold markings and fine taste
Sweet melon 'Oliver's Pearl Cluster'	sow sow sow	transplant harvest harvest harvest	harvest	sow	Fantastic texture, juicy and sweet cassaba
Watermelon 'Sin F1'	sow sow sow	transplant harvest harvest harvest	harvest	sow	Reliable and vigorous. Popular variety
Watermelon 'Florida Favorite'	sow sow sow	transplant harvest harvest harvest	harvest	sow	Juicy flesh, melts in the mouth
Watermelon 'Sugar Jade'	sow sow sow	transplant harvest harvest harvest	harvest	sow	Sweet, refreshing flavour

 transplanting   harvest   sowing

Kiwi fruit

*Actinidia
deliciosa*

Formally known as the Chinese gooseberry, the kiwi fruit's present name gives a clue as to where most of the world's stock comes from – New Zealand. Packed full of Vitamin C, the kiwi fruit travels well, and can be kept for a long time.

Kiwi fruit grow on attractive trailing vines, which need an extremely warm, sunny, sheltered site if they are to be grown out of doors. They fruit more successfully if grown under cover, however due to their length – they can reach 9m (28ft) – ordinary greenhouses are not large enough. Long, standing room polytunnels are much more suitable for undercover growing.

The vines need supporting and are quite easily trained as espaliers. This is an especially good method if you have a warm, sheltered wall which will retain the sun's heat. A less decorative but equally successful solution is to train them along overhead wires strung from posts in the same fashion as the horizontals of a pergola.

The kiwi is a vigorous plant, given the right conditions, and can be distracted from the business of producing fruit by putting on too much foliage growth. Careful pruning is,

soil	Deeply dug, plenty of well rotted manure and well drained. Ideally pH 6–7
site	For best results, plant in a hot, sunny and sheltered position
watering	Regular watering is important, especially during dry periods in the growing season
feeding	The ground should be well manured before planting
general care	Keep the area around the plants weed free and mulch heavily in the spring. Provide support
pests and diseases	Apart from root rot, thrips and scale insects, kiwis are relatively trouble-free from pests and diseases

Kiwi 'Hayward'

therefore, essential. When pruning it is important to remember that the fruit are borne on wood that is a year old. Fruited sideshoots can be cut back to three or four buds when the vine is dormant, and while it is growing in the summer, you can cut excessive growth back to just above any fruit.

Like tree fruit, you must have a male and female vine for the flowers to be fertilized and so produce fruit. The kiwi takes a little while to get started, so do not expect any fruit until about four years after planting.

The vines can be propagated through softwood and hardwood cuttings. Take the softwood cuttings during spring and the hardwood cuttings in late summer.

Propagate in late spring, as long as no late frosts are forecast.

	SPRING	SUMMER	AUTUMN	WINTER	
Kiwi fruit 'Allison'	✂		🥝🥝🥝		Female. Extremely vigorous, with attractive foliage
Kiwi fruit 'Hayward'	✂		🥝🥝🥝		Female. Very reliable. Good flavour
Kiwi fruit 'Tomuri'	✂		🥝🥝🥝		Male. Can cope with light frosts when dormant

✂ planting   🥝 harvest

Passion fruit

Passiflora spp.

These exotic fruit have beautiful flowers – white with a striking purple centre – and are so pretty that they can be forgiven their tenderness. The vine's tenderness would imply that they are only suitable for growing under cover. However, they actually grow better out in the open, as long as they are given a really sheltered, sunny site.

Passion fruit need rich, well drained soil and can be grown quite successfully in large containers, although they must be kept well fed and watered. A dose of general purpose fertilizer every few months is ideal. Add well-rotted organic matter and sharp sand to the planting hole.

For container-grown plants, use a fertile compost with a high organic content. Preferably choose a container that is over 35cm (14in) in diameter.

Just like kiwi fruit, the passion fruit is a trailing climber, capable of reaching great lengths and height. It therefore needs serious support, which can be provided successfully by means of a sturdy trellis or else wires strung overhead between tall, upright posts. They thrive in beds against the back wall of a greenhouse or indoors in a conservatory.

Pruning is relatively simple. In early spring, pinch out the tips of side shoots once they have reached about 15cm (6in), and in winter cut back shoots that have borne fruit that year. Otherwise pruning should be to keep the vine from becoming too overgrown.

The passion fruit is officially self fertile, however like many supposedly self fertile fruit trees it is always a good idea to grow more than one plant to ensure fertilization (hand pollination by means of a soft brush has been proven to boost yield).

The most common variety available is 'Ruby Gold', which has a red skin and mouth-watering, pulpy yellow flesh. Like many passion fruit, they are so attractive in the garden they could be grown for the beauty of their flowers alone.

The best time of year to plant out is in late spring, as long as there is no danger of a late frost. Harvesting is normally in autumn. Replace every six years or so as a precaution against wilt.

Passion fruit 'Ruby Gold'

soil	Deeply dug, with plenty of well rotted manure and well drained. Ideal soil – pH6
site	A hot, sunny and sheltered site is most preferable for best results
watering	Regular watering is important, especially during dry periods in the growing season
feeding	The ground should be well manured before planting to achieve best growth
general care	Keep the area around the plants weed free and mulch heavily in the spring. Provide good support
pests and diseases	Passion fruit are prone to various wilt diseases, fruit flies, aphids and red spider mite

Citrus Fruit

Citrus trees are more than novelty plants, introduced to create an instant Mediterranean feel. With a good understanding of their requirements and some tender loving care, there is no reason why you should not enjoy a crop of oranges or lemons, whichever climate you live in.

Citrus are an extremely attractive group of trees. Firstly they are evergreen, with lovely, dark glossy leaves which are scented, and secondly they are extremely shapely to look at. As an extra bonus, the tree bears fruit and blossom at the same time. This oddity is caused by the fact that the fruit take so long to mature – about a year – so while the previous year's fruit is ripening, the new year's flowers are bursting open.

They are generally self fertile, which saves any worry about choosing the correct varieties to pollinate each other. As sub tropical fruits they need warmth – a temperature of between 15–30°C (58–86°F) is just right – and as such are best grown under cover. They are classic conservatory plants, where it is easier to keep them at the correct temperature and humidity (60–70 per cent). However, unless you have a large, old fashioned conservatory it is easier to grow them in containers, which will allow you to take the trees in during winter and early spring, then move them back outside into a sunny spot once the frosts have finished.

Citrus trees are unusual in that they do not work to set seasons. While other fruit trees have a biological clock set by the time of year – if it is spring then it's time to bear blossom, while if it is autumn it's time for the fruit to ripen – citrus trees flower as soon as they get the correct amount and combination of the essential elements of warmth, water and light. This makes it possible for gardeners growing trees under cover to play God and to stimulate the tree by creating suitable – albeit synthetic – conditions.

Sweet orange
Citrus sinensis

Seville orange
Citrus aurantium

Oranges, both sweet and Seville, have a golden glow reminiscent of long, hot days and a taste like bottled sunshine. Most gardeners are put off growing this fruit because of its association with much warmer climates. However, if you do live in more temperate regions – even areas prone to frost – they can still be grown quite successfully in a greenhouse or conservatory.

There are three groups of sweet oranges – Common or Valencia, Navel and Blood. Valencia oranges are the most widely available, especially the variety 'Jaffa', however Blood oranges have undergone a surge in popularity in recent years. Navel oranges differ from the other two types in that they bear miniature secondary fruit at the end of the fruit. They also have the advantage of being slightly easier to peel, as well as splitting into segments.

There is little to choose between the three categories of sweet oranges in terms of flavour as all are delicious. As far as suitability to more temperate climates is concerned, of the three, Navel oranges are the ones most suited to cooler weather conditions.

Although most sweet oranges can be propagated from seed, amateur growers can easily buy a container-grown young tree. Be sure to check carefully for any sign of disease – the leaves are a good indicator of this – and also make sure that the tree is not pot bound, in other words there are no roots coming out of the holes at the bottom of the container. Finally check that the compost is weed free and that the tree has been kept well watered – if it has been allowed to dry out the roots will be damaged and it will not thrive (see pages 24–5).

If you are growing more than one tree, then the planting distance will depend upon the variety you have chosen. If you are growing the trees in pots then gradually pot on during winter, increasing the size of container as the tree grows.

soil	Very well drained and fertile soil preferred. Ideally slightly acidic – pH 6–6.5
site	A warm, sheltered and sunny position is best or under cover
watering	Water thoroughly during dry periods, especially during flower and fruit growth
feeding	In summer, high in nitrogen; in winter/spring, foliar feed with magnesium, zinc and iron
general care	Keep the area weed free and don't forget its year-round feeding regime. Prune to shape
pests and diseases	Particularly prone to aphids, red spider mites, scale insects, mealybugs, root and crown rot

Orange 'Navelina'

Wait until the tree is virtually pot bound before potting on, as oranges quite like their roots being slightly constricted – another reason why they do so well in containers – and will produce a great deal of foliage but barely any fruit if the container is too large.

When the tree is in its final container, then it is important to remember to replace the top 5cm (2in) of compost every spring and to feed regularly, all year round.

Sweet oranges are curious in the fact that they can bear two crops simultaneously. This is because of the fruit's long ripening period, which means that a new crop will often be developing at the same time as the previous crop is nearing the point of picking.

Sweet orange 'Valencia'

Orange 'Seville'

The Seville oranges are physically slightly different to sweet oranges and certainly differ in taste. While sweet oranges are often quite thin skinned and are, obviously sweet, Seville oranges have thick skins, tend to be fairly acidic and are very bitter.

They are certainly not suitable for eating raw, but instead they can be made into the most delicious marmalade. Seville marmalade is a classic which far surpasses all other marmalades in taste, making the fruit hugely popular.

Below: Planting/harvesting times for citrus fruit will vary according to the amount of heat and light that they receive

	SPRING	SUMMER	AUTUMN	WINTER	
[SEVILLE] Orange 'Bouquet'					Classic Seville taste
Orange 'Bouquet de Fleurs'					Most commonly available variety
Orange 'Chinotto'					Sour, with thick peel
[SWEET] Orange (Valencia) 'Hamlin'					Consistently well flavoured
Orange (Valencia) 'Jaffa'					Most well known variety
Orange (Navel) 'Navelina'					Easy to peel. Juicy
Orange (Navel) 'Robertson'					Lovely fresh flavour
Orange (Blood) 'Malta Blood'					Ruby red colouring
Orange (Blood) 'Moro'					Popular and wonderfully juicy
Orange (Blood) 'Ruby'					Striking deep red veins

Mandarin

Citrus reticulata
and hybrids

The common mandarin (*Citrus reticulata*), nowadays called tangerine, has spawned a number of imitators – the hybrids. Among these are crosses with lemons, the lemon-mandarin (*Citrus* x *meyeri*) and kumquats, the mandarin-kumquat, sometimes called the calamondin, (*Citrus* x *Citrofortunella microcarpa*, syn. *C. mitis*), and many more are being bred all the time.

Mandarins, or tangerines can, like sweet oranges, be divided into different groups – Satsuma, Cleopatra, King and Common Mandarin.

Not all fruit within these groups is edible. It is the Satsuma and Common Mandarin groups which are normally cultivated for crops, rather than being ornamental.

The success of the mandarin and hybrids may have something to do with the small size of the fruit and the ease with which they can be peeled. The fruit also have a strong, fresh perfume and a distinctive flavour, quite different from sweet oranges.

They are an excellent choice for containers, as their small fruit seem perfectly in proportion with the size of the tree, and many will start to bear fruit while quite small.

Like the other citrus trees, temperature is vital to fruit production and must be above 18°C (64°F) for successful fruiting.

soil	Very well drained and fertile soil preferred. Ideally slightly acidic – pH 6–6.5
site	A warm, sheltered and sunny position is best, or under cover
watering	Water thoroughly during dry periods, especially during flower and fruit growth
feeding	In summer, high in nitrogen; in winter/spring, foliar feed with magnesium, zinc and iron
general care	Keep the area weed free and feed year-round, varying the composition according to the season. Prune to shape
pests and diseases	Particularly prone to aphids, red spider mites, scale insects, mealybugs, root and crown rot

Common Mandarin 'Clementine'

Below: Planting/harvesting times for citrus fruit will vary according to the amount of heat and light that they receive

	SPRING	SUMMER	AUTUMN	WINTER	
Common mandarin 'Clementine'					Small, sweet with unequalled flavour. Fast growing
Common mandarin 'Dancy'					Popular variety, juicy and sweet
Lemon-mandarin 'Meyeri'					Unusual, but delicious taste. Slow growing

Lemons

Citrus limon

Limes

Citrus aurantiifolia

The fruit of both these trees has a sour taste, yet with a strangely sweet undertone. This is especially true of the lime, which has an exceedingly distinctive flavour. Both lemons and limes are wonderfully juicy fruit and make excellent pot specimen trees for either indoors or outside in more sunnier climes.

Lemon and lime trees look wonderful in terracotta pots. Their yellow and green fruit glow against the background of dark green leaves.

Limes are especially suited to containers being very neat, compact little trees. The lime variety 'Bearss' is a particularly good specimen.

There have been various crosses made between lemons and limes. The most successful hybrid is the Lemonime, which will only succeed grown as an ornamental tree outside in subtropical areas.

Limes fall into two groups, generally separated according to whether they are acidic or sweet. They are generally quite thin skinned fruit without too many seeds.

Many varieties of lemon do not turn yellow as they mature, despite this common belief. Instead, they stay green, even when fully ripe. This can cause a great deal of confusion between the two fruits.

soil	Both prefer very well drained and fertile soil, ideally slightly acid – pH 6–6.5
site	Lemons and limes thrive in warm, sheltered and sunny conditions or under cover
watering	Water trees thoroughly during dry periods, especially during flower and fruit growth
feeding	In summer, high in nitrogen; in winter/spring, foliar feed with magnesium, zinc and iron
general care	Keep the area weed free and don't forget its year-round feeding regime. Prune to shape
pests and diseases	Particularly prone to aphids, red spider mites, scale insects, mealybugs, root and crown rot

Not all varieties of lemon turn yellow when ripe

Limes are especially suited to containers

Like the other citrus trees, temperature and light is vitally important for growth and crop production. Lemons, for example, need a pretty constant temperature, which should not drop below 20°C (68°F).

Temperature control can be hard to get right. Modern conservatories are often little more than an extra room in a house and may be far too hot and stuffy, while it is expensive to heat a greenhouse. Too much heat in winter can affect flowering and yet so can too little. Frost can easily kill a lemon or lime tree.

Getting the watering right is also very important. Lemons and limes hate waterlogged soil, so a free draining mix of equal measures of loam, sharp sand and coir, with a mulch of compost, is ideal. They like to be soaked thoroughly when watered, but at the same time they cannot bear to sit in water, so always water from above and carry on with the watering until the water is running straight through the pot. Apply feed to them in the same way as oranges (see pages 141–2).

Like oranges, lemons and limes do not need much pruning. A simple clip to keep them in shape is all that is necessary, although you may need to trim new growth back in spring.

Below: Planting/harvesting times for citrus fruit will vary according to the amount of heat and light that they receive

	SPRING	SUMMER	AUTUMN	WINTER	
Lemon 'Garey's Eureka'					Wide, spreading shape
Lemon 'Lisbon'					Lovely shining fruit and leaves
Lemon 'Primafiori'					Extremely juicy, with few seeds
Lime 'Bearss'					Juicy and bursting with flavour. Seedless
Lime 'Persian'/'Tahiti'					Sweet variety. Delicious taste
Lime 'West India'/'Mexican'					Popular, acidic variety

Grapefruit

Citrus x *paradisi*

Grapefruit trees need a fair amount of space as they are fast growing and capable of reaching heights of 10m (30ft). This factor may well make growing this citrus fruit not very practical for the gardener with an average-sized greenhouse. However, if you are able to provide enough space and warmth, the rewards are plenty.

The grapefruit's yellow fruits are also large. In fact, they are the largest citrus fruits, and can reach 10–15cm (4–6in) in diameter. Like the other citrus fruits, grapefruit trees have attractive oval shaped leaves, which are quite leathery, with a glossy sheen.

In the past only white fleshed varieties of grapefruit were commonly available to both grow and buy in the shops to eat. These are very juicy, yet taste quite sour and so are excellent made into marmalade or eaten with a sprinkling of sugar. Recently, however, varieties with pink flesh have become far more popular. These are equally juicy, yet they taste quite sweet.

Grapefruits require a higher temperature than many of the other citrus fruits – they will not do well if the temperature is below 25°C (77°F). They also like high humidity

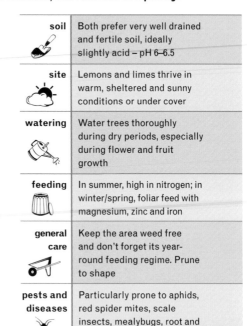

soil	Both prefer very well drained and fertile soil, ideally slightly acid – pH 6–6.5
site	Lemons and limes thrive in warm, sheltered and sunny conditions or under cover
watering	Water trees thoroughly during dry periods, especially during flower and fruit growth
feeding	In summer, high in nitrogen; in winter/spring, foliar feed with magnesium, zinc and iron
general care	Keep the area weed free and don't forget its year-round feeding regime. Prune to shape
pests and diseases	Particularly prone to aphids, red spider mites, scale insects, mealybugs, root and crown rot

Grapefruit 'Duncan'

White grapefruit

Red grapefruit

levels of about 60–70 per cent, which presents a problem for temperate areas.

Being larger trees, grapefruits need slightly more pruning. When first planted, their main branches should be cut back by about a third during their first year and thereafter any dead, diseased or overcrowded branches should be removed, but only after fruiting. Aim for a rounded shape, quite light and open, with no overlapping branches.

If you are growing grapefruit in a container, use a soil-based potting mix made up of about 20 per cent perlite and 80 per cent free-draining soil with added slow-release fertilizer. Top dress in spring.

Below: Planting/harvesting times for citrus fruit will vary according to the amount of heat and light that they receive

	SPRING	SUMMER	AUTUMN	WINTER	
Grapefruit 'Golden Special'					Sunny colouring and bittersweet taste
Grapefruit 'Duncan'					Pink. Extremely juicy and full of flavour
Grapefruit 'Marsh Seedless'					Variety with white flesh

Herbs

Nobody can call themselves a serious cook if they have a garden yet do not grow fresh herbs. The flavour is so superior to dried herbs that once discovered there is no going back.

Luckily, most herbs are happy growing in containers, so it does not matter if your garden is the size of a postage stamp – you can still enjoy the vibrant flavours and heady aromas of the fresh plants.

Two of the most popular herbs are certainly mint and parsley, with rosemary and bay coming a close second. However, these plants represent only a tiny fraction of the herbs available to the kitchen gardener. Many are so ornamental that it is unlikely they will ever make it to the kitchen garden, being used instead in the flower borders. The height and foliage of fennel, make it invaluable, while many others, including the decorative sage and thyme, look beautiful edging a garden path and beds. Some also feature again in the Edible Flowers section on page 156, as their flowers also have a culinary use in the kitchen.

Herbs are more than just attractive plants with the potential to be used as flavourings. Most have medicinal uses and they also attract beneficial insects – such as bees, to pollinate plants, and hoverflies, to eat up insect pests. They are also irresistible to butterflies. In fact, herbs are an all round winner.

Annuals & biennials

Coriander

Coriander has a delicious, distinctive aroma and unequalled flavour, and is a vital ingredient in Mediterranean, Mexican and Thai dishes. The flat leaved, parsley-like leaves are harvested while the plant is young, then later the seed is collected to be used in curries and spicy dishes, as well as in cakes and biscuits, and the leaves are chopped as garnish. If you want to use the leaves rather than the seeds, choose a large-leaved variety such as 'Cilantro', bred specially for that purpose. Sow the seeds in situ at the start of spring, thinning to 30cm (12in). Seeds are ready to harvest in late summer. Treat as cut and come again (see p45).

Angelica

Angelica is a very decorative, tall, stately biennial, whose root is used to make tea and whose aromatic stems have traditionally been candied and used on cakes. Even its leaves are edible, and are delicious added to salads. Angelica can grow to 1.8m (6ft) and will spread itself widely through its seeds. It prefers cool, moist soil and will cope with sunshine, but is happiest in light shade. Grow from seeds sown out of doors in mid-spring or early autumn, thinning the seedlings to 30cm (12in).

Parsley

There are many varieties of parsley. One of the most common is the curled, for example 'Moss Curled' and 'Curlina', which are very compact with tightly curled leaves. There is also flat parsley, sometimes called plain, French or Italian, which has exceptional flavour and softer leaves. Parsley is propagated from seed, which can be sown in situ in late spring and late summer. It likes rich, moist soil, so should not be allowed to dry out. Cut sprigs as required. Good in pots.

Aniseed

The leaves of aniseed make an unusual addition to fruit salad, while the seeds have been used to add distinctive flavour to confectionery and cakes for centuries. Aniseed is half hardy and requires a sheltered site in full sunshine to thrive. It is grown from seed sown in situ in late spring. To harvest aniseed, start by picking the lowest leaves, then gather the seedheads in the autumn to dry and save the seed to be used over the winter.

Chervil

With its aniseed taste, chervil is often used in place of parsley, although it has a more delicate flavour. It is popular in French-style sauces and in bouquet garni. At one time, chervil was grown not only for its leaves but also its roots, which were boiled and mixed with oil and vinegar to make salads. It is a fast growing herb with attractive, lacy fern-like leaves, and is ready to be harvested only six weeks or so after sowing. It is happiest growing in light shade and should be sown in drills in succession from late winter to late summer.

Borage

With a flavour reminiscent of cucumber, the pretty blue flowers of borage are very attractive to bees and can be added, along with the young leaves, to salads or drinks, such as Pimm's. This herb also has medicinal uses: even now, its leaves are sometimes used as a poultice on skin inflammations. Borage is very easy to grow – simply sow the seed in drills 30cm (12in) apart from spring to early autumn, ready to harvest after eight weeks. Borage likes light, well drained soil and a sunny site. It will grow up to 60cm (24in).

Basil

Basil is a half hardy annual. There are numerous types, including: 'Lemon' (compact, superb flavour); 'Red Rubin' (very decorative, bronze leaves); 'Cinnamon' (pale green leaves, tastes of cinnamon); 'Thai' (light and spicy); 'Sweet' (large leaves, very good with tomato); and 'Siam' (used in Thai stir fries and soups). But the most well known are probably 'Minette', a very aromatic dwarf variety, often used in pizzas, and 'Sweet Genovese', which has large leaves, a strong, spicy flavour and clove-like perfume. Grow from seeds sown indoors in spring, transplanting outside after the last frosts.

Marigold

The bright orange flowers of the marigold last throughout the summer. The flowers have long been harvested for medicinal purposes and the petals can be used as a colouring as well as a flavouring in many dishes, besides being eaten raw in salads. The leaves can also be eaten, shredded and added to salads while still young and tender. Grow marigolds from seed sown in early spring or autumn. Once established, they will self seed freely.

Cumin

A tender herb, cumin needs a really warm, sunny spot in order to thrive. It is grown for its aromatic seeds, which are an essential ingredient in many curries and Middle Eastern dishes. To propagate, sow seeds in situ as soon as the soil warms up. The seedheads are ready to harvest once they start to ripen and turn brown. Cut them down carefully and dry them indoors in a warm, airy place. Remember that dried cumin has a far more intense flavour than fresh cumin, so use only a pinch or a teaspoonful when using it to flavour dishes.

Caraway

Caraway is a hardy herb which can grow to about 75cm (30in) high. The roots can be eaten boiled or the leaves used to garnish soups, salads and casseroles. Keep the seeds and roast them, then add them to cakes and bread. Sow caraway seed in situ in mid- to late spring or in late autumn, in well drained soil. The seedheads will appear the following spring and will be ready to harvest by early to mid-summer.

Nasturtium

The dark green leaves, pretty yellow, orange and red flowers and even the seeds of a nasturtium can all be eaten. Nasturtiums have a peppery taste, which varies in strength according to the part of the plant – the seeds are by far the hottest. This herb is particularly useful for interestingly flavoured salads. Grow in a sunny site, sowing seed in situ in spring 1cm (⅓in) deep. Poor soil will produce a better crop of flowers than rich soil, which is better for leaf growth. Nasturtiums have a reputation as companion plants, keeping pests away from the vegetable garden as they attract aphids from other plants and they repel ants and whitefly.

Dill

Good with fish and chicken, but also with cheese and pickles, the leaves and stronger seeds of dill have a similar but slightly sweeter taste than fennel. Dill is quite hardy and can grow to 90cm (36in) tall, and its flat headed yellow flowers are very attractive to beneficial insects. Its feathery foliage makes a dramatic feature in mixed beds and contrasts well with other, fleshier foliage. Sow dill directly outside in a sunny position from mid-spring to early summer and harvest the leaves in spring and summer before the plant sets flower.

Perennials

Bergamot

A hardy perennial, sometimes called Bee Balm, bergamot has large bright red flowers which are very attractive to beneficial insects, such as bees. It can grow up to 90cm (36in) high and is a versatile plant, having edible leaves and flowers. The leaves and flowers are delicious raw in salads, while the leaves can also be made into tea or used as a fragrant addition to pot pourri. Bergamot needs cool, moist soil and should be well watered during dry periods. Grow from seed sown in spring, cuttings of the stem taken in the summer, or division in early spring.

Chives

A hardy perennial with a mild onion taste and pretty flowers, chives are very easy to grow. Sow seeds in shallow drills in spring, in full sun or light shade. Chives like moist, fertile soil, so should be watered regularly during dry periods. You can buy chives from herb stockists, but it is worth propagating your own once you have a basic stock of plants, as this is very easily done. Once established, the plants may be divided in the autumn. Do this by simply digging up a clump carefully, prizing the bulbs apart and then re-planting them in groups of four or five. It is worth repeat sowing every few years as the flavour becomes milder year by year. A less common variety is 'Garlic chives', which differs from common chives in that it has flat leaves which have a mild garlic taste.

Chamomile

Chamaemelum nobile, otherwise known as lawn chamomile, is hardy and evergreen and has been used for many hundreds of years for lawns and seats. The foliage and flowers release a delicate aroma when crushed. *Chamomile matricaria*, the annual form, looks almost identical and makes fantastic tea which has been used for centuries to aid digestion and as a cure for insomnia. It is also dried and added to pot pourri as well as rinsed through hair for its cleansing properties. Chamomile is propagated through cuttings taken in the summer or division in spring or autumn.

Common fennel

Common, or sweet, and bronze fennel have such highly decorative, feathery foliage that it is tempting to grow them in an ornamental border rather than in the kitchen or herb garden. Bronze fennel marginally wins in the decorative stakes, due to its spectacular colouring, although both have an upright form and spread which is the envy of many plants in the mixed border. Fennel has a mild aniseed flavour – bronze fennel tastes like liquorice. Use the leaves to complement fish and cheese, while the seeds add an extra dimension to soups, cakes and bread. This herb is hugely attractive to beneficial insects. Propagate by sowing seed in the spring or by division in the autumn.

Feverfew

Traditionally used as a highly effective medicine to lessen the pain of arthritis and migraine, the aromatic leaves of feverfew are dried and made into tea. However, this plant is so versatile that it can also be used as a moth deterrent, while the pretty, white chrysanthemum-like flowers with their distinctive scent are added to pot pourri. Feverfew is an extremely easy plant to grow. Sow seeds in a seedtray in early spring or outdoors in situ in mid-spring. Feverfew can also be propagated by division and stem cuttings, and will self seed freely. It likes full sunshine.

Tarragon

There are two types of tarragon, Russian and French. Russian is a very hardy, easy to grow variety which has a slightly milder flavour than its more tender French cousin. Tarragon's distinctive flavour complements chicken and fish particularly well, and is excellent added to vinegar. French tarragon is propagated from cuttings or runners, while Russian tarragon should be grown from seed. Both types need a sheltered site in full sun with free draining soil. To prevent the herb becoming invasive, plant it in a bottomless bucket or pot.

Horseradish

With its large dock-like leaves, horseradish is not the most decorative plant, but the wonderful peppery flavour of its roots more than makes up for any aesthetic shortcomings. It is often made into a creamy sauce which is particularly popular with beef dishes and sushi. Horseradish needs a deeply dug ground that is well prepared and manured in order to thrive. It can be invasive and should be lifted every year as a precaution. Store the roots in moist sand or soil then replant the following spring. Twelve roots should be quite sufficient for an average sized family.

Ginger

The exceptional flavour of ginger is guaranteed to add zest to countless dishes and drinks, from stir fries to preserves and ginger ale. As well as being used for its instantly recognizable flavour, ginger is often selected for its equally distinctive scent, being a common constituent of pot pourri and pomanders. It also has medicinal properties and has been used for centuries as a cure for upset stomachs. A tender, delicate looking plant its looks belie the powerful punch it packs, courtesy of its tuberous rhizome. These rhizomes can be used fresh or else sealed in an airtight jar in a syrup. To propagate ginger, divide the rhizomes as soon as they begin to sprout.

Lovage

Lovage is a very vigorous, hardy plant, whose leaves can be harvested to give flavouring to soups or casseroles, or used raw for salads while young. The seeds are used in baking. Lovage has a taste reminiscent of celery. Sow seed indoors in spring, then transplant out of doors in early summer into moist, rich soil. Alternatively divide in early spring or take stem cuttings in the summer. Lovage is happy growing in sun or light shade.

Lemon balm

Lemon balm is a vigorous, hardy plant, perfect for a sunny border among the flowers as well as in the kitchen garden. Use the sweet, lemon scented leaves to make tea, which will soothe headaches, or else in salads and as a flavouring in cooking. Lemon balm leaves also have a soothing effect when they are rubbed on insect stings. Grow lemon balm from seed sown in the spring or else propagate by division in the autumn.

Orris

If you plan to make your own pot pourri, then you must grow orris. Its thick rhizome, if left to dry then ground up, makes a fantastic fixative for all the perfumed flowers, petals and leaves of that mixture, ensuring that their aroma remains undiminished even months later. Harvesting orris is a long term project. The rhizomes should be a minimum of three years old before being harvested, then they should be left for a couple of years to dry out before being ground up. Propagate by division in the spring or autumn.

Sorrel

Sorrel has a quite sharp lemony flavour, and is grown for its dock-like leaves, which can either be eaten raw in salads or cooked. Of the two main types of sorrel available, French sorrel should be your first choice; its taste is milder than that of the more acidic, common garden sorrel. Remove all flowering stems to ensure a good supply of leaves. Sorrel needs well drained soil and is happy in sun, although it prefers light shade. Propagate by sowing seed sparingly between early spring and early summer in rows about 30cm (12in) apart, thinning to half that distance, or by division in spring or autumn.

Marjoram

Often called oregano, wild marjoram is a vital flavouring in many Mediterranean dishes. It has a strong pungent flavour, and can be used in a bouquet garni or added to pot pourri. Different forms include sweet marjoram (*O. majorana*), which has grey green leaves, and pot marjoram (*O. onites*), which is slightly milder than oregano. In the past the herb was attributed with medicinal qualities, being prescribed for conditions as diverse as snakebites, toothache and stomach disorders. Marjoram likes a sunny position with well drained soil and can be propagated by softwood cuttings (taken in the spring) or by dividing plants (in the autumn or spring).

Sweet cicely

Hardy and herbaceous with fluffy, fern-like leaves and flat heads of tiny star-like white flowers in the summer, sweet cicely looks like a smaller, infinitely more delicate, cow parsley. It is pretty all year round, as its delicate flowers are followed by distinctive and large mahogany-coloured seeds. Its leaves, root and seeds can all be eaten, and have a slight aniseed flavour. Sow sweet cicely seed in mid-spring and water well during dry periods to ensure the ground remains moist. Once established, sweet cicely will self seed freely.

Mint

A perennial herb with countless varieties – all delicious and all extremely invasive in the herb garden if given the opportunity – mint is an essential flavouring for serious cooks. This herb goes perfectly with lamb, new potatoes and the summer drink, Pimm's. Mint is happiest growing in light shade, in rich, moist soil, and is propagated from cuttings taken in the spring or autumn. To avoid it taking over the kitchen garden, plant it in a bottomless bucket or pot; this will restrict the roots.

Shrubby

Bay

Although generally thought of as tender, bay is actually quite a hardy plant if it is allowed to develop naturally. It needs a position in full sun with well drained soil and is often grown in a large container – which is thoroughly practical, as it allows it to be moved to a sheltered position in harsh weather. Bay leaves have been used for centuries for decorative purposes – the ancient Greeks used them to make wreaths for poets and heroes. Bay responds well to clipping – a classic design being the mophead standard. To propagate, take cuttings of side shoots with a little old wood attached. Bay leaves are harvested and can be used at once or dried to add flavour to any number of different dishes.

Cotton lavender

Cotton lavender, more usually known by its proper name of Santolina, is a favourite of flower gardeners due to its stunning combination of attractive, silver grey foliage and bright yellow flowers. It is evergreen and hardy and makes an excellent edging to a path or divider of beds. As a herb, it is its scented leaves which are of interest, these being a vital ingredient in pot pourri. Santolina is propagated by means of sideshoot cuttings, which are taken in the late summer.

Rue

Rue is a hardy, attractive evergreen subshrub, which grows to about 60cm (24in) high, and looks just as good in the flower garden as the kitchen garden. An especially decorative and striking variety is 'Jackman's Blue', which has leaves of a deep grey-blue colour. It is these leaves which rue is grown for. They are used while still young and tender to flavour soups and sauces, as well as in salads. Rue is either propagated through seed sown in the spring or by cuttings of semi ripe sideshoots, which should be taken in late summer.

Lavender

Lavender is the queen of the herbs – a hardy, evergreen, bushy shrub so attractive and with such fragrant foliage and flowers that it is one of the most popular plants in horticulture. It has many uses, from culinary to pot pourri, and its oil can be extracted and used to soothe aches and pains and aid sleep. Always pick in the early morning on a dry, sunny day – just before the flowers open is the ideal time. Hang in a dry, airy place to dry. Propagate by taking cuttings of semi-ripe, non-flowering shoots in the summer.

Lemon verbena

Lemon verbena originates from Chile and has long, narrow, pointed leaves which taste and smell strongly of lemon. These are used fresh or can be dried to flavour drinks – most notably tea – puddings and jams. Lemon verbena is tolerant of most soil types; however, being half hardy it needs a sheltered position and good protection from frost. Lemon verbena is propagated through softwood cuttings, which should be taken in the spring.

Rosemary

The pungent, narrow leaves of rosemary served with lamb, make one of those classic culinary combinations. It is a very useful plant in the garden as it is hardy and evergreen and responds well to clipping. This makes it invaluable as a structural plant, especially in the winter. Rosemary needs a sunny, sheltered position and well drained soil. It is not hardy, so it should be brought under cover or thoroughly protected in cold winters. Sow indoors in spring and transplant out of doors when the young plants reach about 7.5cm(3in) high. Keep rosemary plants in shape by pruning after flowering.

Hyssop

Hyssop bears pretty purple flowers and is a semi evergreen subshrub, ideal for growing as a low hedge. The leaves have a minty flavour with a bit of extra zest, and can be used fresh in salads or in soups and casseroles. The strong flavour works especially well combined with rich game dishes. It needs a light soil and sheltered site in full sun, and can be propagated from division or softwood cuttings taken in the spring, or else be grown from seed.

Sage

Although these days sage is used primarily as a culinary herb, for centuries it was credited with medicinal properties, as its Latin name, *Salvia*, testifies. A very aromatic herb with a pungent flavour, sage likes a position in full sun, sheltered from cold winds. This herb also needs a fertile, well drained soil. All, apart from the common green forms, can be propagated from cuttings of side shoots, taken in the summer. The green forms should be grown from seed, sown in situ in late spring. Harvest early autumn and renew every three or four years or as the plants become woody. Apart from the common plant, there are other more decorative types. These include the attractive purple sage and the green/gold variegated sage.

Wormwood

Wormwood is a hardy, decorative, grey-leaved plant which grows to about 90cm (36in) high and is mainly cultivated for its scented foliage, which is used in flower arrangements, herbal wreaths and posies. These leaves are poisonous, so should not be used as a flavouring, although they were once popular as a garnish to drinks. Wormwood looks attractive grown in the flower border or along paths. It is also suitable for scree beds and rockeries, contrasting well with the ground cover and mat-forming plants which are generally found in these types of garden. Propagate through softwood cuttings taken in the summer.

Thyme

Garden thyme has a robust flavour and is used as a flavouring for food as well as a medicine. It is the perfect herb to complement vegetables, such as onions and carrots, and can be used to flavour stuffings and soups, or in beef and fish dishes. It can also be made into tea. As if all that were not enough, its pretty pink flowers and fragrance are reasons enough to grow it. Creeping thyme, as its name suggests, is a very low growing plant which is perfect in a rockery or will quickly carpet an area. It is evergreen and shares its relative's pretty pink flowers, which can be cultivated into a stunning pink lawn effect over a period of years. This extremely versatile herb likes full sun and well drained soil and can be grown from seed in the spring, by division, from cuttings and even layering.

Winter savory

A hardy, dwarfing bush with a strong flavour, winter savory is the cousin of the annual summer savory (*S. hortensis*), which has a milder flavour and can be harvested throughout the summer. Pinch off flowerheads as they appear because when they flower, the leaves quickly lose their flavour. Summer savory should be grown from seed sown in mid- to late spring. Sow at a distance of 30cm (12in), thinning to 15cm (6in) apart. Winter savory is propagated from cuttings taken in the spring or root division. Savory needs a light, rich soil and sunny position.

Southernwood

Southernwood – also known by its alternative common names of Lad's love and Old man – has lovely feathery, silver green leaves and is not dissimilar in looks to cotton lavender (see opposite). The distinctive leaves have a fantastic sweet lemony aroma and can be used in pot pourri or as a very effective insect repellent and antiseptic. This herb is hardy and semi evergreen, and as a fairly compact, bush-forming subshrub makes an excellent low hedge. Southernwood prefers a sunny site, having originated in southern Europe. It produces clusters of small, yellowish flowerheads in late summer. Southernwood is propagated from softwood cuttings, taken during the summer, and also from woody cuttings, taken in the autumn.

Edible Flowers

It is sad but true that our ancestors had, in many ways, a far more adventurous diet than us. Admittedly, they did not have access to the wide range of tropical fruit and vegetables we are so familiar with – unless they lived in the grand style with huge hot houses and a team of gardeners. Nevertheless, they commonly ate things that we would shy away from as being 'not food'.

Edible flowers are a good example of this syndrome. We have fallen into the trap of placing plants into strict classifications: this is for eating; this is for flavouring; this is for decoration; and so on. That is a shame, as many plants defy these definitions. Here are just a few of them.

Viola

Sweet violet (*Viola odorata*) and heartsease/violas (*Viola tricolor*) have tiny delicate, star-like flowers which are a welcome addition to any garden, and what a bonus that they are edible. Both the leaves and flowers can be eaten raw – the whole flower looks pretty decorating a salad and the petals are spectacular sprinkled on top of a risotto. In addition, the flowers have also traditionally been crystalized and used in cake making for decoration.

Nasturtium

Possibly the best known edible flower, both the leaves and brightly coloured flowers of *Tropaeolum majus* are edible raw, as are the buds and semi ripe seeds. Nasturtiums have a pleasant, peppery taste and look very attractive in a salad or omelette. They are best eaten raw, as they lose much of their flavour when cooked. This flower is particularly useful for adding interesting flavours to salads. Grow in a sunny site, sowing seed in situ in spring 1cm (½in) deep. Poor soil will produce a better crop of flowers than rich soil, which is better for leaf growth.

Calendula

Calendula, commonly called pot marigold (*Calendula officinalis*), has vivid petals which will add a burst of sunshine to any dish. Simply pull them away from the flowerhead and sprinkle raw on top of anything from casseroles and rice to pasta and salads, or use cooked in soup or a white sauce. Grow pot marigolds from seed sown in early spring or autumn. Once established, they will self seed freely.

Carnations

Carnations and pinks (Dianthus) and Sweet William (*Dianthus barbatus*) have pretty, colourful pom pom flowers and a rather spicy flavour, reminiscent of cloves. They are extremely good when they are infused in oils and vinegars and they can also be crystalized for use as attractive decorations for cakes and puddings.

Daisy

The humble little flower of the daisy (*Bellis perennis*) has such an unassuming and cheerful face that it is welcome in every garden. It comes in many different colours, has bright green leaves and will enliven even the dullest planting scheme. What is not commonly known is that the petals of the daisy are edible and can be used to decorate puddings, while the leaves can be chopped up and used in salads.

Elderflower

Elderflower cordial has undergone an amazing resurgence in popularity recently. From being a fusty, old fashioned drink, it has suddenly become immensely popular and the drinks makers cannot get enough of the pretty, creamy white flowerheads. Luckily for us, elders grow like weeds anywhere and everywhere. Just remember to avoid plants beside roads, which may be contaminated with carbon monoxide from car exhaust fumes. The flowers of the elder can also be used to make tea, while the fruit can be used in jam.

Roses

Most people will be familiar with crystalized rose petals used as cake decorations, but these fragrant petals have many more uses besides. They can be made into jams and jellies, added to sorbets as well as to honey, and infused in vinegars. The only downside is that their spiky thorns can be a hazard when you are removing the flowerheads!

Sunflower

Guaranteed to bring a smile to anyone's face, the sunflower (*Helianthus annuus*) has edible petals, seeds and buds, all with a delicious nutty flavour. The petals and buds can be eaten raw in salads, while the seeds can be eaten raw as a snack or roasted. Hang a few flowerheads upside down from trees once they start to fade to give the birds a tasty treat.

Vegetable & herb flowers

It is not only the foliage of herbs which is valuable in the kitchen – many herbs have pretty flowers which are also edible. Similarly, many of the flowers which go on to develop into tasty vegetables are delicious in their own right. So be adventurous: instead of discarding herb flowers, put them to use; and whenever you have a glut of any of the following vegetables, experiment with the flowers. One of the greatest pleasures of growing vegetables, herbs and edible flowers is to see every part of the plant used once the crop has made it into the kitchen.

CAUTION

Never use flowers picked from the side of the road or bought from florists, as these may have been contaminated with harmful chemicals. Only ever use flowers that have been grown in the garden specifically for eating. Begin by serving only small amounts, to ensure no adverse or allergic reactions from your diners.

Basil	Like the leaves, the flowers of the basil plant have a wonderfully sweet, yet almost spicy, flavour. They can be eaten whole and go very well with all tomato dishes, as well as being excellent candidates to be infused in oils and vinegars. Also, try them cooked with roasted Mediterranean vegetables or in soup.
Hyssop	Hyssop looks very like lavender, with its shrubby, long spiky stems and, most commonly, blue flowers (there are also varieties with white, pink and purple flowers). It has a very strong flavour and the dried flowers combine well with numerous foods.
Bergamot	This perennial herb has extremely decorative bright red or pink flowers with long narrow petals. These look spectacular when they are sprinkled raw on salads, infused as tea or cooked with fish, rice or pasta. The flavour they impart is quite strong and sweet.

Rocket	When your rocket runs to seed do not despair, as the flowers are edible in their own right. They pack the same punch as the leaves, with their strong peppery flavour, which will be even stronger if you eat the semi ripe seed capsule along with the flower. Sprinkle on salads or infuse in oils and vinegar. For a really unusual touch, blend into butter and serve with any red meat.
Borage	The clear blue flowers of borage look spectacular against the dark green leaves of spinach in a salad and the leaves are a vital ingredient as a garnish to that classic summer drink, Pimm's. Borage has a cooling flavour, quite like cucumber.
Chamomile	Chamomile tea, made from the leaves and flowers of this daisy-like plant, has been used for centuries to aid relaxation. The whole flower is used in tea; however, generally only the petals are used. They have a very strong, and rather bitter flavour, so they are often sweetened with honey.

Chicory	The many petalled flowers of chicory come in startlingly clear blue, a pure white and pink, according to variety. The petals can be eaten raw in salads, along with the leaves, while the flower buds are excellent when added to pickles.
Sweet cicely	Sweet cicely looks very much like cow parsley, with similar shaped leaves and open heads of tiny white flowers. These little flowers have a flavour like aniseed, and, unusually, they go equally well with savoury fish dishes as well as sweet dishes, such as fruit salads.
Chives	Like the other members of the allium family, the flowers of chives are edible and have, not surprisingly, a flavour reminiscent of mild onions. They combine well with fish and cheese dishes, and can also be used to pep up a range of dishes from omelettes to pasta.
Dill	The delicate, lace-like flowers of dill are pretty used as a garnish for salads and cold dishes, and can give zest to fish recipes as well as sauces and pickles.
Courgette & Squash	The large, bright yellow trumpet-like flowers of courgettes have long been popular in Mediterranean countries. They should be cooked, and can then be eaten hot or cold. They are excellent stuffed, in the manner of vine leaves, or battered and fried. They can also be used to add colour to stir fries, pasta dishes and omelettes. The flowers of the other members of the squash family can be treated in the same way.
Fennel	The bright yellow flowers of fennel have been used by herbalists for centuries in the treatment of digestive problems. Fennel flowers have a very strong flavour which goes well with fish and patés, they can also be infused in oil.

Lavender *Lavandula* 'Marshwood'

Lavender	Once an extremely important ingredient in cooking, lavender has lost much of its popularity over the centuries, although it has retained its importance in homeopathy. This is a shame, as the flavour of lavender flowers goes extremely well with meats such as chicken and lamb, and can be added to bread and ice cream, or made into a jelly.
Rosemary	Rosemary is one of the most popular herbs; however, it is usually the foliage rather than the flowers which are used for cooking. The flowers, although small, should not be ignored, as they have a lovely flavour, which complement many different roast and casserole dishes, as well as salads, especially tomato.
Beans & Peas	The pretty flowers of the bean family are a great delicacy which are best enjoyed with ingredients whose taste will not overwhelm them. Try them with omelettes and scrambled eggs, or added to a white sauce. Alternatively, add a few to a risotto or salad.
Onion family	The flowers of the many members of the allium family are all edible. They have a similar oniony or garlic taste, differing in levels of intensity. Use the flowers raw in salads or as a garnish to risotto and fish dishes, or cook and add to vegetable dishes, patés and sauces. They also all go well with eggs and cheesy pasta recipes.
Thyme	The flowers of thyme taste very like the leaves, so they can be used in much the same way, either in stuffings or with vegetables and infused in vinegar and oil. Also, spice up an omelette by sprinkling some on top.
Salsify	The flowering shoots and buds of salsify and its close relation scorzonera, have a very attractive delicate flavour, while the petals of the pretty daisy-like flowers can be used to decorate salads and risotto.

Chives (*Allium schoenoprasum*)

159

Vegetable Troubleshooting

This troubleshooting chart should help you diagnose common vegetable problems. (For help with fruit, see page 162.) To use it, start with the part of the plant that appears to be most affected – leaves, stems or roots and tubers – and by answering successive questions 'yes' [✓] or 'no' [✗], you will quickly arrive at a probable cause. Problems specific to certain vegetables or groups of vegetables are highlighted in a separate diagnostic table opposite. Once you have identified the cause, turn to the relevant entry in the directory of pests and diseases for details of how to treat the problem.

LEAVES

have leaves been eaten? → [✗] do new leaves open out deformed? → [✗] are there coloured markings on the leaves?

have leaves been eaten? → [✓] eaten right down to the base?

do new leaves open out deformed? → [✓] plant growing in greenhouse / under cover?

are there coloured markings on the leaves? → [✓] are the leaves mottled?

eaten right down to the base? → [✓] **RABBITS**

eaten right down to the base? → [✗] have holes been eaten?

plant growing in greenhouse / under cover? → [✓] **APHIDS**

plant growing in greenhouse / under cover? → [✗] **EARWIGS**

are the leaves mottled? → [✓] is the mottling yellow?

have holes been eaten? → [✓] tiny, round holes?

tiny, round holes? → [✓] **FLEA BEETLE**

tiny, round holes? → [✗] large holes, sometimes leaves stripped?

is the mottling yellow? → [✓] is there also a fine webbing?

is there also a fine webbing? → [✓] **RED SPIDER MITE**

large holes, sometimes leaves stripped? → [✓] also slime trail?

also slime trail? → [✗] flowers and buds also eaten?

also slime trail? → [✓] **SLUGS/SNAILS**

flowers and buds also eaten? → [✗] **CATERPILLARS**

flowers and buds also eaten? → [✓] **EARWIGS**

STEMS

white mould around base of stem? → [✓] **SCLEROTINIA**

white mould around base of stem? → [✗] stems and leaves swollen?

stems and leaves swollen? → [✗] is the plant wilting?

stems and leaves swollen? → [✓] **EELWORMS**

is the plant wilting? → [✓] stem base partially eaten?

stem base partially eaten? → [✗] prolonged spell of dry weather, no extra watering?

prolonged spell of dry weather, no extra watering? → [✗] patches on leaves and stems?

stem base partially eaten? → [✓] dark grubs in soil around plant?

dark grubs in soil around plant? → [✗] longer, light brown grubs?

dark grubs in soil around plant? → [✓] **LEATHERJACKETS**

longer, light brown grubs? → [✓] **CUTWORMS**

prolonged spell of dry weather, no extra watering? → [✓] **DROUGHT**

patches on leaves and stems? → [✓] **FUSARIUM WILT or BOTRYTIS (see LEAVES)**

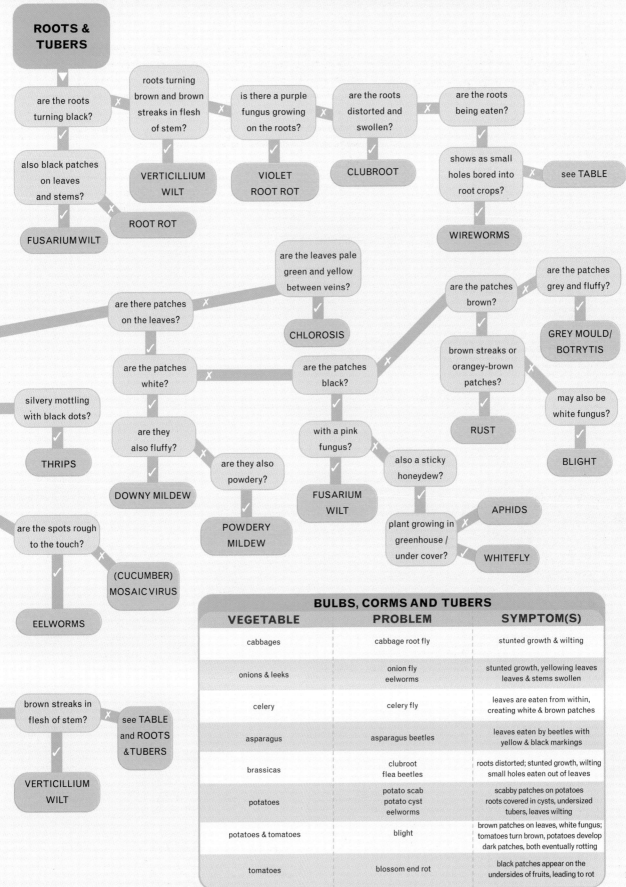

ROOTS & TUBERS

are the roots turning black? ✗ → roots turning brown and brown streaks in flesh of stem? ✗ → is there a purple fungus growing on the roots? ✗ → are the roots distorted and swollen? ✗ → are the roots being eaten? ✓ → shows as small holes bored into root crops? ✗ → see TABLE

are the roots turning black? ✓ → also black patches on leaves and stems? ✓ → FUSARIUM WILT
also black patches on leaves and stems? ✗ → ROOT ROT

roots turning brown and brown streaks in flesh of stem? ✓ → VERTICILLIUM WILT

is there a purple fungus growing on the roots? ✓ → VIOLET ROOT ROT

are the roots distorted and swollen? ✓ → CLUBROOT

shows as small holes bored into root crops? ✓ → WIREWORMS

are the leaves pale green and yellow between veins? ✓ → CHLOROSIS

are there patches on the leaves? ✗ → are the leaves pale green and yellow between veins?
are there patches on the leaves? ✓ → are the patches white?

are the patches brown? ✗ → are the patches grey and fluffy? ✓ → GREY MOULD/ BOTRYTIS
are the patches brown? ✓ → brown streaks or orangey-brown patches? ✓ → RUST
are the patches grey and fluffy? ✗ → may also be white fungus? ✓ → BLIGHT

are the patches white? ✓ → are they also fluffy?
are the patches black? ✗ → (to brown streaks / orangey-brown patches)

silvery mottling with black dots? ✓ → THRIPS

are they also fluffy? ✓ → DOWNY MILDEW
are they also fluffy? ✗ → are they also powdery? ✓ → POWDERY MILDEW

are the patches black? ✓ → with a pink fungus? ✓ → FUSARIUM WILT
with a pink fungus? ✗ → also a sticky honeydew? ✓ → plant growing in greenhouse / under cover? ✗ → APHIDS
plant growing in greenhouse / under cover? ✓ → WHITEFLY

are the spots rough to the touch? ✗ → (CUCUMBER) MOSAIC VIRUS
are the spots rough to the touch? ✓ → EELWORMS

brown streaks in flesh of stem? ✗ → see TABLE and ROOTS &TUBERS
brown streaks in flesh of stem? ✓ → VERTICILLIUM WILT

BULBS, CORMS AND TUBERS

VEGETABLE	PROBLEM	SYMPTOM(S)
cabbages	cabbage root fly	stunted growth & wilting
onions & leeks	onion fly eelworms	stunted growth, yellowing leaves leaves & stems swollen
celery	celery fly	leaves are eaten from within, creating white & brown patches
asparagus	asparagus beetles	leaves eaten by beetles with yellow & black markings
brassicas	clubroot flea beetles	roots distorted; stunted growth, wilting small holes eaten out of leaves
potatoes	potato scab potato cyst eelworms	scabby patches on potatoes roots covered in cysts, undersized tubers, leaves wilting
potatoes & tomatoes	blight	brown patches on leaves, white fungus; tomatoes turn brown, potatoes develop dark patches, both eventually rotting
tomatoes	blossom end rot	black patches appear on the undersides of fruits, leading to rot

Fruit Troubleshooting

This troubleshooting chart should help you diagnose common fruit problems. (For help with vegetables, see page 160.) To use it, start with the part of the plant that appears to be most affected – leaves and stems or fruit and buds – and by answering successive questions 'yes' [✓] or 'no' [X], you will quickly arrive at a probable cause. Once you have identified the cause, turn to the relevant entry in the directory of pests and diseases for details of how to treat the problem.

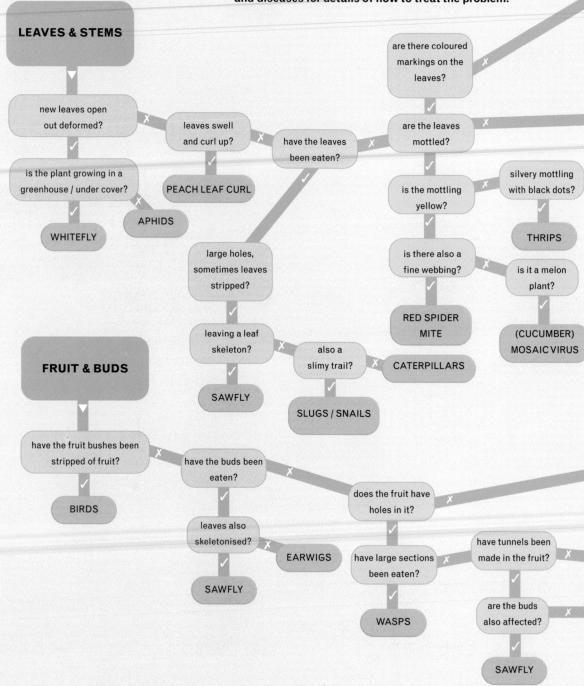

LEAVES & STEMS

new leaves open out deformed?

is the plant growing in a greenhouse / under cover?

WHITEFLY

APHIDS

leaves swell and curl up?

PEACH LEAF CURL

have the leaves been eaten?

are there coloured markings on the leaves?

are the leaves mottled?

is the mottling yellow?

silvery mottling with black dots?

THRIPS

is there also a fine webbing?

is it a melon plant?

RED SPIDER MITE

(CUCUMBER) MOSAIC VIRUS

large holes, sometimes leaves stripped?

leaving a leaf skeleton?

also a slimy trail?

CATERPILLARS

SAWFLY

SLUGS / SNAILS

FRUIT & BUDS

have the fruit bushes been stripped of fruit?

have the buds been eaten?

BIRDS

leaves also skeletonised?

EARWIGS

SAWFLY

does the fruit have holes in it?

have large sections been eaten?

have tunnels been made in the fruit?

WASPS

are the buds also affected?

SAWFLY

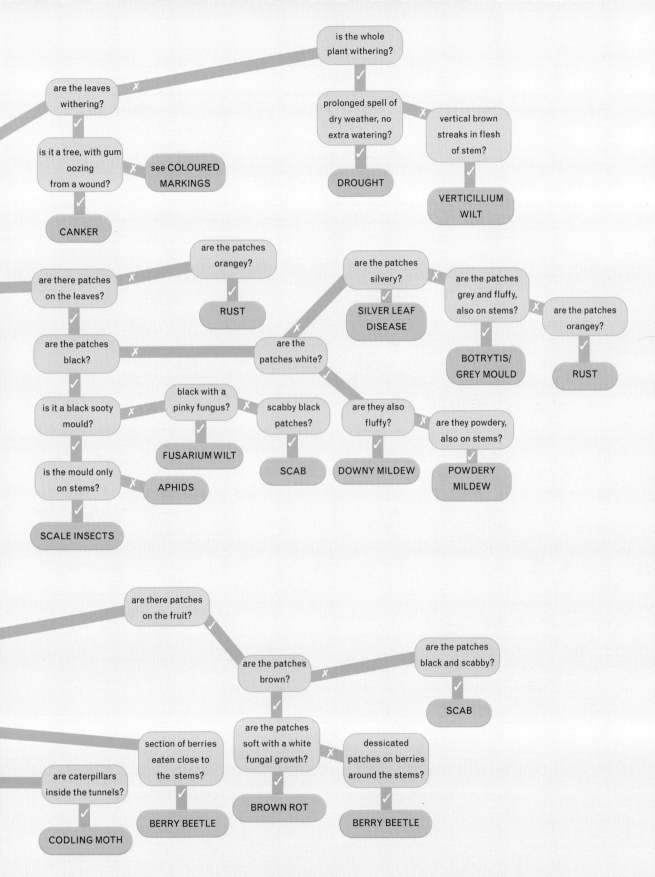

is the whole plant withering?

are the leaves withering?

prolonged spell of dry weather, no extra watering?

vertical brown streaks in flesh of stem?

is it a tree, with gum oozing from a wound?

see COLOURED MARKINGS

DROUGHT

VERTICILLIUM WILT

CANKER

are the patches orangey?

are the patches silvery?

are the patches grey and fluffy, also on stems?

are the patches orangey?

are there patches on the leaves?

RUST

SILVER LEAF DISEASE

BOTRYTIS/ GREY MOULD

RUST

are the patches black?

are the patches white?

are the patches grey and fluffy, also on stems?

is it a black sooty mould?

black with a pinky fungus?

scabby black patches?

are they also fluffy?

are they powdery, also on stems?

FUSARIUM WILT

SCAB

DOWNY MILDEW

POWDERY MILDEW

is the mould only on stems?

APHIDS

SCALE INSECTS

are there patches on the fruit?

are the patches black and scabby?

are the patches brown?

SCAB

section of berries eaten close to the stems?

are the patches soft with a white fungal growth?

dessicated patches on berries around the stems?

are caterpillars inside the tunnels?

BERRY BEETLE

BROWN ROT

BERRY BEETLE

CODLING MOTH

Pests & Diseases

Most fruits and vegetables will at some time suffer from pests and diseases. There are many different ways of approaching the disease and pest control issue, and not all of them involve reaching for the chemical spray. Remember the maxim 'prevention is better than cure', and often you will keep problems to a minimum. Most of the common fruit and vegetable pests and diseases are listed here, with advice on how to deal with them. You should also keep a close eye on animals and birds.

Fruit & vegetable pests

Aphids

Among the most troublesome garden pests. They weaken plants by sucking their juices, making new growth deformed and spreading viruses. Aphids breed fast, so immediate action is required. They live in colonies under leaves and around new growth; sooty mould is a tell-tale sign. Physically wash them off – with broad beans, pinch off the tops before colonies form. Lightweight horticultural fleece also provides good protection, after pollination. The aphids' natural predators are hoverflies, lacewing larvae and ladybirds, so hang up ladybird nesting boxes to encourage these. If all else fails, spray with contact insecticide.

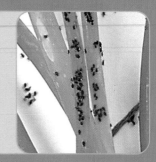

Whitefly

Whitefly are related to aphids and cause the same sooty mould with their honeydew, but they tend only to attack plants in the greenhouse. Set sticky traps and vacuum up. If you spot them in the early stage, then introduce *Encarsia formosa*, a parasitic wasp which lays its eggs inside the whitefly's larvae, between mid-spring and mid-autumn.

Slugs & Snails

Slugs and snails will rapidly munch through foliage, leaving large holes and tell-tale silvery trails of slime. Collect them at night with a torch, and drop them into a bucket of salty water. Jam jars full of beer buried to their neck in the ground are also good; they are attracted to the beer, fall in and drown. Do not use slug pellets as these get into the food chain, i.e. a bird will either eat it or take it to feed baby birds. Encourage natural predators, frogs, hedgehogs and thrushes, or water soil with the biological control nematodes.

Cabbage root flies

Cabbage root flies affect not only cabbages but all brassicas, as well as radishes. Damage is caused by the little white grubs which bore into roots causing stunted growth and wilting. They can be prevented from reaching the plant by fixing collars around the stems, 15cm (6in) in diameter, or covering with horticultural fleece.

Onion flies

Onion flies attack all types of onions and leeks, eating the roots and tunnelling into the bulb, causing poor growth and yellowing leaves. Prevent these from becoming established by practising strict crop rotation, protecting emerging seedlings with fleece and control by destroying all affected plants.

Celery fly

The white grubs of the celery fly burrow into celery leaves, especially in the spring. White or brown areas appear within the leaves, blotching or discolouring them. Control by removing and destroying all infested leaves when the damage is first noticed.

Thrips

Thrips are tiny flies which lay their eggs on greenhouse plants. The adults and nymphs attack the top of leaves, weakening the plant and spreading viruses. Affected leaves take on a silvery mottling with black dots. As they thrive in hot, dry conditions, the best course of action is to damp down the greenhouse and water the plants regularly, as well as to open windows to ventilate it. There are sprays available.

Carrot flies

Carrot flies lay eggs which hatch and eat into the carrots, creating brown tunnels. To prevent them, sow in early summer to avoid the flies; cover with horticultural fleece or erect a barrier – a sheet of polythene about 1m (36in) high around the carrots is effective as the flies fly low. Sow sparingly to avoid thinning. If you must thin, do it late in the evening when the flies are less likely to smell the carrots.

Red spider mites

Red spider mites attack plants in the greenhouse. Leaves take on a yellow mottling and at an advanced stage, mites cover the tops of plants with fine cobwebs. Spray plants regularly with water mist and damp down the greenhouse on warm days to stop mites becoming established. You can also buy their predator, the mite *Phytoseiulus persimilis*. Disinfect the greenhouse during the winter.

Earwigs

Earwigs eat through leaves, flowers and buds. The best way to control them is to clear away any debris, and also set traps. Fill upturned flowerpots with straw and place upside down on top of canes among the affected produce. The earwigs will crawl into the flowerpots during the day, which you can empty every evening.

Eelworm

Eelworm. There are several types of these which attack the roots of various plants, including potatoes, tomatoes, onions and leeks, causing leaves to turn spotted or stems to swell up. Choose resistant varieties of plant wherever possible and practise a strict crop rotation. If vegetables are attacked, then the only course of action is to burn the affected plant.

Millipedes

Millipedes attack tubers and seedlings, and can be prevented from becoming a problem by good hygiene – in other words clearing away all plant debris. Turning over the soil around affected plants will reveal the millipedes, which can then be caught and destroyed. Do not destroy centipedes; these are our allies not foes. Centipedes have one set of legs per body segment, whereas millipedes have two.

Caterpillars

Caterpillars can cause a great deal of damage, sometimes stripping leaves entirely. They particularly like the leaves of cabbages, cauliflowers and Brussels sprouts. One method of control is to crush the eggs or simply remove by hand any that hatch while still small. A dusting of derris powder is also very effective for serious infestations.

Cutworms

Cutworms are moth caterpillars which live in the soil and come out at night to feed off the base of plants, especially lettuce. Stems of affected plants will be partially eaten, causing poor growth and wilt. Prevent the moths from laying eggs in the soil with a covering of fleece; however, if they are already established collect them at night and destroy or, if desperate, use a soil pesticide.

Leather jackets

Leatherjackets (cranefly larvae) cause damage similar to cutworms, but are more difficult to control as their eggs are laid the previous autumn. Roots are eaten and stems severed at ground level, causing plants to turn yellow, wilt and eventually die. At the first sign of damage, dig around the affected plants and uncover the dark grubs to the elements; these should then be eaten by birds.

Asparagus beetles

Asparagus beetles are small beetles with distinctive yellow and black markings, whose larvae feed on asparagus leaves, destroying plants. Damage occurs between late spring and early autumn. Prevent by scrupulously clearing all debris from asparagus beds and control by removing by hand. If all else fails, spray with a contact insecticide.

Wireworms

Wireworms are click beetle larvae, which live in the soil and feed on the roots of vegetables, boring small tunnels and causing foliage to wilt. Potatoes and other root vegetables are particularly affected. Apart from causing small, bore-like holes through the root crops, wireworms can cause small, young plants to wither and die. Prevent by keeping the kitchen garden weed free. Where the damage can be seen, try to look for the culprits and destroy them. Lift root crops as soon as possible.

Codling moth

The caterpillars of the codling moth tunnel into ripe apples and pears, making them inedible by the time the fruit ripens; you can see exit holes at the end opposite the stalk or indeed elsewhere on the fruit. Prevent these pests becoming troublesome by suspending pheromone traps from the trees in late spring to mid summer to catch the male moths, thus preventing egg fertilization.

Scale insects

Scale insects attack the stems of apples, bay, cherries, citrus, figs, peaches and vines. They do not cause major damage, although they slow down plant growth and cause sooty mould similar to aphids by excreting honeydew. Most outdoor species hatch around mid-summer, but you can get scale insects under glass at any time of the year. Control by spraying trees with a cold tar wash in winter.

Sawfly

Sawfly come in various types whose larvae attack apple, plum and gooseberry flower buds and leaves, destroying them. Apple sawfly larvae also tunnels through the fruitlets, causing them to drop off the tree. You can easily spot the tell-tale sign on apples – the fruit has a ribbon-like scar on its skin. The only cure is spraying affected trees, preferably at dusk to avoid harming bees.

Flea beetles

Flea beetles are tiny black insects which jump high into the air when disturbed, and will eat holes in the foliage of all types of brassicas. Prevent them becoming a problem by clearing away all plant debris, where they overwinter, and protecting with fleece. Early and late sowings are safe from attack. Dusting with derris powder is another solution.

Fruit & vegetable diseases

Blight

Blight affects potatoes and outdoor tomatoes, especially in wet seasons. It can be identified by the brown patches which appear on the leaves and lead to rot. Prevent it by growing disease resistant varieties, and control by spraying in the very early stages – any later, then the plants must be pulled up and burnt.

Scab

There are various forms of scab. Potato scab manifests itself by growths on the tubers and is more of a problem where the soil is light. Again, choose disease resistant varieties and practise good husbandry by clearing away plant debris in the autumn.

Clubroot

Cabbages, cauliflowers, sprouts, swedes and turnips are among the plants prone to this disease which causes growths to appear on the roots, wilting and rot. It is caused by spores which can remain dormant in the ground for a couple of decades waiting for a suitable host. Prevent by liming the soil and adhering to a strict rotation plan. As there is no cure, remove and burn all affected plants.

Blossom end rot

Blossom end rot affects tomatoes in particular, especially those grown in pots or growbags, as this problem is commonly caused by underwatering. The first sign is the appearance of black patches underneath the fruit, which then rot. It cannot be cured, only prevented by regular watering and feeding.

Root rot

Root rot primarily affects beans, peas, tomatoes, cucumbers and container-grown vegetables. It is a fungus which causes roots to turn black and the plants to wilt and die. Prevent the disease by practising crop rotation, using sterilized compost and watering with mains water. Pull up and burn any diseased plants, and dig up and remove the soil around their roots, which will harbour spores.

Damping off

Damping off can affect all seedlings, which collapse and die, and is caused by fungi in the soil or water. Whole trays of seedlings can die within a few days. There is no cure, however it can be prevented by ensuring seed trays and compost are sterilized and that the seeds are sown thinly and kept well ventilated. It is thought that sowing seed too thickly causes overcrowding and inadequate light. Do not over water.

Fusarium

Fusarium wilt can strike many types of vegetables, turning their roots black and killing them slowly. The early signs are black patches on the leaves and stems, often coated with a pinky fungus. At the first sign of disease remove and destroy all affected plants to minimize spread, as well as removing the surrounding soil. Do not put on the compost heap. Clean all garden tools. To prevent the disease try and buy disease resistant stock. There is no chemical cure.

Verticillium

Verticillium wilt is a fungal infection mainly affecting plants grown in the greenhouse and will kill them after a few seasons. At the first sign of the disease – brown markings on the stems and roots – remove and destroy all affected plants; at other stages of the disease, plant foliage wilts and leaves may turn yellow or brown. Also clear away the surrounding soil, as this will harbour the fungus, and clean all gardening tools, paying special attention to secateurs and loppers.

Cucumber mosaic

Cucumber mosaic virus can affect all members of the cucurbit family. It is spread by aphids and causes leaves to turn a mottled, mosaic-patterned yellow and the plant to languish. Flowering is reduced or non-existent. There is no cure and plants must be destroyed. Reduce the risk of infection by controlling aphids and clearing up weeds. Prevention involves cleaning off aphids as soon as they appear.

Downy mildew

Downy mildew appears as white fluffy spots on foliage and, besides stunting growth, leads to other infections. It affects all the brassicas, lettuces, courgettes and onions and can be prevented by choosing disease resistant varieties, practising crop rotation, leaving plenty of space between plants and ensuring there is good drainage. Remove all affected material and burn, then water plants at their base to prevent the disease spreading. If all else fails then spray with a fungicide.

Powdery mildew

Powdery mildew is caused by a variety of fungi which attack a range of vegetables, and can be identified by powdery white spots on the foliage, which will eventually turn yellow and drop off. The fungal spores spread through the air or by water splash and particularly attack plants growing on dry soil. Prevent by adequate watering and mulching, and control by removing all affected material and burning. A fungicide spray is useful if all else fails.

Grey mould

Grey mould or botrytis attacks a range of vegetables, including lettuces, cucumbers and tomatoes, especially those grown in the greenhouse. Those with a cut or injury are especially vulnerable. It appears as a fluffy grey mould and spreads through the air and also via water splash and physical contact. It is very resilient and will remain in the soil to re-infect plants later. Prevent it spreading by clearing up all plant debris and removing and burning all affected material. Ensure there is plenty of space between plants for air to circulate and, if all else fails, spray with a fungicide.

Rust

There are numerous forms of rust, which affect many types of fruit. They cause orangey patches to develop on the foliage and stems, which then drops off. Rust can be prevented by adhering to a strict crop rotation and by leaving plenty of space between plants and tree limbs for air to circulate. Once rust strikes, remove all affected material and burn, including any foliage which has fallen on the ground. Spray with a fungicide if all else fails.

Chlorosis

Chlorosis causes foliage to turn yellow and is caused by lack of iron and manganese, nitrogen or magnesium. It can also be caused by waterlogging, low temperatures or weedkiller contamination. It affects acid loving plants and can be prevented by ensuring that they get enough acid and, if necessary, giving them a top up in the form of an acidic mulch.

Violet root rot

Violet root rot is a very similar disease to root rot (see page 167) and attacks asparagus, beetroot, carrots and parsnips. The fungi cause leaves to turn yellow and wilt, while a violet fungus coats the roots. Prevent by practising crop rotation, and to control an outbreak remove all the affected plants, plus the soil around them and destroy. Do not put on the compost heap.

Peach leaf curl

Peach leaf curl is a fungus that also attacks nectarines, causing the leaves to curl up, turn a deep red, then drop off. The diseased leaves will be replaced by a fresh, non-diseased batch. However, if a tree suffers repeated attacks it will die. Prevention is better than cure, and to prevent infection protect wall trained trees by erecting a polythene covered frame around and over them. Pick off all diseased leaves from affected trees and destroy.

Silver leaf disease

Silver leaf disease particularly attacks cherries, peaches and plums, and is very serious – it can eventually kill the tree. It is spread by spores, which enter damaged wood, and can be recognised by the silver marks which appear on the leaves. Control by removing all affected material, plus about 30cm (12in) of adjoining healthy wood and burning immediately. Prevent by pruning in the summer and then protecting the wounds with wound paint.

Sclerotinia

Sclerotinia appears as a white mould which grows at the base of the stems of vegetables such as artichokes, celery, carrots and parsnips. Most of the above-ground tissues can be affected, turning brown and slimey as they rot. Prevent it by sticking to a strict rotation schedule and, as there is no treatment, remove affected plants and burn them.

Mosaic virus

Mosaic virus affects lettuces, beans, potatoes and has a similar appearance to cucumber mosaic virus (see page168), although it is spread by seeds not aphids. There is no cure, except to remove and burn all affected material. Always use a new site for planting replacement crops. Try to buy disease resistant plants where possible.

Canker bacteria

Canker bacteria attack apples, cherries and plums, entering the tree through cuts or wounds and causing the leaves and flowers to wither. The stem also starts to deteriorate. The first sign of canker bacteria is a golden gum oozing from the cut or wound. Immediately cut off and burn all affected limbs and treat the wounds with a wound paint. Spray the foliage with a copper fungicide in late summer or early autumn.

Gardener's Calendar

This calendar provides an overall look at the gardening tasks throughout the year, and is useful for planning ahead. However, it is only a guide and should not be seen as a gardener's bible. Local conditions must be taken into account, as spring can arrive much earlier and winter can be much more severe, depending upon where you live. The weather for each season can also change considerably from year to year. Use this calendar as a quick reference and keep an eye on weather forecasts.

Winter

Complete digging, manuring and preparation of the ground. Continually inspect stored fruit, discarding those showing any sign of decay. Force rhubarb and chicory.

	Early winter	Mid-winter	Late winter
Vegetables	Dig over beds to break up the soil in preparation for planting in the next few weeks. Leave large clods near the surface and allow the frost to break them up naturally.	Plant rhubarb and cover with manure for protection. Sow peas and plant shallots in sheltered areas. Sow early crops of Brussels sprouts and broad beans.	Continue sowing early broad beans and peas in sheltered areas. Continue planting shallots. Buy early potato tubers and leave them to sprout. Sow carrots in a cold frame.
Herbs	Protect bay, rosemary and marjoram from extreme cold by wrapping them in some kind of protection such as horticultural fleece.	Time to plan the planting scheme and order seeds from catalogues.	Sow parsley during spells of dry weather. Propagate mint runners.
Tree Fruit	Continue planting and pruning. Spray tender trees with tar-oil winter wash. Cut back new apple, pear and cherry trees.	Plant bare-rooted trees if the ground is not frozen. Prune established trees. Feed with a nitrogen fertiliser if necessary, especially bushes and trees growing in grass. Check ties and stakes.	Continue to plant and prune, weather permitting.
Soft Fruit	Cut back new blackberry, currant, loganberry, gooseberry and raspberry bushes.	Rewire soft fruit frames if necessary. Prune newly-planted gooseberry and currant bushes, cutting back the leader shoots by a third. Cut newly-planted blackcurrant bushes back hard.	Newly-planted raspberry, blackberry, loganberry and hybrids should be cut down to about 30cm (12in) above soil level.
Vegetables in season	Beetroot, seakale, Brussels sprouts, cabbage, carrots, chicory, Jerusalem artichokes, leeks, marrows, onions, parsnips, salsify, scorzonera, spinach, winter radishes, turnip.	Brussels sprouts, cabbage, carrots, chicory, Jerusalem artichokes, leeks, onions, parsnips, salsify, scorzonera, swede, winter radishes.	Brussels sprouts, cabbage, carrots, chicory, Jerusalem artichokes, leeks, onions, parsnips, spring broccoli, salsify, scorzonera, swede, turnips, winter radishes.

Spring

Water during dry spells and after planting. Hoe between crops on a weekly basis to keep weeds under control. Apply a thick layer of mulch around plants, bushes and trees to preserve moisture and keep down weeds.

	Early spring	Mid-spring	Late spring
Vegetables	Finish planting shallots and main-crop onions. Plant asparagus, Jerusalem artichokes, Kohl rabi and early potatoes. Sow summer spinach, salad onions, radishes, maincrop Brussels sprouts, parsnips, late summer cabbages. Sow carrots in a cold frame/under glass. Some lettuce can go directly into soil.	Sow Oriental vegetables (Pak Choi, Mizuna, Chinese cabbage, spinach mustard etc). Also, beetroot, broccoli (including purple sprouting), maincrop carrots, lettuce, winter cabbages. Sow French beans under glass. Plant artichokes (both globe and Jerusalem), late summer cabbages, onions.	Sow beetroot, broccoli, French, dwarf and runner beans, radishes, spinach, seakale, scorzonera, salsify and sweet corn. Plant out French beans sown under glass. Continue sowing Oriental veg, lettuce, summer spinach etc. Prepare sites for outdoor tomatoes, marrows and other squash.
Herbs	Once soil has warmed up sow chervil, chives, dill, marjoram, parsley and sorrel. Sow basil under glass. It takes a large amount of fresh herbs to make a small amount of dried herbs so sow in quantity. Some herbs, such as clumps of sorrel, bergamot and chives can be divided.	Sow dill, fennel, hyssop, marjoram, rue, thyme and more parsley. Continue sowing basil under glass. Plant lavender and rosemary.	Continue sowing chervil, dill, fennel, hyssop and parsley. Plant out basil and sow more seed directly into the ground. Take cuttings of marjoram, rosemary, sage and thyme.
Tree Fruit	Finish planting and pruning. Top-dress newly-planted trees with well-rotted manure or similar. Feed trees planted amongst grass. Spray apples, cherries, peaches, pears, plums and nectarines.	Protect the blossom of soft fruit from frost (light-weight horticultural fleece is ideal). Spray blackcurrants and strawberries. Pick off flowers from autumn-fruiting runners.	Feed apples, pears, cherries, peaches, nectarines and plums. Begin to thin fruit on trees growing against walls. Spray apples, cherries, pears, peaches and nectarines. Remove any suckers.
Soft Fruit	Plant strawberries and raspberries. Tie blackberry and loganberry shoots on to wire. Feed established bushes.	As trees start to blossom watch out for any signs of pests and diseases. Protect trees growing against walls from frost with horticultural fleece. Mulch newly-planted trees. Spray apples, peaches, nectarines, pears and plums.	Feed blackberries, loganberries, gooseberries, raspberries and redcurrents. Spray blackcurrents, gooseberries and strawberries. and mulch raspberries – removing any excess shoots. Spread protective straw around strawberry plants.
Veg/ Fruit in season	Brussels sprouts, carrots, Jerusalem artichokes, leeks, purple-sprouting broccoli, radishes, spinach.	Asparagus, broccoli, lettuce, radishes.	Asparagus, broad beans, spring cabbage, Kohl rabi, leek, lettuce, radish, salad onion, summer spinach.

Summer

Water during dry spells and after planting. Hoe between crops on a weekly basis to keep weeds under control. Apply a thick layer of mulch around plants, bushes and trees to preserve moisture and keep down weeds. Start sowing in earnest.

	Early summer	Mid-summer	Late summer
Vegetables	Sow French dwarf beans, chicory, courgettes, lettuce, peas, radishes, spinach beet, rocket and swede. Plant broccoli, Brussels sprouts, celery, chicory, leeks, marrows, tomatoes, savoy and winter cabbages. Earth up potatoes. Water during dry spells (especially salad vegetables).	Sow swedes, winter radishes and turnips. Continue sowing salad vegetables, chard and spinach, beetroot and carrots. Finish planting leeks, Brussels sprouts, winter cabbages and spring broccoli. Pinch out side shoots from tomatoes, apart from bush tomatoes – these should have straw spread around the fruit.	Sow Brussels sprouts, spring cabbages. Continue sowing lettuce.
Herbs	Continue sowing dill and chervil. Continue to take cuttings from rosemary and sage. Begin to harvest herbs. Dead-head and mulch as necessary.	Continue sowing chervil, dill and parsley. Harvest just prior to herbs coming into full bloom. Dry (in airing cupboard) and freeze.	Continue harvesting and freezing or drying. Take cuttings of woody herbs, for example bay, mint, rosemary, rue and sage, then start cutting back.
Tree Fruit	Look out for signs of pests or disease. Thin crop if heavy to ensure large fruit after natural shedding. Water and mulch apples and pears. Tie in shoots of new peach and nectarines growing against walls. Net plum and cherry trees against birds.	Summer prune trees where you want to restrict growth. Support limbs of apples, pears and plums weighed down with fruit. Finish thinning apple and pear fruits to encourage growth. Watch out for wasp and earwig damage on peaches; net fruit trees.	Continue summer pruning any trees of which you want to limit growth. Support any limbs of plum trees weighed down with fruit. Pick early apples and pears.
Soft Fruit	Look out for signs of pests or disease. Harvest strawberries. Water and mulch blackcurrants. Tie in blackberry and loganberry shoots. Summer prune goose-berries and outdoor vines. Net redcurrants, raspberries and strawberries against birds. Pin down strawberry runners.	Harvest fruit as it ripens. Tie in new shoots of blackberries and loganberries. After picking raspberries cut back old canes. After picking blackcurrants prune bushes. Dig up any strawberry plants which have produced three crops. Continue summer pruning vines.	Separate and plant pinned down strawberry runners which have rooted. Net against birds, especially early autumn-fruiting raspberries. Harvest loganberries and then remove fruited shoots, tying in all new shoots.
Veg/Fruit in season	Asparagus, broad beans, broccoli, chard, lettuce, Oriental vegetables, peas, potatoes, salad onions, spring cabbage, radishes, summer spinach. Fruit in season: gooseberries, strawberries.	Beetroot, carrots, courgettes, cucumber, globe artichokes, Kohl rabi, lettuce, marrow, runner beans, shallots, summer squash. Fruit in season: blackcurrants, cherries, raspberries, redcurrants.	Celery, chard, cucumber, shallots, sweetcorn, dwarf French beans, onions, Oriental vegetables, radishes and mange tout. Fruit in season: apple, blackberry, red, white and blackcurrants, pears.

Autumn

Harvest and store and/or preserve crops immediately. Clear and manure ground following harvesting. Plant new trees and begin the winter pruning of any established trees.

	Early autumn	Mid-autumn	Late autumn
Vegetables	Continue harvesting and clear away all traces of crops which have been harvested, for example cabbages and peas. Sow carrots and winter lettuce under cover. Earth up and stake brassicas.	Continue harvesting and clear away all traces of crops which have been harvested, for example marrows and courgettes or peas. Plant garlic and plant out spring cabbages, winter and spring lettuces. Force rhubarb. Sow peas and broad beans under cover. Protect plants as necessary.	Sow broad beans, peas and winter lettuce under cover.
Herbs	Sow parsley and chervil. Take cuttings of bay and rue and keep under glass.	Continue taking cuttings of bay and rue. Divide chives and mint.	Clear chervil, dill, fennel and parsley. Protect early autumn-sown parsley and chervil under glass (cloches or similar).
Tree Fruit	Continue harvesting. Finish summer pruning.	Continue harvesting. Prepare sites for new trees (if planting new trees on ground where old trees stood then sterilize the soil to guard against disease). Put grease bands around apple and cherry trees to trap winter moths.	Prepare soil, plant new trees and prune when planted. Start winter pruning established trees.
Soft Fruit	Harvest early autumn-fruiting raspberries, blackberries and loganberries, then remove all old growth before tying in new shoots. Plant strawberries under cover.	Continue harvesting (for example autumn-fruiting strawberries). Remove fruited blackberry and loganberry canes, then tie in new shoots. Take gooseberry cuttings.	Start planting new bushes. Divide raspberry suckers and sow alpine strawberries.

	Early autumn	Mid-autumn	Late autumn
Veg/ Fruit in season	Beetroot, cabbage, carrots, cauliflower, celery, chard, cucumber, dwarf French beans, artichokes, lettuce, marrows, Oriental vegetables, peas, onions, radishes, runner beans, sweetcorn, shallots and tomatoes. Fruit in season: apple, apricot, blackberries, blackcurrants, cherries, gooseberries, loganberries, peach, pears, plums and raspberries.	Dwarf French beans, Brussels sprouts, cabbage, carrots, cauliflower, celery, chard, cucumber, globe artichoke, lettuce, marrows and courgettes, onions, Oriental vegetables, peas and mange tout, potatoes, radishes, runner beans, shallots, spinach beet, sweet corn, tomato, turnip. Fruit in season: apple, grapes, peaches, pears, plums, strawberries.	Beetroot, cabbage, carrots, chard, chicory, Jerusalem artichokes, marrows and courgettes, salsify, scorzonera, swedes, sweetcorn, parsnips, radishes.

Index of Plants

General Index

Acknowledgements

Author's acknowledgements:
This book is dedicated to Isabel, Antonia and Cicely.

The majority of photographs in this book were taken by Tim Sandall. A number of others were kindly contributed by S.E. Marshall & Co Ltd, as well as one picture by John Feltwell/Garden Matters on page 117.

The publishers would like to thank Coolings Nurseries for their cooperation and assistance with the photography in this book, including the loan of tools and much specialist equipment. Special thanks go to: Sandra Gratwick, Garry Norris, Ian Hazon, and Brian Archibald. Coolings Nurseries Ltd, Rushmore Hill, Knockholt, Kent, TN14 7NN. Tel: 00 44 1959 532269; Email: coolings@coolings.co.uk; Website: www.coolings.co.uk